MIDRASH & MEDICINE

Also Edited by Rabbi William Cutter, PhD

*Healing and the Jewish Imagination: Spiritual and Practical
Perspectives on Judaism and Health*

Also Available from Jewish Lights

*Facing Illness, Finding God: How Judaism Can Help You and
Caregivers Cope When Body or Spirit Fails*
By Rabbi Joseph B. Meszler

*Healing of Soul, Healing of Body:
Spiritual Leaders Unfold the Strength & Solace in Psalms*
Edited by Rabbi Simkha Y. Weintraub, LCSW

*Jewish Paths toward Healing and Wholeness:
A Personal Guide to Dealing with Suffering*
By Rabbi Kerry M. Olitzky; Foreword by Debbie Friedman

*Jewish Visions for Aging: A Professional
Guide for Fostering Wholeness*
By Rabbi Dayle A. Friedman, MSW, MAJCS, BCC
Foreword by Thomas R. Cole, PhD
Preface by Dr. Eugene B. Borowitz

MIDRASH & MEDICINE

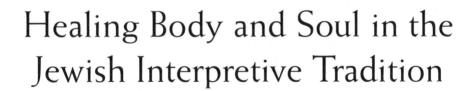

Healing Body and Soul in the Jewish Interpretive Tradition

Edited by Rabbi William Cutter, PhD

Preface by Michele F. Prince, LCSW, MAJCS

JEWISH LIGHTS Publishing

Woodstock, Vermont

Midrash & Medicine:
Healing Body and Soul in the Jewish Interpretive Tradition

2011 Hardcover Edition, First Printing
© 2011 by William Cutter

Library of Congress Cataloging-in-Publication Data
Midrash & medicine : healing body and soul in the Jewish interpretive tradition / edited by William Cutter ; preface by Michele F. Prince.
    p. cm.
 Includes bibliographical references.
 ISBN 978-1-58023-428-3 (hardcover)
 1. Health—Religious aspects—Judaism. 2. Human body in rabbinical literature. 3. Rabbinical literature—History and criticism. 4. Midrash. 5. Medicine—Religious aspects—Judaism. 6. Suffering—Religious aspects—Judaism. 7. Death—Religious aspects—Judaism. 8. Bioethics—Religious aspects—Judaism. 9. Spiritual life—Judaism. I. Cutter, William.
 BM538.H43M53 2011
 296.3'76—dc22

2010029951

10 9 8 7 6 5 4 3 2 1

Manufactured in the United States of America

Jacket Design: Jenny Buono
Jacket Art: © iStockphoto.com/Manuela Krause, modified by Jenny Buono
Interior Design: Kristi Menter

Published by Jewish Lights Publishing
A Division of LongHill Partners, Inc.
Sunset Farm Offices, Route 4, P.O. Box 237
Woodstock, VT 05091
Tel: (802) 457-4000   Fax: (802) 457-4004
www.jewishlights.com

CONTENTS

9 THE NARRATIVE TURN IN JEWISH BIOETHICS

10 WHAT TAKES PLACE AND WHAT CAN BE CHANGED

Michele F. Prince, LCSW, MAJCS, is the director of the Kalsman Institute on Judaism and Health of Hebrew Union College–Jewish Institute of Religion. She specializes in oncology and is cofounder of the Los Angeles Jewish Bereavement Project. Her work is partially supported by a grant from the John Templeton Foundation.

PREFACE

Michele F. Prince, LCSW, MAJCS

The present volume was inspired by the "Midrash & Medicine: Imagining Wholeness" conference cosponsored by the Kalsman Institute on Judaism and Health and the Bay Area Jewish Healing Center and held in Monterey, California. One hundred and fifty people from throughout North America and Israel participated in the conference, which combined Rabbinic texts, contemporary storytelling, and interpretive process. Norman Cohen, Lewis Barth, and Dayle Friedman keynoted the conference by applying their deft midrashic minds to well-known biblical stories and rendered their sense of "midrash" for the many rabbis, physicians, artists, musicians, therapists, and educators who both studied midrash and ventured to create some of their own. My own appreciation for the creativity inherent in the midrash was greatly enhanced.

In a physical setting of immense beauty, we inhabited the landscape of illness and wholeness with partners from across the country and across the religious spectrum, and we all learned new things about the way in which midrash can be a part of our healing work.

The Kalsman Institute on Judaism and Health

The Kalsman Institute is privileged to sponsor this book, whose theme grew from the Monterey conference. Kalsman was founded by William Cutter, editor of this book and one of its authors. I am proud to be the institute's director. We concentrate on the connections between Judaism and health. We are a catalyst for interaction among spiritual leaders, health-care providers, and Jewish community professionals and members;

we coordinate pastoral education for Hebrew Union College students. We strive to teach our students how to listen, how to ask the right questions, and how to simply be present. We believe these skills are enhanced by midrashic training.

Kalsman conferences and workshops provide opportunities for engagement and education—to teach professionals these same skills of presence and discernment. Our gatherings generate ideas and projects on Jewish spirituality and healing, Jewish medical ethics, illness and wellness, and the health of the health-care system. Kalsman has an international network of two thousand friends and partners, and in union with them, the institute makes positive contributions to Jewish thought and practice through training, collaboration, and dialogue.

We focus on educating and motivating Jewish health-care providers and providing consultation to congregations and health organizations. A critical underpinning of all our work is building a scholarly foundation for our field, through efforts like this book, and now with the support of the John Templeton Foundation, through a research roundtable to identify research priorities for the field, to catalyze applied research and evaluation, and to publish articles and other scholarly products.

"Midrash & Medicine: Imagining Wholeness"

We convened the "Midrash & Medicine: Imagining Wholeness" conference to foster collaboration through an exchange of learning and best practices among participants—to help them do the work of Jewish healing. Every Kalsman Institute gathering is built on the same model—to educate, exchange, and energize. At the conference, participants stimulated and nourished their personal and professional growth through text study and a retreat. With our partners from the Bay Area Jewish Healing Center and the many conference committee members from around the country, we engaged midrash as an interpretive and creative process to accomplish this growth, and we studied the intersection of Judaism and health through the prism of Jewish commentary—adding visual arts, song, poetry, and movement to the customary forms of commentary.

Hebrew Union College midrash professors teach that midrashic texts are viewed as a rich treasure for contemporary preaching and teaching. As Philip Cushman states later in this book, the process of midrash "emphasizes interpersonal engagement, critical interpretive processes, and playfulness." Cushman suggests that midrashic process takes place within a group—the "antithesis of hyperindividualism." This engagement came to life at the conference from which this set of essays is derived. Reflection on midrashic interpretation through the arts was a focus of our learning and play. Singer and songwriter Debbie Friedman created a healing song with her students before our very eyes. Andrea Hodos used movement to embody the midrash by helping participants think with their bodies and move with their minds. Elizheva Hurvich borrowed from Jo Milgrom's torn-paper midrash exercises to help conference attendees fill in the blanks of our texts and visually portray the poetry of the retreat experiences.

In addition to engaging the arts, another facet of "imagining wholeness" during the conference was the interdisciplinary nature of our *kahal*—our community. Conference attendees came from across the spectrum of Jewish religious and spiritual life and represented a wide variety of Jewish and medical disciplines.

In preparation for the conference, Natan Fenner, conference faculty and Bay Area Jewish Healing Center staff member, defined interpretive midrash as a creative process for drawing out meaning from a central text or experience using different modes of expression.

The Field of Judaism, Health, and Healing

The Kalsman Institute has sponsored numerous publications and forums since its inception. Articles, position papers, and theses by our colleagues and students chart the territory of health and Judaism, adding to a growing body of literature and scholarship. *Quality of Life in Jewish Bioethics* came out in 2006 through the institute's partnership with a coalition of Jewish bioethicists. The predecessor to this book was Dr. Cutter's *Healing and the Jewish Imagination: Spiritual and Practical Perspectives on Judaism and Health* (Jewish Lights). Several of the essays in that book were commissioned as keynote speeches for another international Kalsman conference, "Mining the Jewish Tradition." Some of the conference scholars noted that the exposure to our contemporary field was the first time they had extracted nuggets of insights on health and healing from Jewish traditions of prayer, ritual, narrative, and presence. Rabbi Arthur Green, distinguished scholar of theology and Jewish mystical thought, abandoned a lifelong distance from the healing aspect of Kabbalah to ponder the power of prayer and presence.[1] Bible professor Tamara Eskenazi had always been less resistant and established that "the Bible is a book of hope and a book of healing." She argued that texts traditionally used to punish or reject were actually balanced by depictions of restoring bodily and spiritual wholeness and integrity. Professor Eskenazi pointed out that the "Bible began as a response to crisis. Its early compilers aimed at restoring hope and providing healing to a people whose world had come undone."[2]

The work of the Kalsman Institute and other groups devoted to the field of Judaism, health, and healing is a modern version of this response to crisis. Social service agencies, grassroots groups, and synagogues developed health-related services and resources to meet the needs of contemporary Jews. Initial efforts of the Jewish healing movement were spearheaded by professionals and lay leaders who came to realize that, as a consequence of modern life, many Jews no longer had easy or meaningful access to the spiritual and communal supports that had sustained previous generations of Jews through difficult times of illness and loss. As noted by the leadership of the Jewish healing movement, these initiatives draw on wellsprings of Jewish thinking that speak to the religious tradition as a resource for comfort and solace.[3] Surely the vision of our generous founders, the Kalsman family, has been realized.

Second Generation

I am one of the Jews who did not have access to the support that could have sustained me in my family's time of illness and loss. I am the daughter of two Holocaust concentration-camp survivors. When prompted to reflect on my life, I consider being a "second generation" among the most significant elements of my identity. Both my parents, David and Regina Burdowski, of blessed memory, survived years of violence, starvation, and degradation. Their experiences framed the way they looked at the world and shaped my upbringing and outlook. The horrors they survived scarred them—and toughened me.

The legacy of being a child of survivors encourages me—forces me, really—to reflect continually on what I am supposed to do with my life, how to be a Jew, and how the world operates after the Holocaust.

My parents built a family after the horrors of their experiences. They both died too young. My mother died when she was only fifty-five (and I was sixteen). My mother's death and her pain and suffering during the majority of my lifetime significantly affected my growth and development. It also significantly affected my career. In high school, I saw myself headed for a career in medicine, but after too many years spent next to her hospital beds, I turned from that direction and moved toward the business world.

I needed twenty years to find my way back to the intersection of Judaism and health. During the many days spent at my mother's bedside, my family and I were never visited or called on by a member of the Jewish community or a health-care provider to offer support or comfort. No chaplain, social worker, rabbi. I never knew such a possibility existed, and when I discovered the concept, I made it my life's work to ensure that others would not live without this particular form of Jewish communal support.

A Tale of Healing

One of the pleasures of working in community to bring Jewish wisdom to the medical and Jewish communities is that the teacher learns while preparing to teach. While planning the "Midrash & Medicine" conference, faculty and committee members studied together frequently. I joined planning-committee members to gain exposure to the midrashic process, narrative, and Rabbinic texts from William Cutter, Eric Weiss, and Natan Fenner from the Bay Area Jewish Healing Center. Elliot Kukla and Julie Pelc (now Julie Pelc Adler), were key conference staff and faculty, and they chose a central text for the preparation stage of the conference, "Tilling Our Souls," based on part of Psalm 103: "The days of the human life are like grass in the field, indeed like grass" (Psalm 103:15).[4]

Kukla and Adler taught that in traditional midrash, the Rabbis layered meaning on a text by excerpting another text and linking the two through a common thread. The Rabbis used this line from Psalms to expound on a thought suggested in the book of Samuel. The midrash is a tale of healing. Pelc Adler and Kukla provided this translation and interpretation of the midrash:

> It is told of Rabbi Yishmael and Rabbi Akiva that, while they were walking through the streets of Jerusalem accompanied by a certain man, a sick person confronted them and said, "Masters, tell me, how shall I be healed?" They replied, "Take such-and-such, and you will be healed." The man accompanying the sages asked them, "Who smote him with sickness?"
>
> They replied, "The Holy One."
>
> The man: "And you bring yourselves into a matter that does not concern you? God smote and you would heal?"
>
> The sages (to the man): "What is your work?"
>
> The man: "I am a tiller of the soil...."
>
> The sages: "Who created the vineyard?"
>
> The man: "The Holy One."
>
> The sages: "Then why do you bring yourself into a matter that does not concern you? God created it, and you eat the fruit from it!"
>
> The man: "If I did not go out and plow the vineyard, prune it, compost it, and weed it, it would have yielded nothing."
>
> The sages: "Have you heard the verse, *'the days of the human life are like grass'* [Psalm 103:15]? A tree, it will not grow if not given water to drink, it will die—will not live. So, too, the human body is a tree: a healing potion is the compost, and the physician is the tiller of the soil."
>
> MIDRASH SAMUEL 4[5]

Comparing the human body to a living tree, and healing potions to compost, Rabbis Adler and Kukla drew from our Rabbinic sages to teach that our physicians and health-care providers are God's assistants responding to illness, pain, and crisis:

> No matter how rich the soil is by itself, if it's not tilled and broken up, the nutrients won't get in. This is the practice of studying texts ourselves and "breaking up" our own level of understanding. It is

also interesting to think of the image of parched earth: when there is a drought, the ground hardens and the healing elements of water and other nutrients just run off. When we are in pain, our "earth" can become hardened, too. We must "till" our soil in order for true healing to enter. Soil can only be tilled in relationship. We help one another "till," so that the healing potions can seep in.[6]

Our quest for spiritual intimacy, the holy work that Dayle Friedman offers in her essay, is satisfied by the work we do to facilitate health and healing. From the fourth prayer of the *Amidah* or *Shemoneh Esrei* (the nineteen central daily Jewish prayers and blessings), we pray for understanding:

> You graciously endow mortals with intelligence, teaching us wisdom and understanding. Grant us knowledge, discernment, and wisdom. Praised are You, *Adonai*, who graciously grants intelligence.[7]

Much work remains in the field of Judaism, health, and healing. I believe we will find the knowledge and discernment to draw on a deeply rooted wisdom that has much to say about the effects of illness even as it celebrates wellness of body, mind, and spirit.

ACKNOWLEDGMENTS

The author-editor is grateful to his many students, to Michele Prince, to Scarlet Newman-Thomas, and to Nanci Newman for support. Rabbi Joseph Hample brought wit and style to his work on this volume. Along the way, so many have made my work possible, including, of blessed memory, the men who first trusted me—my father, Jacob ben Ze'ev, and Alfred Gottschalk, who knew I would work out—and my mother, who somehow believed I had it in me. I trust that this current work is an adequate token of thanks. Thanks are due, also, to the folks at Jewish Lights: Stuart M. Matlins, Emily Wichland, and Lauren Hill, talented professionals who have been tolerant and patient.

Michele Prince brings her personal experience to bear on the institutional commitments of the Hebrew Union College–Jewish Institute of Religion. Coming later in life to the world of rabbinic thinking and Jewish communal work, Ms. Prince demonstrates that with deep sensitivity, lofty mind, and proper intention, one may grasp the spirit of the Jewish tradition that is alien to so many.

To my family: patriarch and matriarch, the son who is "all four sons," and to the true rabbi in our family, newest member and friend. To Mark and Peachy, kin of a kind, who make most things possible. Dedicated to the memory of the wise and witty Henry Levinson.

INTRODUCTION

It is a pleasure to present *Midrash & Medicine: Healing Body and Soul in the Jewish Interpretive Tradition*. Each author in this collection has a rare relationship to the world of care and healing and to the work of interpretation in religious community. The authors accept the reality that is the human condition, and yet they remain eager to modify that reality; they are critical of the way in which health care is conceived and delivered but deeply respectful of the caring men and women who have brought us to our amazing clinical successes. Their literary offerings here describe an effort to move beyond those successes. The reader will see in these pages—in essays on disparate subjects—a stubborn attention to the radical presence of individual people.

Two landmarks of past and present stand on either side of this volume. The first, a philosophical and historical monument, is the work of Moses Maimonides, physician, philosopher, and codifier of Jewish law. Whenever we think of healing in Judaism, we stand on the Rambam's shoulders. The other monument is the current situation in which we find ourselves: a time when the American people have decided to work toward making health care available to more people. Whenever we have hoped for healing, our current economic dilemmas have bedeviled us. My hope is that the spirit of Maimonides informs the aspirations of the American people to provide more physical cures and a fuller spiritual healing to more people. And I affirm, on behalf of the Kalsman Institute for Judaism and Health, that science and faith can be partners.

In this very year, the Kalsman Institute has begun to study the relations between science and faith and to explore the reaches and limits of empirical science in the world of healing. Through a grant from the Templeton Foundation, we will be able to continue that exploration.

The *Sugyot*/Pairings

Metaphors and Side Effects

In this pairing of essays, two remarkable spirits tackle well-known questions in an unusual way. Metaphors add meaning to experience, Simkha Y. Weintraub argues, and they even direct us to the healing needs of those who are suffering or in pain; Stuart Schoffman responds with a unique twist, noting that metaphors have side effects, just like medicines and even like our national movement, Zionism. The relationship among these three phenomena—metaphors, side effects, and the Jewish national home—adds a dimension to healing inquiry that few, if any, have thought of before. Rabbi Weintraub has been a leader of the Jewish healing movement for nearly two decades and has conducted workshops in which metaphor making is at the heart of the healing enterprise.

The Narrow Place from Which Healing Comes, and the Expansive Edge of the Continent

Rabbi Norman J. Cohen tackles two aspects of our total subject: a particular set of midrashim, and the more general way in which the literature of midrash works. In one sense, then, he suggests something about the relationship between medium and message, which has been the case he has made so often—sometimes in the pages of books published by Jewish Lights. In *Midrash & Medicine,* he brings the rhetorical illuminations of our public conference to the intimacy of our printed pages. His essay is joined to remarks from Rabbi Eric Weiss, director of the Bay Area Jewish Healing Center, which cosponsored the original conference in Monterey. Rabbi Weiss provides informal historical notes about the healing movement while considering the idea that language, like social movements, has an organic internal development that creates new ways of looking at things.

Lyric and Community

The author-editor of this volume joins with distinguished rabbi-pastor-poet Sheldon Marder to argue that poetry is especially strong when it helps people create reality—especially when reality is threatened by advanced age or illness. Here we see instances of creating a communal awareness of struggle and the rebound from struggle that humans are called upon to experience. In the case of each essay, the poetic form in question is often far from too many people's consciousness. It should be noted that both Rabbis Marder and Cutter enter into a field where distinguished physicians have already entered: Marc Straus, Rafael Campo, Robert Carroll, William Carlos Williams, and others for whom the pill, the scalpel, and the pen have been partners.

God in the Doctor's Office: Some Midrashic Elaborations

Abraham Joshua Heschel argued years ago that doctors shouldn't stray so far away from God. In that charge, Heschel's particular and romantic theology represented a bit of a threat to empirically oriented clinicians. But in this grouping of two essays some new thinking about the "God idea" comes to the foreground. The author-editor expresses his concern that a kind of literal anthropomorphism has created an embarrassment about what God might do in the doctor's office, while suggesting that thinking about God is an opportunity to contemplate the meaning of full communication and maximum discourse. Dr. Ronald M. Andiman challenges that solution by presenting a frank and concerned picture of the problems doctors face in their work— problems that may keep them from spiritual contemplation and theological fulfillment. It is noteworthy that I, the rabbi, am something of a spiritual skeptic, while Ron Andiman is a faithful synagogue Jew for whom the words of poetry have often served as keys to spiritual understanding. Dr. Andiman has actually used poetry in his training of young resident physicians.

Contexts of Suffering, Contexts of Hope

Ruhama Weiss's book *Committing My Soul* created a stir in Israel several years ago, but until now that book has not reached the English reading public. The translation gives us a look into a new reading (although shared with some scholars) of the meaning of a well-known Talmudic story about a famous case of visiting the sick. Was there really a secret society against the idea that suffering was noble? Whether or not there was, the Rabbis (as Professor David Kraemer of The Jewish Theological Seminary has also argued) clearly promoted a countercurrent to Judaism's effort to see suffering as having positive value. Rabbi Aryeh Cohen deepens our reading of

Dr. Weiss's essay with a justification for the way in which her material is presented. He celebrates and applauds Ruhama Weiss's effort to instate her argument in the midst of a real and living situation through her own dialogues with her study partner. Through this pairing, we can see that Dr. Weiss participates in *chavruta* in the ultimate sense.

Midrashic Renderings of Age and Obligation

This unit brings together two colleagues who have always appreciated each other's work and who have often referenced it in their other public oral and written presentations. Dr. Thomas Cole is a world famous thanatologist, gerontologist, and medical educator and has written as widely as he has read in the literature of aging. In this essay, he adds a rich comprehension of Christian thinking to the topic, coupled with his active engagement in Jewish life and literature. Both he and Rabbi Dayle A. Friedman urge now and have urged in the past that full recognition of the needs of the elderly be accompanied by an equally strong sense of elders' obligation to continue to serve society and to participate fully in society's problems and projects. Both thinkers have changed the landscape of aging in the United States.

Narrative and Loss

Eitan Fishbane's memoir comes out of personal tragedy and offers a perspective that is at one and the same time intimate and universal. As a scholar of Jewish thought, Dr. Fishbane's loss is reflected in his deep attachment to and occasional skepticism about the great tradition that enlivens his life and that he and his late wife shared so profoundly. His story includes improvised "midrash," while retaining as its main focus the particulars of experience over and against literary device. Dr. Linda S. Raphael demonstrates in her response that she can both be analytical and have compassion and empathy for the object of her academic study. Dr. Raphael is part of the new movement of narrative thinking that applies literature to the work of healing and the experience of loss. It has been a privilege to bring these two minds together, a privilege modified only by the sadness of our protagonist's loss.

The Dilemmas of Psychotherapy, the Healing Response of Midrash

This is an unusual pairing by two important students and thinkers—both engaged in one or another aspect of "hermeneutic psychology." For Dr. Philip Cushman, however, the interpretive turn is accompanied by a profound concern that most forms of psychotherapy perpetuate some of the problems they are designed to address. For Dr. Cushman, midrashic ways of thinking respond brilliantly to precisely what has been missing in much psychotherapy. Rabbi Lewis M. Barth, himself engaged in the school of psychotherapy that Cushman admires, believes that Cushman's insights are colored by a hopefulness that may not be fulfilled. The disagreement between people who agree is—in itself—somewhat "midrashic."

The Narrative Turn in Jewish Bioethics

Two ethicists try their hands at critiquing the dominant approaches to Jewish bioethics. Dr. Leonard A. Sharzer, rabbi and physician, brings his personal experience in the clinic to bear on his elegant understanding of the importance of *aggadah* for the way in which decisions are actually made when a case is "at hand." Dr. Jonathan Cohen probes further into the very theory of what narrative is and the limits of authority for resolving our deepest moral dilemmas. Narrative work, for Dr. Cohen, is a hedge against authoritarian excess and, in that view, he echoes from a different perspective the contentions of many authors in this collection. But Dr. Cohen argues that much Jewish aggadic thinking bears some of the same problems that liberals feel are evinced in *halakhah*.

What Takes Place and What Can Be Changed

Inspired by the work of Rabbi Richard Address, the Reform movement in Judaism has fostered deep attachment to healing communities and institutions that serve people whose needs are beyond the services of existing organs. In that spirit, Rabbi Julie Pelc Adler's call for new prayers represents the best of Reform thinking among the younger generation of leadership that is blessing the work of the American Jewish community: prayers for persistence in the face of difficulty. This case provides material for precisely the communities that Rabbi Address is helping to create.

1

Metaphors and Side Effects

Rabbi Simkha Y. Weintraub, LCSW, serves as rabbinic director of the Jewish Board of Family and Children's Services (JBFCS) and has led workshops on Jewish spiritual resources in confronting illness, trauma, and loss for rabbis and health professionals. Rabbi Weintraub edited *Healing of Soul, Healing of Body: Spiritual Leaders Unfold the Strength and Solace in Psalms* (Jewish Lights), and his book *Guide Me Along the Way: A Jewish Spiritual Companion for Surgery* was published by the National Center for Jewish Healing of JBFCS. Ordained by The Jewish Theological Seminary, he holds a master's degree in clinical social work from Columbia University.

L'Mashal
Metaphor and Meaning in Illness

Rabbi Simkha Y. Weintraub, LCSW

Let not a man say, "The Psalms are not Torah";
they are Torah, and the Prophets, too, are Torah,
and the riddles and the parables are also Torah.
MIDRASH PSALMS, ON PSALM 78:1

Do not underestimate the parable,
for it leads to the Torah's true meaning.
A penny wick may help to find a lost pearl.
SONG OF SONGS RABBAH 1.1.8

We are stories. Since you awakened this morning (and even before, asleep), you have been living today's story. Not only that, you have told yourself your ongoing story, consciously or not—who you are, what you are supposed to do, what challenges you face, what just happened and what might happen, and what your motivations and resources are.

An important part of your story, at various points in your unfolding narrative, is *metaphor*—the description of one thing in terms of another, such as when Shakespeare has Jaques say, "All the world's a stage."[1]

Dr. Mardy Grothe writes, "When people speak metaphorically, they make a connection between two conceptual domains that, at first glance, don't appear to have much in common with each other. A metaphor is a kind of magical mental changing room, where one thing, for a moment, becomes another, and in that moment is seen in a whole new way."[2]

Metaphors, of course, have powerful and far-reaching potential—for example, to encapsulate experiences, expectations, and emotions. We humans draw on metaphor even when we don't know it because we rely on metaphors to manage our lives—to digest what is going on in and around us, to reach for some influence on what is happening, and often, to reframe events and search for new perspectives.

Some years back, at St. Vincent's Medical Center in New York City, a group of doctors and other health-care professionals met in a monthly "Jewish Healing Torah Study Group." One month Dr. Lawrence A. Hoffman of Hebrew Union College–Jewish Institute of Religion in New York addressed "Prayer, Healing, and Metaphor" and commented that "medicine can address symptoms, and it can even cure illnesses, but you need a metaphor to make it through." Indeed, metaphor is a critical tool in confronting symptoms, tests, diagnoses, treatments, and all the trying points in navigating illness and disease.

This, of course, is not news to Jews and Judaism. The very essence of midrash—the seeking of more meaning from sacred texts and the lives of our forebears—depends on the tools of metaphor (along with its literary siblings: allegory, fable, personification, satire, and simile). Consider the following statements by two of the top healers in the Talmud:

> Rabbi Yehoshua ben Levi said: The Israelites are compared to an olive tree, because as the olive never sheds its leaves whether in winter or summer, so will the Israelites never cease to be, whether in this world or in the world to come. Rabbi Yochanan said: The Israelites are compared to an olive tree, because as the olive yields its oil only by hard pressure, so the Israelites do not return to righteousness except through suffering.
>
> BABYLONIAN TALMUD, MENACHOT 53B

Consider what the olive-tree metaphor might accomplish. For one thing, Rabbi Yehoshua ben Levi gives a morale-boosting context, a frame of reference: we Jews are as much a part of the natural ecology as the ubiquitous olive tree.[3] And in that olive tree, which holds its ground and flourishes its leaves year-round, we can imagine our collective blossoming and durability, our national identity and timelessness, which extends beyond this life. And Rabbi Yochanan, who buried ten children and sought to make sense of the great suffering in this life, uses the olive tree to reach for a narrative that is somehow intelligible and meaningful, even if, in some very real ways, ultimately unacceptable.[4]

Now, Jewish spiritual and pastoral care is dynamic and fluid; we would never "prescribe" a metaphor or rigidly insist on one. *It is the helpful nature of metaphors to shift and grow, to morph and expand in a chameleonlike manner.* See what happens in this famous narrative about Moses's resistance to his impending death:

> When Moshe heard his fate, he summoned every argument to secure a remission of his sentence.
>
> Among other things, he said, "Master of the universe! Arise from the Seat of Judgment and sit on the Throne of Mercy, so that I do not die. Let my sins be forgiven by reason of the bodily sufferings that may come upon me. But put me not in the power of the Angel of Death. If you will do this, then will I proclaim your praise before all the inhabitants of the world, as David said, 'I shall not die but live, and declare the works of *HaShem*' [Psalm 118:17]."
>
> Then God said to Moshe, "Hear the rest of the verse, 'This is the gate of *HaShem*, through which the righteous shall enter' [Psalm 118:20]."
>
> For all creatures death has been prepared from the beginning.
>
> PARAPHRASE OF *TANCHUMA*,
> BUBER EDITION, *VA-ET'CHANAN* 6A

Moses thought that he could utilize the "heavenly architecture" for his case, his argument, urging God to shift from the Seat of Judgment to the Throne of Mercy. The sufferings (Judgment) that may come upon him, he reasoned, could happily serve an atoning function and pave the way for continued life (Mercy). And like the rest of us, perhaps, Moses throws into the bargain a bribe of flattery—"I will proclaim your praise," giving as his proof text the words of King David the Psalmist, "I shall not die but live."

Brilliantly, God—the Rabbi, after all, of our Rabbi Moses—then does two things: (1) God directs Moses to read on in the psalm he has quoted, to see the ultimate disposition that awaits the righteous— Death; but (2) *God also enters and redirects the "heavenly architecture" metaphor that Moses has highlighted.* "Death," God says, "is a heavenly *gate* through which the righteous, such as yourself, Moses, shall [must] enter." The issue is no longer God's *seats* of Judgment and Mercy but God's *gate.* As the Kotzker Rebbe put it centuries later: "Fear not death. It is just a matter of going from one room to another, ultimately to the most beautiful room."[5]

In our contemporary society, I have experienced quite a variety of metaphors for people's illness journeys. Here are seven voices/vignettes from the field:

"Seven years ago, I went through all the tests, the surgery, the treatments, like a real trooper. And I not only negotiated the needs of my spouse and kids, but complied with all that everyone told me I had to do ... and I got a clean bill of health as my reward. But now it's back, and I just don't have the energy to enlist again—I want to be discharged from the service, and return to civilian life—but I can't, I'm not allowed to."

A MEMBER OF A SYNAGOGUE, FACING A CANCER
RECURRENCE, SPEAKING TO A *BIKKUR CHOLIM* VOLUNTEER

"I'm on my knees; an abject servant of the Almighty. I'll do anything He wants. But without my mom, my world is collapsing. So I acknowledge my lowliness and seek only to do what the Master wants, if only He will spare her."

THE ADULT CHILD OF A WOMAN (NOW CLINGING TO LIFE
IN THE ICU, AFTER A HORRIBLE ACCIDENT), TO A RABBI

"I showed up at the 'repair shop' today. I arrived at 1:00—I was scheduled for 1:10, and at 1:07 the '1:20' checked in. The receptionist-foreman at the front desk didn't look up when I spoke my name to her. Moments later: 'Shapiro! Copay twenty dollars!' Soon, I was led to the examining room and hoisted myself up, waiting to have my 'oil change.'"

A PATIENT REPORTING ON A RECENT MEDICAL
APPOINTMENT AT A JEWISH SPIRITUAL SUPPORT GROUP

"Shul has been impossible for me, ever since I heard those words on *Yom Tov*—'Who shall live and who shall die; who in the fullness of years and who before his time....' Ever since our son was diagnosed with cancer, I'm a box of kindling wood, saturated with gasoline, and I feel like all around me are matches waiting to set me off. Not just 'what kind of God is this?!' but 'why are people complaining about their bad haircuts, worried about their cash shortfall, pained by their inability to take vacations?'"

THE PARENT OF A SON IN CHEMOTHERAPY,
SPEAKING TO A RABBI

"It was the death of my final dream. I had thought that I would be a mother, but I didn't meet Al until I was thirty-nine. And, of course, he packed his bags just as I turned forty-three. And now, at forty-five, this diagnosis!? I am witnessing my own funeral."

C., WHOSE RECENT BIOPSIES ARE POSITIVE, SUMMARIZING
HER STORY IN A JEWISH SPIRITUAL SUPPORT GROUP

"In my whole life I have never felt like this. There are people like you who try to help, but I am living in a thick plexiglass container that nobody can truly penetrate. Sometimes I see lips moving but the words don't convey anything. I'm cut off from the world of the living and now reside in the world of the suspended, looking out at life."

A SIXTY-THREE-YEAR-OLD WOMAN, NOW COPING
WITH ILLNESS, TO A *BIKKUR CHOLIM* VOLUNTEER

"Throughout Mom's illness, as throughout her life, I was subject to abuse. Though the community saw her as a generous, and even selfless, public servant, she treated me like [expletive]. She insisted that I do this and that, and then criticized anything I tried to do. She maligned me to everyone, and she pitted my brother and his family against me. She wiped her shoes on me. I was her doormat."

AN ABUSED DAUGHTER, WHOSE MOTHER WAS
NOW IN HOSPICE CARE, TO A RABBI

In fact, at the New York Jewish Healing Center, we once made a list of metaphors that have been used in discussing/exploring suffering and/or illness: war, battle, struggle, fight; journey, travel; maze, puzzle; script, play, dramatic role; race, competition, marathon; challenge, test, trial, exam; punishment, sentence; exile, homecoming; purge, cleansing, purification; story, narrative, poem, verse; storm, earthquake; burden, weight, cross to bear; gardening, landscaping, pruning; building, construction, renovation.

If we seek to be present for those who are suffering, and perhaps to help them in some way, we need to know their unique and shifting metaphors. Our task, and our privilege, is to be open to each individual's metaphors, to be curious about their shape, meaning, and evolution, and to be sensitively reflective in response.

Which brings us to the role of the healer, or the helping one. Here, too, the possible metaphors are many; the list might include the following: advocate, intermediary; choreographer, conductor; witness, audience; sparring partner, punching bag; *Tzelem Elokim,* image of God; *shaliach,* agent, messenger; donkey, burden sharer; fellow traveler.

Those of us who want to be present and helpful to those who are suffering need to know our own metaphors, to name/carry our "calling," purpose, tasks, and activities—and like the metaphors of the individuals we are trying to help, they must, generally, be somewhat flexible and permeable. Witness this classic Jewish narrative, again involving the third-century scholar and healer Rabbi Yochanan:

Rabbi Yochanan had the misfortune [lit., "was chastised," from heaven] to suffer from gallstones for three and a half years. Once Rabbi Chanina went to visit him. He said to him, "How do you feel?" He replied, "My sufferings are worse than I can bear!" He said to him, "Don't speak so, but say, 'The faithful God.'" When the pain was very great he used to say, "faithful God," and when the pain was greater than he could bear, Rabbi Chanina used to go to him and utter an incantation that gave him relief. Subsequently Rabbi Chanina fell ill, and Rabbi Yochanan went to see him. Rabbi Yochanan said to him, "How do you feel?" Rabbi Chanina replied, "How grievous are my sufferings!" Rabbi Yochanan said to him, "But surely the reward for them is also great!" Rabbi Chanina replied, "I want neither them nor their reward." Rabbi Yochanan said to him, "Why do you not utter that incantation that you pronounced over me and that gave me relief?" Rabbi Chanina replied, "When I was out of trouble I could be a surety for others, but now that I am myself in trouble, do I not require another to be a surety for me?"

SONG OF SONGS RABBAH 2:46

Once again we have two "top healers" of the Talmud interacting and, in this case, exploring their roles. Rabbi Chanina first gave Rabbi Yochanan a kind of mantra to utilize—"the faithful God"[6]—but when the pain persisted and intensified, he utilized an incantation that brought Rabbi Yochanan relief. When the tables were turned, and Rabbi Chanina became the one visited by Rabbi Yochanan, the latter wondered why Chanina didn't utilize the same incantation for himself. And Rabbi Chanina responds with a powerful metaphor—that of a "surety," in Hebrew, *eiravon*, which suggests a guarantee, a deposit, a bond, or a pledge. It seems that the understanding was that the *bikkur cholim* visitor, in a certain sense, "stands in" for the one who is ill, perhaps, by "representing his/her interests," advocating both on earth and vis-à-vis the One Healer of All, in heaven.

This same metaphor surfaces in a powerful *aggadah* (Rabbinic narrative) about five disciples coming to visit Rabbi Yochanan after the death of one of his children. Four of them step forward, open their mouths and get it wrong—they each suggest, in effect, that Rabbi Yochanan can "pull himself out of it," pointing to the biblical stories of Adam, Aaron, Job, and King David, who each lost children and somehow went on. Deep in his grief, Rabbi Yochanan cannot tolerate their words and rebuffs them each with "Is not my own sorrow enough for me, that you have to make mention of Adam's!" But then the fifth disciple, Elazar ben Arak, enters:

"Let me tell you a parable," he said to Yochanan. "A king gave a man an object in trust. Day by day the man wept and cried out, 'Woe is me! When can I be free from the responsibility of this trust?' You, too, my Master, had a son, a scholar of Torah, learned in the Five Books of Moses, in the Prophets, and in the Writings, as well as in Mishnah, *halakhah*, and *aggadot*. He has departed sinless from this world. You should receive comfort for having restored your trust whole."

Yochanan replied, "You have comforted me as far as any man can."

AVOT D'RABBI NATAN 14

To be sure, there are many factors here, but surely the thoughtful metaphor of a trust, and of the restoration of that trust to its (divine) Owner, seems to have carried some meaning for Rabbi Yochanan.

In this connection it is worthwhile to point to the metaphor of *hashavat aveidot*, "the return of lost possessions," an important *mitzvah* in our tradition:

If you see your fellow's ox or sheep gone astray, do not ignore it; you must take it back to your fellow. If your fellow does not live near you or you do not know who he is, you shall bring it home and it shall remain with you until your fellow claims it; then *you shall restore it to him*. You shall do the same with his ass; you shall do the same with his garment; and so too shall you do with anything that your fellow loses and you find: you may not hide yourself.

DEUTERONOMY 22:1–3

Maimonides, the leading twelfth-century rabbi, physician, legal expert, and philosopher, uses these verses from Deuteronomy 22 as the basis of a binding religious obligation to render medical care:

It is obligatory from the Torah for the physician to heal the sick and this is included in the explanation of the scriptural phrase *"and you shall restore it to him,"* meaning to heal his body.

MAIMONIDES, *MISHNAH COMMENTARY*, ON *NEDARIM* 4:4

Earlier scholars had used other biblical texts to establish the physician's obligation to heal the sick, but Maimonides chose to utilize this source—and this metaphor.[7] If we pause for a moment to consider it, the metaphor of returning lost possessions may trigger some thought-provoking questions for our work with those who suffer:

- What loss might I restore to this person who I am trying to help/to heal?
- Even if I cannot restore what I would like, what loss can I address, can I mollify?
- Is there an aspect of the lost possession, or an equivalent, that I can reasonably aim to restore?
- Losses need to be grieved. How can I be present for or facilitate some grieving?

Now, curiosity is a, if not *the*, major tool in Jewish pastoral care and Jewish spiritual healing. Relating to another person as a fellow image of God, we want to know what makes him tick, how she has faced previous challenges in life, when life has shone and when it has been shrouded in darkness. And metaphors are critical in this exploration.

Let's illustrate this with one of the "voices" above. Let's call her "J" and the healer/helper "H."

"In my whole life I have never felt like this. There are people like you who try to help, but I am living in a thick plexiglass container that nobody can truly penetrate. Sometimes I see lips moving but the words don't convey anything. I'm cut off from the world of the living and now reside in the world of the suspended, looking out at life."

A SIXTY-THREE-YEAR-OLD WOMAN, NOW COPING
WITH ILLNESS, TO A *BIKKUR CHOLIM* VOLUNTEER

Here's how the ensuing conversation began to unfold:

H: You said "cut off" and "suspended"—how does it make you feel?
J: Lonely, hurt, and angry ... and without any hope.
H: Because the people, like me, can't change your situation?

J: I guess I don't expect you to change it ... but what's hard is that I can't expect you to really "know" it, to "get" it. It's like I'm on another planet.

H: I wish I could know it more and help you more.

J: I know. That's when there's a kind of window in this thick plexiglass, I guess.

H: I can listen to anything you want to tell me, if that can help.

J: That really, really helps.

In this exchange, the "restoration" that takes place is obviously not one of physical health, but of relationship. J had powerfully illustrated her isolated, cut-off existence, and H did not challenge J's metaphor, conceptually, but rather "entered" it, experientially. The restoration that both J and H truly want cannot happen, at least not immediately, but sincere and respectful human connection can be reaffirmed. The thick plexiglass container is still there, but a window has been discovered and opened.

Recently, in a Jewish spiritual support group for Jewish survivors of a loved one's suicide, one of the traumatized participants, trying to gain a foothold in unsteady ground after a relative's suicide, expressed the idea that she, herself, "was not courageous enough" to take her own life "in the face of all this pain and suffering." "Do you think he was *heroic*?" someone challenged, earnestly and respectfully. "No—he isn't a hero," she replied, to which the questioner said, "I think you're *too courageous* to do something like that, to yourself and those who love you. It takes *courage* to live on." And the group, in various ways, affirmed that living on is both necessary and heroic. A metaphor "metamorphosed"!

We can, in fact, glean much guidance from the world of midrash for our work in Jewish healing, in Jewish pastoral and spiritual care. There are over 550 times, in *Midrash Rabbah* alone, that our Rabbis, in expounding on the biblical text, say "*l'mashal /* as an example ..." and offer a thought-provoking parable or metaphor. Though their intent is certainly to offer insights, perspectives, and teachings, these narratives or images are never offered as "You must view it in this particular way" but rather "Consider this angle on the situation." In fact, in the midrash, the Rabbis sometimes pile these up, one on top of the next, without concern for how they might conflict with, or even dismantle, each other.

And that's because they are all needed. Torah is life, and life is stories. And stories—yours, mine, and the next person's—depend on metaphor. What's yours?

Stuart Schoffman, MPhil, is a fellow at the Shalom Hartman Institute in Jerusalem and editor of *Havruta: A Journal of Jewish Conversation*. A graduate of Harvard and Yale, he has worked as a Hollywood screenwriter, a journalist for *Time* and the *Jerusalem Report*, and a teacher at several American universities. His translations from Hebrew include books by David Grossman and A. B. Yehoshua.

From Heaven to Hypochondria
Metaphors of Jewish Healing

Stuart Schoffman, MPhil

The World to Come

Let us begin in Babylonia:

> Moreover, it has been taught: A scholar should not reside in a city where the following ten things are not found: a court of justice that imposes flagellation and decrees penalties; a charity fund collected by two and distributed by three; a synagogue; public baths; a convenience; a circumciser; a surgeon; a notary; a slaughterer; and a schoolmaster. Rabbi Akiva is quoted [as including] also several kinds of fruit, because these are beneficial to the eyesight.
>
> BABYLONIAN TALMUD, *SANHEDRIN* 17B,
> SONCINO TRANSLATION

In the Hebrew, that final phrase is *me'erin et ha-einayim*, which literally means "to light up the eyes" and metaphorically means whatever you choose: wisdom, illumination, discovery, enlightenment, revelation. "Fruit" surely does not mean only pomegranates, with their salubrious free radicals and antioxidants that control your blood sugar, but also the fruits of Torah, which elsewhere the Rabbis compare to a fertile, multiseeded pomegranate. The Soncino translators quoted above took a more scientific approach, turning Rabbi Akiva into an ophthalmologist. In biblical Hebrew, the word for "pomegranate" is *rimon*. In modern Israeli Hebrew, it also means "hand grenade." In a famous Talmudic parable, it is explained that Rabbi Meir, who learned Torah from the brilliant apostate rabbi known as Acher ("the other"), "found a pomegranate, ate the insides, and threw away the peel" (Babylonian Talmud, *Chagigah* 15b).

I have not traveled widely in Tractate *Sanhedrin*. My only systematic study of that text was twenty years ago, when I was undergoing chemotherapy for acute T-cell non-Hodgkin's lymphoma. I had free time on my hands and so did my father, a retired professor of Hebrew, and we decided to study a little Talmud together in *chavruta*, and he picked the eleventh chapter of *Sanhedrin*, known as *Perek Helek*. My brain was somewhat addled by drugs, which may be why I didn't protest. *Perek Helek*, you see, deals with the afterlife. *Perek* means "chapter"; *helek* means "portion." Here's how it famously begins:

> All Israel have a portion in the world to come, for it is written, "Your people are all righteous; they shall inherit the land for ever, the branch of my planting, the work of my hands, that I may be glorified" [Isaiah 60:21]. But the following have no portion therein: he who maintains that resurrection is not a biblical doctrine, the Torah was not divinely revealed, and an *epikoros*. Akiva added: One who reads uncanonical books. Also one who whispers [a charm] over a wound and says, "I will bring none of these diseases upon you which I brought upon the Egyptians: for I am *Adonai* who heals you" [Exodus 15:26]. Abba Saul says: Also one who pronounces the divine name as it is spelled.
>
> BABYLONIAN TALMUD, *SANHEDRIN* 90A

In other words, every Jew gets an afterlife, except for the ones who don't. Heretics and fake healers need not apply. Only those who believe in the afterlife deserve to partake of it. Ergo, to be on the safe side, one may as well believe. This is known in the philosophical trade as Pascal's Wager and has been aptly summarized by Woody Allen: "I don't believe in an afterlife, although I am bringing a change of underwear."[1] Now you see why my father, the rationalist professor, chose this chapter. He was about eighty at the time, and I with my aggressive cancer was eighty in a metaphorical sense, and he was telling me what to pack, just in case.

My father was a modern Orthodox Jew with a love of Greek and Latin classics, which means he flunked Rabbi Akiva's stipulation about reading uncanonical books. But it was always clear which side he was on. His favorite legend (*aggadah*) in *Perek Helek* describes an encounter between Queen Cleopatra and Rabbi Meir, which uncannily prefigures Woody Allen's midrash on Pascal. Cleopatra (a shapely Talmudic trope for Greek civilization) asks the rabbi: When the dead are resurrected, "shall they arise nude or in their garments?" The rabbi wins:

> He replied, "You may deduce by *a fortiori* argument [the answer] from a wheat grain: if a grain of wheat, which is buried naked, sprouts forth in many robes, how much more so the righteous, who are buried in their raiment!"
>
> BABYLONIAN TALMUD, *SANHEDRIN* 90B

A fortiori is Latin for the Talmud's *al achat kamah v'khamah*, which means "all the more so" or "it is even likelier to be the case." The Latin, literally, is "from the stronger." A Hebrew equivalent, *kal vakhomer*, may be translated legalistically as "lenient and severe," but I prefer "light and heavy," a metaphor that suggests not only trumping, but an ongoing dialectic of body and soul. And surely Rabbi Meir, when he speaks of "raiment," is using a metaphor for the gossamer garb of the spirit, not the material weave of Cleopatra's knickers. Garments disintegrate, memories endure.

Hundreds of years later, in his commentary on *Perek Helek*, Moses Maimonides enumerated his famous Thirteen Principles of Faith, incumbent on every Jew, the last of which is belief in the resurrection of the dead. Ever since then, Jews have argued over whether he really meant it. In that same introduction to "Chapter 11," the wise doctor wrote of the bankruptcy of literalist thinking:

> You must know that the words of the Sages are differently interpreted by three groups of people. The first group is the largest

one.... They accept the teachings of the Sages in their simple literal sense and do not think that these teachings contain any hidden meaning at all. They believe that all sorts of impossible things must be. They hold such opinions because they have not understood science.

The second group, says Maimonides, also take the Rabbis literally, but in the opposite sense: they dismiss these "impossible" things as poppycock, proof that science overrules faith. "Most of those who have stumbled into this error are involved with medicine or astrology," he says. The third group is tiny, and "consists of men to whom the greatness of our Sages is clear." These people know, says the Rambam,

that the Sages did not speak nonsense.... Thus, whenever the Sages spoke of things that seem impossible, they were employing the style of riddle and parable which is the method of truly great thinkers. For example, the greatest of our wise men [Solomon] began his book [Proverbs] by saying: "To understand an analogy and a metaphor, the words of the wise and their riddles."[2]

Maimonides, a medical man, understood science. He also understood that the afterlife itself, for his patients and everyone else, is a beautiful metaphor—spiritual therapy for the human condition. Whatever else it may be, we may never know. In any event, *dayenu*.

Metaphor as Therapy

I picked up the Rabbi Akiva fruit-recommendation story from *Sanhedrin* 17b via a footnote in a book of jokes. This was no ordinary book of jokes, but *The Book of Jokes and Wit* (*Sefer HaBedikha VeHaKhidud*), a classic three-volume compendium first published in 1922 in Tel Aviv by the Hebrew writer Alter Druyanov, who had lately made *aliyah* from Odessa.[3] There are more than three thousand jokes in the collection, many of them dated and unfunny. Like metaphors, jokes need to be refreshed.

Druyanov's footnote cites just a few words from that passage in *Sanhedrin*, the bit about the doctor, to explain the setup of the joke:

Guy goes to the town rabbi, says, "Rabbi, we have learned in the Talmud that scholars are not permitted to live in a town with no doctors, so how come we can live here, in a town with no doctor?" The rabbi answers, "Relax, there's a guy in town who everybody *thinks* is a doctor," but then the joke gets convoluted, so I'll skip to a better one, while we're on the subject of Latin:

> Why is Latin called a dead language? —Because the doctors, the partners of the Angel of Death, use it.[4]

Ouch. That midrash is too close to home. My high-octane chemotherapy had many nasty side effects, some of them life-threatening, the worst of which kicked in five years later: leukemia. This meant more chemo, plus radiation, a stem-cell transplant, and a new raft of side effects. The whole time, it felt like I was fighting the treatment as well as the disease, and I expressed my feelings in an avalanche of metaphors. I e-mailed friends that my many weeks in the hospital were like being a prisoner of war in the Hanoi Hilton, only with slightly better food. I used to refer to chemo as "leechcraft"—brutal, effective, and destined (one hoped) for speedy obsolescence (though I now gather that leeches are making a comeback). My battles with cancer and its attendant maladies, I used to imagine, were like thwacking enemies with a heavy iron sword on a rickety footbridge over a bottomless ravine. When you're as sick as I was, you don't care how many metaphors you mix. If the cocktail gets you through the day, the stronger the better.

For many patients, metaphor is integral to healing. But such metaphors have their own side effects. Here I invoke the late Susan Sontag, whose *Illness as Metaphor*, penned during her first bout with breast cancer, is an elegant polemic against the entire notion. Illness is bad enough as it is, she said. It does not need to be anything else:

> My point is that illness is *not* a metaphor, and that the most truthful way of regarding illness—and the healthiest way of being ill—is one most purified of, most resistant to, metaphoric thinking. Yet it is hardly possible to take up residence in the country of the ill unprejudiced by the lurid metaphors with which it has been landscaped.[5]

Sontag, as a woman of the left, was especially opposed to the military imagery of cancer and its treatment. That comparison, she said, valorizes violence, and she wanted no part of it. As an inveterate Israeli peacenik, I get what she meant. But as a cancer survivor, an unexpired passport holder of the country of the ill, I draw strength from the knowledge that I once fought like a tiger. It feels good to be a battle-scarred survivor. And as a Jew, I like feeling tough. God knows, it beats being weak. But there are side effects to this, too.

Is it lurid to liken cancer to a multiclawed crab? Perhaps, but that's how the disease got its name, back in ancient Greece. (In Hebrew, *sartan* means both the crustacean and the disease.) Sontag argued that the mythologizing of illness gives rise to dangerous misunderstanding. Cancer, she wrote, is thought by some to "stem from the repression" of emotion, just as tuberculosis in the nineteenth century was ascribed to "being too full of passion." Such thinking turns cancer into a disease of the spirit, encouraging patients to believe that a failure of character had caused it in the first place, and this is a bad thing.

Here I agree. When I was sick in the 1990s, well-intentioned friends brought me best-selling books about spiritual healing and cancer. I opened one or two and discovered they were predicated on an argument I could not accept: since cancer patients had in some way brought the illness upon themselves, they could make themselves well by thinking positively and being hopeful. I put the books on a shelf, ignored the self-blaming bit, and went straight to the hopeful part.

Of all the metaphors that helped me through that difficult time, the one that worked best is an ancient trope that worked its way into Kabbalah and Hasidism, as well as various Jewish heresies—*Yeridah letzorech aliyah*, which means going way down so you can rise way up. The phrase is originally Talmudic:

> Rabbi Abbahu asked Rabbi Yochanan, "If while a person is going up a ladder, a rung giving way under him comes down and kills somebody, how would this be taken? Was the death to be considered [a result] of an upward or a downward movement?" He replied, "You have indeed laid your finger on a downward motion

as a prerequisite of an upward movement [*yeridah tzorech aliyah*]." To this Rabbi Abbahu objected.

BABYLONIAN TALMUD, MAKKOT 7B

This is the kind of hair-splitting *pilpul* (Talmudic argumentation) that drove me mad as a yeshiva boy in Brooklyn. But the arid legalism became a soaring metaphor, and I embraced it avidly in the depths of my cancer treatment. It is used to great poetic effect in Chaim Nachman Bialik's Hebrew translation of S. Ansky's famous Yiddish play *The Dybbuk*, also known as *Between Two Worlds*. At the beginning of the play before the curtain rises, mysterious voices are heard:

> *Al mah v'lamah yoredet haneshamah*
> *Me'igra rama l'vira amikta?*
> *Yeridah tzorech aliyah hi*
> *Yeridah tzorech aliyah hi*

I translate freely: "Why, oh why, does the soul plummet from on high, down to the deepest pit? Here is the descent that enables the arising." *Me'igra rama l'vira amikta* is not Hebrew but Aramaic, a marvelous image that originates in a comment about the book of Lamentations from Tractate *Chagigah* and means "from a high roof to a deep pit." Do Ansky's "two worlds" conjure sickness and health? Is getting cancer like being possessed by a dybbuk, and is chemo a kind of exorcism? Maybe, if that helps the patient. For most people, it's the chemo itself that flings you into the muddy pit and wrings you out like a *shmateh* (a wet rag), but then (one can only hope) you are lifted up— way, way up—to sway gently on the clothesline, like a nice clean sheet on a warm, sunny day, and get well.

Our tradition is replete with stories of *yeridah letzorech aliyah*: Abraham going down to Egypt in Genesis 12, and Joseph and the whole House of Jacob many years later; Jonah in the belly of the big fish; Jewish exiles in Babylon, who dreamed of Zion and returned there. *Yeridah letzorech aliyah* was also how the followers of Sabbatai Zevi, the charismatic false messiah of the seventeenth century, explained his shocking conversion to Islam, and maybe they were right: his heresy, some have argued, enabled the rise of political Zionism, which usurped the Orthodox messianic tradition.

In common usage, the words *aliyah* (going up) and *yeridah* (going down) are of course Zionist metaphors. Am I suggesting that my own *aliyah*, my being an Israeli, is a factor in my recovery? As Chou En-lai said of the French Revolution, it's too early to tell, but I will say this: living in Jerusalem does envelop me in the up-and-down worlds of Jewish spiritual dialectics—the *Yerushalayim shel matah* (earthly Jerusalem) of quotidian concerns and fears, the *Yerushalayim shel malah* (heavenly Jerusalem) of undying hope and magical thinking. What comes down, we make ourselves believe, must also go up. And this too: here in Israel, we have universal health insurance.

Freeing Our Minds

Finally, we arrive at the trickiest, most perilous application of illness metaphors. Until now we have discussed the use of metaphor to describe the disease, which if practiced with care, can yield healthy results. But what happens when people use the disease as a metaphor for something else? Here, we run into big trouble, not least from a Jewish perspective.

In the Middle Ages, Jews were accused of poisoning wells and causing plague. Centuries later, elaborating on the same toxic theme, Hitler in *Mein Kampf* ranted about the Jewish infection of German society:

> Was there any shady undertaking, any form of foulness, especially in cultural life, in which at least one Jew did not participate? On putting the probing knife carefully to that kind of abscess one immediately discovered, like a maggot in a putrescent body, a little Jew who was often blinded by the sudden light.... Here was a pestilence, a moral pestilence, with which the public was being infected. It was worse than the Black Plague of long ago.[6]

In his book *The Nazi War on Cancer*, the Stanford University historian Robert N. Proctor writes of the proliferation of Nazi disease metaphors—"Joseph Goebbels routinely castigated the objects of his contempt as 'cancers' or 'malignancies'"—and describes a lecture in

Frankfurt in 1936 in which an SS radiologist compared cells to Jews, and "the X-rays launched against these tumor-Jews as Nazi storm troopers."[7] In our own day, a few moments of googling will turn up a website called "Palestine Monitor," claiming that "Israel is a malignant cancer because of the many ways it invades, intrudes upon, and destroys Palestinian lives," and also a Jewish website called "Masada 2000," which brands Israel's Arab citizens as a "cancer [that] has been left to fester much too long already." Susan Sontag, with cool precision, identified the larger problem:

> No specific political view seems to have a monopoly on this metaphor. Trotsky called Stalinism the cancer of Marxism.... John Dean explained Watergate to Nixon: "We have a cancer within— close to the Presidency—that's growing."... The cancer metaphor seems hard to resist for those who wish to register indignation.... But the modern disease metaphors are all cheap shots.... Only in the most limited sense is any historical event or problem like an illness. And the cancer metaphor is particularly crass. It is invariably an encouragement to simplify what is complex and an invitation to self-righteousness, if not to fanaticism.[8]

Again, she is right. To call something a cancer is to demand a radical cure—amputation, excision, perhaps nuking. But does this disqualify the use of any disease as a metaphor for something political? How about the plague of anti-Semitism? Years ago, at a conference, I heard Elie Wiesel say that anti-Semitism is a gentile disease from which Jews die. It's a fine one-liner that brings to mind a trenchant argument that was laid out in 1882 by Leon Pinsker, a medical doctor from Odessa and master diagnostician of the Jewish condition. In his tract "Auto-Emancipation," written in the wake of pogroms that followed the assassination of Czar Alexander II, the Zionist thinker launched a salvo of disease metaphors that may seem as obsolete as Druyanov's jokes. But from where I sit, it's a midrash still worth pondering:

> Among the living nations of the earth the Jews are as a nation long since dead. With the loss of their country, the Jewish people lost their independence.... But after the Jewish people had ceased

to exist as an actual state ... they lived on spiritually as a nation. The world saw in this people the uncanny form of one of the dead walking among the living.... This spectral form without precedence in history, unlike anything that preceded or followed it, could but strangely affect the imagination of the nations.... A fear of the Jewish ghost has passed down the generations and the centuries ... [and] it culminated in Judeophobia....

Judeophobia is a variety of demonopathy with the distinction that it is not peculiar to particular races but is common to the whole of mankind, and that this ghost is not disembodied like other ghosts but partakes of flesh and blood, must endure pain inflicted by the fearful mob who imagines itself endangered.

Judeophobia is a psychic aberration. As a psychic aberration it is hereditary, and as a disease transmitted for two thousand years it is incurable.[9]

Okay, okay, doc, we get the depressing point, but what's the cure for this spooky atrophy, this pit of prejudice and persecution? Pinsker's remedy, as he says in the title, is "auto-emancipation." Jews need to declare themselves a proud nation and seize independence. This is the essence of Zionism, and as any Rastafarian can tell you, the metaphor of Zion transcends ethnicity and religious borders. In the late twentieth century, the Jamaican folk hero Bob Marley captured the idea in his reggae classic "Redemption Song": "Emancipate yourselves from mental slavery, none but ourselves can free our minds." A good chemo tune for the iPod. The stronger the cocktail, the better the odds.

But the Jewish Patient, says Dr. Pinsker, is not so easy to treat:

The greatest impediment in the path of the Jews to an independent national existence is that they do not feel its need. Not only that, but they go so far as to deny its authenticity. In the case of a sick man, the absence of desire for food is a very serious symptom. It is not always possible to cure him of this ominous loss of appetite. And even if his appetite is restored, it is still a question whether he will be able to digest food, even though he desire it. The Jews are in the unhappy condition of such a patient. We must discuss this most important point with all possible precision. We must prove that the misfortunes of the Jews are due, above all, to their lack of desire for national independence; and that this desire must be awakened and maintained in time if they do not wish to be subjected forever to disgraceful existence—in a word, we must prove that *they must become a nation.*[10]

Hungry or not, the reader is pelted by a feast of metaphors, as befits a Jewish food fight. Here's what he means: Judeophobia, also known as anti-Semitism, has deformed the Jew. The deformed Jew must re-form himself, as a proud member of a separate nation—a nation that is Jewish the way Russia was Russian. Indeed the anti-Semitic trope of the diseased nature of the Jew is spun in Zionist discourse into a case of *yeridah letzorech aliyah.* Anti-Semitism pounds the Jew to a pulp, degrades and emasculates him, brings him to the point of self-loathing, which only encourages the loathing of others. The cure: Jewish sovereignty, *aliyah* to Eretz Yisrael.

Such ideas did not sit well with Jews in the democracies of Western Europe or America, who were striving to become upstanding citizens of the Mosaic persuasion, and succeeding quite nicely. They were not inclined to pick up and move to Palestine, a dusty Ottoman backwater. When Theodor Herzl invented the Jewish State in 1897, he met with strong opposition from Jewish leaders and opinion makers, some of whom laughably tried to besmirch him as being into Zionism for the money.

Herzl, a playwright and journalist by trade, returned fire with an essay titled "The Family Affliction," first published in January 1899 in *The American Hebrew*—my very favorite Jewish medical midrash. The very first line sets the stage: "Anyone who wants to work in behalf of the Jews needs—to use a popular phrase—a strong stomach." His Zionist agenda, he writes, has been roundly attacked by Jews who accuse him of being a charlatan, a messianic pretender, a con man. Not so, he says; these Jews are afraid of standing up as Jews and demanding a country of their own. "For they themselves," he declares at the very end, "are the family affliction: the Jews who want to be anything but Jews."

That's the argument. Like any good midrash, Herzl's article comes full circle. But the strongest part is the metaphor in the middle. Herzl quotes from a poem by a brilliant nineteenth-century German apostate

Jew who, to this day, is a hero to many Israelis: Heinrich Heine. The occasion for the poem was the founding in 1841 of a new Jewish hospital in Hamburg by the poet's wealthy uncle, Salomon Heine. "A hospital for poor, sick Jews," it begins, "for human beings suffering threefold." Their three "dire ailments" are poverty, physical pain, and Judaism. Of these three ills, Heine wrote, the last one—"the millennial family affliction"—is the worst.

"Well, then, Zionism is a kind of new Jewish care for the sick," continues Herzl. "We have stepped in as volunteer nurses, and we want to cure the patients—the poor, sick Jewish people—by means of a healthy way of life on our ancestral soil.... When we live there again, we, too, will enjoy a good name!" The "poor, sick Jewish people" has a double meaning, *peshat* and *derash*. The manifest meaning is indigent, sickly shtetl Jews in the Pale of Settlement. The latent meaning is the assimilated Jewish bourgeoisie that fears Jewish nationalism: they are the true "family affliction."[11]

Herzl died in 1904, at the age of forty-four. Four decades later, after his youngest daughter Trude and six million more were killed by Hitler, his Zionist project encountered little Jewish opposition. I need not belabor the phenomenal success story of the plucky Jewish State, today only six decades young. Nor need I spell out the overwhelming irony that the Jewish State, which was intended as an antidote to Judeophobia, is now a powerful magnet for the newest mutations of anti-Semitism. And the most heartbreaking irony of all: that the Jewish Athens imagined by Herzl and his many admirers and disciples, down to our own day, too often resembles a brutal Sparta. "We, too, will enjoy a good name!" exclaimed Herzl. Yes, we do, but not quite good enough.

If Zionism is the ultimate treatment for the Jewish condition, it inevitably has side effects; all therapies do. Call them what you will, euphemize and rationalize them, but they are there. We may excoriate our critics for wielding the *treifeh* (nonkosher) word "apartheid," but as a metaphor, it ought to give us pause. How we, as a community, treat our ongoing side effects constitutes a formidable challenge, because the underlying condition itself, like its doppelgänger, Judeophobia, would seem to be incurable. With all our Nobel Prizes, are we smart enough to heal ourselves? And if we aren't, why not?

Here in Jerusalem, I turn on the TV news and am reminded, night after night, of a poignant, tragic joke (#2081) from Alter Druyanov, the metaphor man from Odessa. A question is put to a *mumar*, a baptized Jew: "You are both a Jew and a *goy*, so tell me, what's the difference between them?" The man answers, "When a gentile is thirsty, he takes three drinks one after the other; when a Jew is thirsty, he checks his blood sugar." The *goy* as drunkard, bracing himself for the next pogrom; the Jew as hypochondriac, checking for diabetes.

There you have it: From the *igra rama* of metaphorical healing to the *bira amikta* of historical hypochondria. Wherever you turn, Amalek is out to get you. Woody Allen reframed the idea in an interview he gave to promote his 2002 film *Hollywood Ending*, a comedy about a movie director who goes blind:

> I'm not a hypochondriac and the character is. I'm an alarmist; a completely different problem. I do not imagine that I get illnesses. Should I wake up one morning with chapped lips or a hangnail, I think I have cancer.

May we construe this condition too as *yeridah letzorech aliyah*? Laughing at hypochondria is a good way to transcend it. But hypochondriacs, not to mention alarmists, also actually get sick. Then what? Rx: Consume healthy fruits, such as midrash and pomegranates, but don't forget to throw away the peel.

2

The Narrow Place from Which Healing Comes, and the Expansive Edge of the Continent

Rabbi Norman J. Cohen, PhD, is professor of midrash and former provost at Hebrew Union College–Jewish Institute of Religion. He has published several works through Jewish Lights Publishing, including *Self, Struggle and Change: Family Conflict Stories in Genesis and Their Healing Insights for Our Lives*; *Voices from Genesis: Guiding Us through the Stages of Life*; and *Hineini in Our Lives: Learning How to Respond to Others through 14 Biblical Texts & Personal Stories*.

Surviving the Narrow Places
Judah and Joseph and the Journey to Wholeness

Rabbi Norman J. Cohen, PhD

The Rabbis of old often reimagined biblical narratives in an effort to find relevance for their time and context. Midrash, the process of finding contemporary meaning in the biblical text, builds on scriptural material, but frequently goes far beyond the bare bones of the ancient stories. Robert Alter has noted, as have other scholars of literary criticism of the Bible such as Erich Auerbach, that the sparsely sketched foreground of the biblical narrative implies a large background dense with possibilities of interpretation.[1]

As the Rabbis interpreted the Bible, among their principle objectives was to provide comfort and support in life's most difficult moments. Their messages of consolation (called *nechemta*), of hope and healing can speak to our needs today as they did to ancient believers. People in every generation ask whether God heals the sick, brings wholeness to the broken, or returns the estranged and rejected. While healing often seems out of reach and achieving wholeness seems impossible, our midrashic texts teach that hope is always there.

As we consider in this essay a portion of the powerful, troubling story of the estrangement and imprisonment of Joseph and his brothers in Genesis 37–50, my hope is that through our immersion in midrash we will come to understand that the pain in Joseph's family, as it is in ours, is remediable.

Biblical characters, especially as enhanced through midrashic interpretation, are like relatives and old friends who are a kind of mirror reflecting back to us who we are, where we have been, how we have changed, and what in our lives remains unchanged. Interpreting the Joseph stories through the process of midrash gives us this gift of recognition (*hakarah*), seeing more clearly how we have hurt others and how we can grow and reconcile, how we have suffered and how we can heal. In this midrashic treatment of Genesis, the reconciliation of Jacob's children is our own reconciliation with those against whom we have struggled.

In this spirit and with this hope, we begin with a piece of the biblical story of Joseph and one powerful midrashic extension of it:

So Joseph went up to bury his father; and all of the officials of Pharaoh went up with him, the senior members of his court, and all of Egypt's dignitaries, together with all of Joseph's household, his brothers, and his father's household; only their children, their flocks, and their herds were left in the region of Goshen. Chariots, too, and horsemen went up with him; it was a very large troop.

When they came to Goren ha-Atad, which is beyond the Jordan, they held a very great and solemn lamentation; and he observed a mourning period of seven days for his father. And when the Canaanite inhabitants of the land saw the mourning at Goren ha-Atad, they said, "This is a solemn mourning on the part of the Egyptians." That is why it was named Abel-Mitzrayim, which is beyond the Jordan. Thus his sons did for him as he had instructed them.

His sons carried him to the land of Canaan, and buried him in the cave of Machpelah, the field near Mamre, which Abraham had bought for a burial site from Ephron, the Hittite. After burying his father, Joseph returned to Egypt, he and his brothers and all who had gone up with him to bury his father.

GENESIS 50:7–14

Joseph led a caravan made up of his brothers and Egyptian officials back to Canaan to bury his father in the Cave of Machpelah
in Hebron. Throughout the entire trip, Joseph couldn't stop thinking about the day some forty years before when his brothers sold
him into slavery and he was carried down to Egypt by a band of
Ishmaelite traders. He believed that he would never have to confront his brothers again and take their abuse, and they thought
that they had finally gotten rid of the haughty dreamer who made
their lives miserable and alienated them from their father. In
effect, they had killed him without ever laying a hand on him;
they had metaphorically buried him in the *bor*, the pit in Dothan.
It was the place of his pain, aloneness, and isolation, as was Egypt
[*Mitzrayim*].[2]

Yet, upon leaving the Cave of Machpelah, instead of moving
southward directly back to Egypt, Joseph led the caravan north-
ward toward Dothan. He had to return to the place of his suffering and terror, the pit in which he languished for three days and
from which he beseeched his brothers to have pity on him
[Genesis 42:21]. One can imagine the fear the brothers experienced when they realized that Joseph was leading them from the
grave [of their father] to the pit of their past, and what might
transpire once they arrived there.[3]

Yet, as Joseph stood over the pit, the site of his pain, he
uttered the following words: "Blessed be God who permitted a
miracle to come to pass for me here."

AN EMBELLISHMENT OF *MIDRASH TANCHUMA, VA-YECHI* 17

But what is the process that enables us to move from the biblical narrative to this midrashic extension? As we answer this key process question, it behooves us to raise the deeper, more poignant issues of how
can we as individuals survive the pit, the narrow places (*meitzarim*) of
our lives, the pit in which we all have dwelt on occasion? Playing
midrashically on the word *bor*, the dry pit, we ask if it can be transformed into a *be'er*, a well of life-giving waters?[4] Can the place of
emptiness and pain become a source of healing? As we address the
issue of how individuals can come to greater wholeness in their lives,
we will focus on the necessary process of change that they must

undergo, which at its core involves coming to a clearer recognition of self. In analyzing the biblical and midrashic passages, we will pay attention to the trope of "seeing" (in Hebrew, *ra'ah*) and its more powerful counterpart, "recognizing" (*haker*), which are present in the biblical text and which will play important literary roles.

In order to help us wrestle with these challenges, let us refocus on the Joseph story in Genesis, paying attention to one key character in particular, Judah, and two central biblical passages, as we read them through the prism of the Rabbinic process of midrash.

Midrash: The Process of Finding Contemporary Answers to Enduring Questions

The term "midrash" comes from the Hebrew root *darash*, which means "to seek, to search." But it also can mean "to demand." For some forty years of work with the process of midrash, I have urged the seeking and searching within these ancient texts in order to see what they demand of us, the readers. As readers of midrash, we succeed when we are keen and dogged in pursuing all that a given text means—like a detective in a mystery story who is not satisfied with the most obvious solution to the crime.

The midrashic process requires three steps: First, we must spend time with the biblical text. We ought not run too hurriedly through the narratives of the Bible. Rather, ours is the task to immerse ourselves in the fabric of the text, imbibing the power and flavor of every lexical and syntactical element. Second, we need to ask all the questions we can about the text: What are the inherent linguistic and literary issues, the historical and sociocultural settings? What must its original religious meaning have been? And finally, when we go about questioning the text, we need to broach the most difficult questions. For us as modern readers, they are the questions of belief and the most challenging human questions. We cannot escape seeing the characters of the Bible as human beings standing at the crossroads of their lives in situations that are very much our own. These questions help us, first of all, to appreciate the simple meaning of the story and its message, but then the exercise of "seeking" invites us to imagine how the message might apply in a different time—perhaps our time.

Steven Kepnes wrote that "interpreting the text must involve the assimilation of the text's meaning into the personal life of the interpreter."[5] As we turn to the first of our two passages, let us realize that our immersion in the texts of old can enable us to come to healing and wholeness.

Genesis 38: The Story of Judah and Tamar

At first blush, Genesis 38 looks like a later interpolation into the ongoing Joseph narrative, since it breaks the flow between Genesis chapters 37 and 39. Chapter 37 ends with Joseph being carried down to Egypt and sold to Potiphar, and chapter 39 picks up the story with the words, "Joseph was brought [*hurad*] down to Egypt." Yet, on closer look, chapter 38 in many ways fits into the story line and resonates with what precedes and succeeds it. It focuses on Judah, the fourth son of Jacob, but the most powerful of Joseph's siblings, and what happens to him while Joseph is in Egypt.

Though Joseph survived the desert journey and was sold into slavery, Jacob believed his favorite son to be dead. The brothers had told their father that a wild animal had devoured him and then insensitively asked their father to recognize Joseph's multicolored tunic, which they had dipped in the blood of a slaughtered kid (*haker na ha-ketonet bincha*—"recognize please the coat" [Genesis 37:32]).[6] At its very outset, the biblical narrative introduces the key trope of the story, to which we already alluded—Judah and his brothers force their father to "recognize" what had happened to Joseph, the altered reality of his life—which will come back to haunt Judah. The brothers not only did away with Joseph, but they also destroyed their father just as they had killed the animal. Jacob mourned for his son the rest of his days and refused to be comforted (*va-yema'ein le-hitnachem*). He felt his life was over, and he cried inconsolably (Genesis 37:35).

Witnessing Judah's Nature

The pain the brothers caused their father was great, and they soon regretted what they had done (Genesis 37:35). According to the midrash, Judah was the one most responsible, since he wielded the most power and his brothers would have listened to him. After all, it was his plan that they had followed! All Judah had to do was to have said, "Let us return [Joseph] to our father" instead of "Let us go and sell him to the Ishmaelites" (Genesis 37:27) and they would have acted differently.[7]

Castigated by his brothers, Judah distanced himself from them, leaving as if he were banished. This is indicated by the atypical expression in Genesis 38:1, "Judah went down [*va-yeired*] from his brothers." The midrash typically pays close attention to the choice of words in the Bible, noticing when a term is used that is unexpected. So here, the Rabbis emphasize that the term *va-yeired* tells us much more about the moral condition of Judah than about his journey southward from Beer Sheba. They suggest that his "descent" was the result of his actions in the selling of Joseph and in his treatment of their father.[8]

Having settled in Adullamite territory, near his friend Hirah, Judah fell in love and married a Canaanite woman, and he fathered three sons, Er, Onan, and finally Sheilah, whom we learn was born at Cheziv. Later, it must have seemed ironic that they named him Sheilah, which means "mislead," and that he was born at Cheziv (the verb *chazav* meaning "deception"), when we have no idea where the other sons were born. When details appear on a selective basis in a biblical passage, they are frequently understood in the midrash as red flags, in this case helping us as readers anticipate the deception on Judah's part that is about to occur (Genesis 38:5). Names of people and places often are plays on words, which provide added meaning for the reader.

In time, Judah found a wife for his firstborn, Er—a Canaanite woman named Tamar. When Er was killed by God for acting in an evil manner, Judah gave Onan to Tamar, thus fulfilling the obligation of the brother to ensure the continuity of his deceased brother's line.[9] However, Onan refused to stand in his brother's stead, and God also took his life. All this caused Judah to fear for his remaining son, Sheilah. Although obliged to give him to Tamar, he counseled Tamar to leave and dwell in her father's house until Sheilah came of age, implying that he would then fulfill his responsibility to her. Yet, he never intended to do so. As a result, Tamar was relegated to living in a state of widowhood, unable to marry again, and tied to Sheilah for the rest of her life.[10] This was not the first time that Judah had not lived up to his responsibility. His previous actions caused Jacob to lose a son; now not only has he lost his two sons, but in his treatment of Tamar, he seems to have sacrificed the core of his humanity.

Ironically, a short time later, Judah's own wife died. He, like Tamar and Jacob, suffered a terrible loss, though unlike his daughter-in-law and father, who would never get over their losses—Tamar could not remarry, and Jacob "refused to be comforted" (*va-yema'ein le-hitnachem* [Genesis 37:35])—Judah went through a period of mourning and was indeed "comforted" (*va-yinachem* [Genesis 38:12]). As we noted, often the midrashic process involves focusing on similar words used in different passages from the Bible.

Judah rose up from his mourning and went up to Timnah to join his friend Hirah and the other men for the sheepshearing festival, where he would be able to sow his oats. The biblical writer chooses the words "Judah went up [*va-ya'al*] to Timnah" (Genesis 38:12) so that the verb *alah* stands in tension with *yarad* (go down), used before in the narrative to describe Judah's leaving his brothers, his descent from them (Genesis 38:1). The contrast between *yarad* (descend) and *alah* (ascend) is understood to indicate that it would be at Timnah that perhaps Judah would be forced to see himself for what he was, to have the mask of respectability removed, just as the sheep would be uncovered, and thereby begin the rise, the return to his higher self.[11]

The Opening of Judah's Eyes:
The Beginning of the Journey to Wholeness

As the narrative develops, let us not underestimate the importance of the theme of truly seeing, having one's eyes opened. The repetitive language in this passage not only highlights the text's message, but helps us understand an essential ingredient in our process of healing.

Hearing that Judah was coming up to Timnah, Tamar became infuriated. She was not able to get on with her life, but her father-in-law could pick himself up after his wife's death and get on with his life. She realized (literally, "saw") that Judah would never fulfill his obligation to her; she would never marry Sheilah. Bent on unmasking him, she took off her widow's garb, veiled herself—she covered herself to expose him—and sat down at the entrance (*petach*) to Einayim, where the harlots congregated. *Petach* literally means "opening," so knowing that *einayim* means "eyes," the biblical place name forces us to ask, "Whose eyes would be opened on the road to Timnah?" Though Tamar recognized the truth and was willing to act upon it, all that Judah was capable of initially "seeing" was a mere harlot sitting at the crossroads (Genesis 38:14–15).

Judah turned aside and sought to engage her. When Tamar asked how much he was willing to pay, Judah replied that he would send her a young kid from his flock.[12] She demanded a pledge to ensure that Judah would keep his promise (Tamar knew that Judah had difficulty keeping promises!). And when Judah inquired about the pledge, the *eiravon*, Tamar demanded nothing less than Judah's seal, cord, and staff. What in fact Tamar demanded was the family status of which Judah had deprived her from the beginning by withholding Sheilah. Yet, unknowingly, as he gave in to his desires and slept with the prostitute on the road, Judah actually had taken Sheilah's place, thus providing his deceased sons with heirs. Tamar conceived and carried twins, which would make up for Judah's two lost sons. Tamar was positioned to teach Judah that the lost brother must be redeemed, something he had not understood when Joseph was thrown into the pit.[13] Judah's sin of sleeping with his daughter-in-law would lead to both Judah and Tamar experiencing healing in their lives.

Three months passed and it became obvious that Tamar was pregnant. Judah, finding out that her condition was the result of her prostitution, ordered that she be killed. As she was being brought out to be burned, she informed him, saying, "I am with child by the man who owns these [objects]," and added, "Recognize please to whom this seal, cord, and staff belong" (Genesis 38:25). When Judah heard her words, he could not help but recall the words he had spoken to his own father when showing him Joseph's coat dipped in the blood of the kid: "Recognize please if this is your son's tunic" (Genesis 37:32). The words sounded eerily similar: *Haker na ... ha-hotemet* and *Haker na ha-ketonet*, as if one was the retribution for the other! Judah was forced to recognize the injustice of his actions and the pain he caused both

Jacob and Tamar. As he stared at the seal, cord, and staff and saw the symbols of who he was—or at least ought to have been—at that moment, perhaps for the very first time in his life, he took an honest look at himself: *Va-yaker Yehudah*, "Judah recognized" (Genesis 38:26). What did he recognize, really see? It was not just the objects, though most translations here read, "Judah recognized them." What Judah finally was able to see clearly was himself, and he said for all to hear, "[Tamar] is more righteous than I, inasmuch as I did not give my son Sheilah to her" (Genesis 38:26).

The Result of Judah's Self-Recognition

This was the turning point for Judah, and we should note that it was fostered by a non-Israelite woman. He took the first step toward personal change and wholeness in his life through his relationship with his daughter-in-law, Tamar. According to the Rabbinic tradition, the change in Judah as demonstrated by his recognition of his responsibility to Tamar is the reason why Judah deserved to have the messianic line of King David emanate from him.[14] Ironically, the Davidic line is traced through one of the twins whom Tamar birthed, who is named Peretz, "the one who made the breach."[15]

Again, a play on a biblical name can enhance the potential meaning of the biblical text for us. The verb *paratz* means "to break boundaries," including sexual boundaries (*peritzut* means "licentiousness"), and underscores that the messianic line flows from Tamar, of all people, the prostitute on the road to Timnah. Like Ruth, who seduced Boaz and whose progeny also stands in the Davidic line, Tamar played a major role in guaranteeing the survival of the nation of Israel.[16] Tamar mirrors for Judah and, by extension, for every reader, not only who we are, but also who we can become. Even a Canaanite of inconsequential lineage can ultimately become the one from whom the Davidic line emerged!

But with all this said, there remains one gnawing question: By what merit did Judah deserve to have the line of kingship emanate from him? If all he did was recognize that Tamar was more righteous than he and that he did not fulfill his responsibilities to her, why is King David descended from the tribe of Judah? Surely, more had to be expected from him.[17]

Genesis 44:18–34: The Confrontation between Judah and Joseph

Judah would eventually demonstrate the essential change in him that would warrant his becoming the progenitor of the Davidic line. But it would take over two decades. As fate would have it, after Joseph emerged as the viceroy of Egypt, his brothers would also travel to Egypt because of the famine in Canaan. Jacob heard that there were stores of food rations in Egypt, and he sent all the remaining brothers with the exception of Joseph's younger sibling Benjamin to procure them (Genesis 42:1–5).

Joseph, having heard that the sons of Jacob were in Egypt, orchestrated a number of meetings with his unsuspecting brothers, all of which could either engender even greater animosity between the sons of Rachel and Leah or rapprochement between them. Joseph and his brothers, like many siblings who are distanced from one another, continued to struggle with what the other once represented. It is difficult to overcome the distance, the animus, the pain; it is carried with us wherever we go like an old suitcase bearing memories from our past. I think the biblical account of the "confrontation" between Joseph and his brothers suggests that only when siblings come face-to-face are they able to *see* themselves in ways they have never done so before.

Benjamin in Egypt: Revisiting Past Actions

After a series of confrontations in which Joseph systematically placed the brothers in situations similar to the ones in which he found himself after leaving his father's house in search of his brothers,[18] Joseph finally made the decisive demand of them: if they wanted food for the family, they would have to bring Benjamin back with them. Twenty-two years after they had been responsible for Joseph being brought down to Egypt, they would now actually carry his full brother, the other son of Rachel, down to Egypt themselves! The symmetry of the story is revealing.

The scene was now set: Joseph insisted that Benjamin remain alone in Egypt, while the other brothers returned in peace to Canaan. However, dramatically Judah took the lead in arguing for Benjamin's life. When Joseph insisted that Benjamin remain with him, Judah, the strongest of Leah's sons, confronted the viceroy of Egypt. His confrontation with Joseph is underscored by the play on the verb *vayiggash* (Judah approached [Joseph; Genesis 44:18]).[19] The root *nagash* can imply both a drawing close as well as conflict. The ambiguity of the verb demands midrashic interpretation; it is as if, in the idiom of the classic midrashim, the text says to the reader, *Darsheni*, "You must interpret me!"

Although Judah addressed Joseph in a rather delicate and supplicating manner—"Please, my lord, let your servant appeal to my lord" (Genesis 44:18)—the forceful intent of his words was clear: one gets the impression that Judah would not have taken no for an answer; he would have done anything necessary to protect Benjamin and return him to their father. Perhaps Judah's plea to Joseph reveals the reason why Judah was willing to put himself on the line for Joseph's full brother. His description of Benjamin as the child of Jacob's old age upon whom he doted (literally, "whom he loves") and how Jacob would die if anything happened to Benjamin (Genesis 44:20–22) could as easily have been said about Joseph himself. The more Judah went on about Jacob's love of Benjamin, the more the reader understands that Judah was underscoring his own guilt and that of his brothers. This paralleling between Judah's words in Genesis 44 regarding Benjamin and the description of Jacob's relationship with Joseph is an example of the process of intertextuality that is often used in the midrash—the drawing together of two disparate passages in an effort to uncover additional meaning in the biblical text. As a result, it is possible to see that the very same Judah who had been chiefly responsible for causing his father to mourn the rest of his life in the aftermath of Joseph's apparent death was now poignantly concerned about his father. A caring Judah lamented, "If I come to your servant, my father, and the boy is not with us, since his soul is bound up with his, he will surely die and [we] will send the white head of … our father down to Sheol in grief" (Genesis 44:30–31). Judah could finally admit that Jacob deeply loved Benjamin (Joseph), seemingly without a touch of jealousy.

The Moment of Truth: Can People Truly Change?

The confrontation scene between Judah and Joseph in Genesis 44 raises the essential question of whether human beings have the capacity to grow in substantial ways over time and move to a sense of healing in themselves and in their relationships, especially knowing themselves as they do. Perhaps as Judah stood before Joseph as Benjamin's advocate, he consciously recalled the fateful day years before at Dothan. Then he was given a chance to save his brother Joseph's life and return him to his father, but all he could do was to utter the words, "Let us sell him to the Ishmaelites and be done with him" (Genesis 37:27). Joseph languished in the pit for three days, and Judah was never moved to intervene on his behalf. Now, twenty-two years later, in a replay of that scene, with Benjamin the one incarcerated, Judah was given another opportunity to fulfill his responsibility. This was the moment of truth for Judah. Would he—we—act differently than in the past? Had he essentially changed? Could he turn/return (the Rabbinic notion of *teshuvah*, "repentance") to a more holistic sense of himself?

Standing before Joseph, haunted by the memories of his past failures—the sale of Joseph and his inability to fulfill his obligation to Tamar—he demonstrated the potential that we all possess. His words, spoken with great humility, yet with forceful commitment, resound across the generations: "Now your servant has pledged [*arav*] himself for the boy [*na'ar*] to my father, saying, 'If I do not bring him back to you, I shall stand guilty [*chatati*] before my father forever.' Therefore, please let your servant remain a slave to my lord instead of the boy [*hana'ar*]" (Genesis 44:32–33). Judah's words just jump off the page and demand that we listen and apply them to our lives, especially the term *arav*, which brings us back to the scene in which Tamar demanded a pledge (*eiravon*) from Judah ensuring that he would fulfill his obligation to her (Genesis 38:17–18). In fact, the "pledge" may be a triple entendre, alluding at one and the same time to the three biblical passages we have mentioned: to the implicit responsibility Judah had in protecting Joseph (Genesis 37), to the pledge he was forced to give to his daughter-in-law to ensure her identity (Genesis 38), and in this case (Genesis 44), to the pledge he made to Jacob to protect Benjamin.

From this perspective, the Joseph narrative cycle has at its core the journey of Judah to greater wholeness even as it focuses on the repair of the relationships within the family. Seven chapters after the sale of Joseph, Judah was again confronted with his responsibility vis-à-vis a half brother, and this time he not only argued for Benjamin's life but was willing to put his own life on the line. In so doing, for the very first time Judah recognized the guilt he bore for his past actions: "If I do not bring him back to you [Jacob] ..., I shall stand guilty [*chatati*] ... forever" (Genesis 43:9). In verbalizing the key word *chatati*, which means "I have sinned," Judah admitted that not only did he not fulfill his obligations as the most powerful brother, but his actions constituted a sin against God, which, I would suggest, means a diminution of his highest self.

Judah could not fathom returning to his father in Canaan without Benjamin, and he even went so far as to articulate in a very poignant way the pain that it would cause Jacob: "Let me not see [*er'eh*] the woe that would overtake my father!" (Genesis 44:34). Judah and his brothers, who in the beginning could not "see" the pain that they caused their father and even forced him to "recognize" Joseph's coat ostensibly covered with his blood (Genesis 37:32), now could not bear seeing their father suffer. Judah's utter concern for his father's well-being, especially as it involved Joseph's brother Benjamin, together with his willingness to give up his life for his half brother, having pledged to protect him, underscore for us as readers that Judah's transformation was complete. Twenty-two years after selling Joseph into slavery, Judah had come full circle as he urged Joseph, of all people, to allow him to remain a slave in Egypt to Rachel's firstborn son (Joseph) instead of Rachel's second son, Benjamin.

The Midrash on Judah's Transformation

Having moved through the Joseph narrative cycle, we can now better respond to the question raised in the Rabbinic tradition as to why Judah, who played such a key role in the selling of Joseph, deserved to be the progenitor of the Davidic line. In fact, according to the *Mekhilta D'Rabbi Yishmael*,[20] the students of Rabbi Tarfon, an important Rabbinic figure in Palestine in the first half of the second century CE, ask this question of their teacher: "Master, teach us, by what virtue did Judah merit the kingdom, that is, having the royal line and, by traditional theological extension, the Messiah, emanate from him?"

Tarfon, in Socratic fashion, asks them to proffer an answer, and they initially suggest, "By virtue of Judah having said: 'What profit is there if we slay our brother?' [Genesis 37:26]." The implication is that instead of killing Joseph, Judah saved his life by selling him to the caravan of traders heading down to Egypt. His basic instinct was to save his life. However, Rabbi Tarfon counters by noting that saving Joseph's life was only sufficient to atone for their selling him into slavery, which constituted a capital offense.

The students then suggest that Judah deserved having kingship come from him because "Judah acknowledged and then said, 'She [Tamar] is more righteous than I' [Genesis 38:26]." Judah publicly recognized what he did; he clearly saw who he had become and in a sense confessed his guilt. A crucial element in the process of transformation is removing the masks we wear and seeing ourselves for who we are. By embracing our past, we, too, can begin to shape our future in more constructive ways. Yet, Tarfon is still not satisfied, and he responds to his students by saying that Judah's confession only atoned for the fact that he inappropriately cohabited with his daughter-in-law.

Finally, the students argue that Judah is worthy of the royal mantle because at the moment of truth in his life, he demanded of Joseph, "Therefore, please let your servant remain a slave to my lord instead of the boy" (Genesis 44:33). Judah's willingness to give his life for Benjamin not only atoned for his inability to truly protect Joseph and fulfill his obligation to Tamar, but demonstrated the essential change that he underwent. He now could live up to his commitment to his father and, in so doing, come to greater wholeness in his life and bring healing to the relationships within his family. Judah moved beyond his limitations so that he was able to acknowledge what he had done.

In the end, Judah internalized the lessons of his past, which enabled him to fulfill his higher destiny. In so doing, I believe that our midrashic reading of Genesis shows that it is possible to transform the place of our pain, isolation, and trauma, the pit into which life can cast us, into a source of healing and growth.

Rabbi Eric Weiss is executive director of the Bay Area Jewish Healing Center, based in San Francisco, California. He is formally trained in Jewish education, clinical chaplaincy, and spiritual direction. He and his husband, Dan, live in San Francisco.

Widening the Boundaries

Rabbi Eric Weiss

"The Jewish healing movement" is a term first spoken by Rabbi Nancy Flam. She used the term with a lowercase "m" as a way to acknowledge that while not a formally structured movement, it represents a significant pursuit in individual lives and in the communal life of the Jewish community. Over the years there have been many conversations over cups of coffee, in larger structured groups, and in significant essays that have appeared in journals and books. These conversations have always searched for words to articulate the experiences of mind, body, and spirit in a Jewish context. Conversations naturally involved issues of health, spirituality, and communal engagement. Clergy, health-care practitioners of all kinds, and interested laity talked to one another. They talked about their own illness experiences as well as about their role as caregivers. From this, for example, came attempts to distinguish between healing and curing. Just one sample of how this conversation has developed can be found in the introduction to *Healing and the Jewish Imagination: Spiritual and Practical Perspectives on Judaism and Health* (Jewish Lights) and its subsequent essays.

Over time, more formalized gatherings were convened. These structured experiences attempted both to nourish the ongoing work in the field and assess how this daily work was functioning among those who engage issues of healing and curing as a part of their vocation, for example, at the bedside, in a caregiver's office, or in a synagogue service. Interestingly, it seems that an early aesthetic formed.

Needless to say, the healing impulses have certainly spread throughout the entire country. Like all movements in Jewish life, the

Jewish healing movement has its own anthropology. Even this early there are ruminations about its origins. Some comment that it is a uniquely Jewish American development: a mixing of rugged individualism with the Jewish insistence that we are a communal organism. Some cite the influence of contemporary response to diseases such as AIDS or breast cancer. Some mention the grassroots spiritual searches that are stimulated by more secular frames such as Twelve Step programs. Still others suggest a shift away from the immigrant's assimilation to a post-Holocaust-centered Jewish identity that tries to form a different way to engage both the Jewish and broader community.

In the theological mix, one can say that when we reflect upon the American understanding of the relationship between God and human beings we realize that Christianity's personal God contrasts with the covenantal Jewish relationship. In this sense, it is possible to suggest that the Jewish healing movement mingles America's rugged individualism and Judaism's eternal triumvirate of God, Torah, and Israel. Where every formal branch in Jewish life frames a hierarchy of these three, the Jewish healing movement has remained transdenominational because it does not maintain any such hierarchy but rather suggests how God, Torah, and Israel may create constellations around issues of healing and spirituality.

Asilomar, an oceanfront conference center in Monterey Bay, California, was the setting for our most recent gathering. We came together during the Omer, the period of time between Passover and Shavuot. We all know the ways in which we respond to various parts of the Exodus story, the themes and liturgy, and sew them to our own ever-developing Jewish identity: the movement from slavery to freedom, the wandering in the desert, the covenantal experience at Sinai. The story has different aspects of meaning specifically because we know the entire narrative. We tell and relive it every year.

Yet, if we imagine that we were ourselves Children of Israel at the time of our liberation, the truth is that we did not know the end of our own story. In the moment, the Children of Israel did not know that the Red Sea would part, that manna would feed them, that there would be a pillar of smoke and fire, that there would be a mountaintop, a set of tablets, even a golden calf. All they did was say "yes" to Moses, to God, perhaps, and to themselves. All they had was their own imagination and the hope for a new life. They took a leap of faith. They put one foot in front of the other, imagining that the next day would be better than the present. The story is an example of how narrative may yet give us templates that apply to our lives, even though each moment is filled with large and small leaps of faith.

The Jewish healing movement weaves narrative and leaps of faith. All we know is this moment of our own story and our hopes for the future. We all have our own story; it may range from what each of us knows in the privacy of our own souls to the ways others speak about us, from the family from which we come to the family we form, from the national story of our America to the awesome story of our collective text, from the way we say "yes" to our own God-given gifts to the ways we use them. None of us knows the end of our own story, yet we hope, we plan, we yearn for a future whose story will evolve.

In the canon of our sacred literature, "midrash" means at its core "interpretation." Because we use sacred narrative as a framework to interpret its application to our own lives, the very nature of midrash invites us to weave the cumulative text of our own lives into a canonized communal story such as the Exodus. And so we ask ourselves questions like: What are modern-day plagues? In what ways am I enslaved today, and how do I become free? By its very literary form, midrash invites us to interpret the cumulating text of our lives.

The notion of reflecting on our own life experience becomes paramount. For some the self-reflective quality is uniquely human, for some it is uniquely American, while for others it is solely the landscape of a bourgeois class. Yet it is uniquely Jewish to understand our communal life in the context of what our past tradition can illuminate today. We look to our past from which to form clues of meaning to the present. At the same time, we understand that interpretation, while it can lead to the making of meaning, nonetheless implies that our very lives, like our sacred texts, are porous. Each story, whether from sacred text or from an individual life, is filled with leaps that demonstrate that we never truly know the meaning of something we experience until we reflect backward over time.

The story of our people, the midrash of our collective lives, is spoken in every counseling office, at every hospital grand rounds, at every staff meeting, at every bedside. It isn't just "Let's reduce [or increase] the dosage of your medication," "I'm depressed," or "Where can I find spirituality while I'm having chemotherapy?" Rather, these are all code for the ways in which we yearn for nurturance, for some kind of anchoring—perhaps a way station of meaning—of our tradition to our individual experience in both happy and challenging times. The midrash—the interpretation—is in the ways we tell our own story and the story of our people.

Midrash becomes the Jewish form that melds the personal with the collective. It is authentically Jewish, allowing simultaneous exploration of the personal and communal God.

"Midrash and Medicine" was the title we gave the gathering at Monterey Bay, California. It represents the many ways in which the rabbi, physician, and patient share their narratives, individually and together, none knowing the end of their own individual or collective stories. All we know is this moment and our hopes for the future. We all have our own imagination. In these pages are the reflections of God, Torah, and Israel as we continue the conversation that advances the Jewish healing movement.

3

Lyric and Community

Rabbi William Cutter, PhD, the editor of *Healing and the Jewish Imagination: Spiritual and Practical Perspectives on Judaism and Health* (Jewish Lights), has been teaching his poetic message for over forty-five years at Hebrew Union College–Jewish Institute of Religion. Therapoetics has been introduced at the Esalen Institute and at numerous forums in synagogues and Jewish centers throughout the United States and Israel.

The Midrashic Impulse in Poems, Our Dialogue with Ecclesiastes, and Other Lyrical Interpretations

Rabbi William Cutter, PhD

Reading poetry is a way into the experience of illness—broadly construed—and an opportunity to describe or interpret the personal story of anyone who is affected in one way or another by illness as patients, family caretakers, nurses, or physicians. A pair of classic voices from the early nineteenth century begin my ruminations about poetry and healing. John Keats believed, as did so many romantics, that there is healing power in poetic words ("… sure, a poet is a Sage; / A humanist, Physician to all men"). And Percy Bysshe Shelley believed that poems arranged human experiences and held them back from being fleeting, on the one hand, or from falling into distance and unfamiliarity, on the other. "Poetry," he insisted in "A Defence of Poetry," "redeems from decay the visitations of the divinity in man."[1]

My task in this brief essay and partnership with Rabbi Sheldon Marder is to describe, in language more of our time, how Percy Shelley's capturing of redemption might occur in practice and what the lyrical humanism of the literary physician can do for us.

Of course I have more concrete—simpler and less metaphysical—notions about the value of poetry, living as I do in the pragmatic twenty-first century. Here I am obligated to be practical and explicit, and that is what I shall try to be in this brief essay. To Shelley's argument that we can make experience pause in poetry, I want to add that poems can offer an opportunity to say the "unsayable," the thoughts that occupy the darkest parts of the mind, or—at least—to reflect on the "unsaid" that keeps being unsaid through a thousand nervous and sometimes rushed experiences in the physician's office by the patient, and in the private ruminations of the physician him- or herself when no one else is around. In addition, poems—as our preeminent communication through words—create a chain of associations and new ways of looking at old reality. There is, in all aspects of reading poetry, an act of creation and of re-creation of old ideas that suits the theme of "midrash" that shapes this book. I call my own work with poetry and healing "therapoetics," a term into which are gathered several meanings, all of which have to do with "making," with change, and with art. I mean to consider in that expression the relationship between healing as a subject and the poetic form in which the subject is encased. It is the relationship between the two—form and theme—that helps move healers beyond their quotidian and practical assignment to a richer relationship with their health projects. Sometimes it is a rhyme, at other times a metaphor that strikes a chord. Often the arrangement of words on a page makes the healer sit up and take notice or the patient find comfort in shared response.

A troubled visit with a friend who is desperately ill may be described through the dialogue within the stanzas in a poem; the unclarity about what the doctor really said might be suggested by a rich play of words that confuse because they sound like other words; the need to see pain as part of the physical world we inhabit might be clarified through metaphors that exaggerate the experience of pleasure and pain. A patient's simple, poetically direct affirmation of friendship may give meaning to the bashful friend who hesitates to "visit the sick." And a long skeptical rumination about faith may symbolize the endurance that the loved one experiences as she watches her beloved suffer. And whatever the specific experience of the caregiver or the sufferer, poetry suggests a community of people behind the "congregation" of words that poems offer up. Each of these examples has a particular poem in mind, and in this essay, we shall see several examples of particular poems. But for starters: is there anyone who has been seriously ill who would fail to understand John Updike's poetic notions from an old poem I read in the *New Yorker* magazine in which humans are seen as living in vales of breakdown, out of warranty?[2] Even Updike's elevated language can bring together the community of people who have experienced that breakdown of warranty and those unrepairable complaints.[3]

As one who has taught poetry for more than four decades, perhaps the most interesting consequence I can propose is that readers of poems often come up with personal meanings in their readings—precisely because of the way words work in poems—personal meanings that may not have been anticipated by the person who offers up the poem in the first place.

When you write poetry (which is not the principal subject of my essay here), you actually create the surprising words and conjunctions of words that help you think about the connections between things you experience and that help you find some form in life as it is lived—beyond the mere words. Writing poems and teaching poetry writing are what Rabbi Marder, in the tradition of Kenneth Koch, describes in his essay from the halls of the Jewish Home of San Francisco. (Is Shelly Marder's first name a symbol of his poetic destiny?) My essay suggests that reading poetry is also a form of making meaning, perhaps as much as writing, and in either case, making meaning can move the healer toward a higher plateau in her practice. I am not suggesting that physicians should be reciting poetry as they examine their patients; but I am suggesting that the physician pause in appropriate moments of composure where experience may be recollected poetically in the quiet between the deployment of the medical artillery involved in the clinical workday. Somewhere in that background resides the quartermaster corps providing food for the soul. As one of those great physician-quartermasters, Rafael Campo, has suggested, "If any mode of human expression can be said to have an almost universal affiliation with illness, it is poetry."[4]

Beyond every health professional's experience and behind every caregiver's constant attention to an ill family member is the need to move from the material and physical necessity of curing a particular malady to the deeper (or higher) purposes of their work, to make the move from "curer" to "healer." And behind every ill person's experience is the need to see the deeper significance of their experience with illness. Poetry, then, can be a form of midrash, for purposes of my thoughts here, that may help patients make some sense out of an experience that so often stuns them into spiritual incoherence. No tired cliché here, that illness is something to be grateful for, or that life is poetry; but in this creation of something not expected, reading and writing poetry is much about life in the largest sense—and beyond particular themes of particular poems. I cannot, in these remarks, speak of the numerous examples of great prose literature where illness and the experience of dying have actually created a literary cosmos of narrative meaning, but critic Sandra Gilbert has, and one only has to reflect on a few of our literary greats to recall what I am talking about.[5]

A Physician's Awareness

The American physician and poet Marc Straus wrote about a doctor's realization after receiving a surprising compliment from a very ill young girl:

> *When I was two, my doctor*
> *had a large house*
> *on Cortelyou Road. The exam room*
> *smelled like a dead frog*
> *and my temperature was taken*
> *rectally. By age five*
> *I was injected with tetracycline*
> *monthly*
> *by Dr. Ryan. He later died*
> *of lung cancer.*
> *Who influenced me*
> *the most? A medical school*
> *interviewer asked. Thirty years later*
> *I still don't know. Today*
> *a sixteen-year-old girl said*
> *she'd like to be*
> *just like me, as I pushed*
> *her third course*
> *of chemotherapy.*[6]

Surprised by the question he was asked as a medical-school applicant, the doctor finds himself surprised that he can't answer it still; and surprised by the young patient's affirmation, we are—as readers—just as surprised at the symmetry and asymmetry that the poem suggests between doctor and patient. Such analogical interest is the very stuff of midrash—no matter how subtle and elusive.

Dr. Straus shares the following intriguing midrashlike recognition from a patient on the fearsome size of a new hospital:

> *A van near the west parking lot sells bagels,*
> *jelly rolls, hot dogs, and soda. I can't read its sign*
> *from here, but I see a workman holding a can*
> *in one hand and with the other eating food*
> *from a paper wrapper. I don't know why*
> *they design these buildings so high. A conference*
> *on hospital architecture should have been convened*
> *to establish the optimum height. I doubt many*
> *have paid attention to this. What if*
> *a patient is acrophobic? Wouldn't it be better*
> *if one were level with a flowering dogwood,*
> *a Japanese maple? From here I look down on sunsets.*
> *Why the eleventh floor? Admissions*
> *is on the first, radiology the second, surgery the third,*
> *pediatrics the fourth, obstetrics the fifth. Everyone knows*
> *what's in the basement. Perhaps that's why*
> *oncology is so far away.*[7]

Do most doctors think about the influence their office buildings have upon their patients? My own physicians, I noted, haven't paid attention to the slow and clumsy elevators, the chairless corridors, and the absence of support bars in their very own office building where old and crippled patients struggle their way—almost crawl, sometimes—to a doctor's office and where patients out of breath struggle to fit into the elevator that is out of room. What a nice vindication for me to meet Marc Straus's poem! I don't want to be like that building. I don't even want to be *in* it!

Each of these poems has a midrashic property, at the very least in the shock of the doctor's hearing, or the noticing of something new, or the conjunction of ideas or people that don't seem to belong together. "Look at this!" Norman Cohen reminds us in his essay. You, the doctor or building administrator, see a tall, efficient office building; your patient sees a clutter of people on the first floor and nothing outside of the bleak space except some very old magazines. Marc Straus—writing in the name of one of his patients—sees something else and echoes the poetry of patient and Israeli poetic genius Abba Kovner, who described Memorial Sloan-Kettering Cancer Center as an "encounter with a trackless wasteland ... that emerges from within itself."[8]

We can't change the shape or size of these buildings, we healers, but it wouldn't hurt to know something about what patients experience when trapped in them.

The Bemused Patient

Here is a delightful poem about a nonmorbid illness, in a uniquely American comic context. Doctors, beware; sometimes your patient writes for television.

From producer-director and writer Benjamin Kukoff:

> *Dr. Fleiss whipped my hip X-Ray up crackling*
> *Toward the light, clipped it,*
> *Jabbed fingers against it, like it was a suspect held at bay,*
> *Smirked at my white, shadowed bones, crowing*
> *I was a perfect candidate for hip replacement.*
> *Like it was a compliment.*
>
> *No doubt about it, look! Bone against bone. Me?*
> *Would have done it years ago.*
>
> *My own efforts? Dismissed:*
> *Acupuncture? Works for a minute.*
> *Glucosamine-sulphate? A failed placebo.*
> *What about that new cranial-sacro stuff?*
> *Or the magnets my sister-in-law*

Swears by, that seemed to relieve.
He cuts me off with a shrug.
Scribbles the name of a surgeon,
A pioneer of prosthesis fused to bone.
Hardly any cement. Hardly any risk.
Maybe one in a hundred die.

That many?

He shook my hand backing out.
If I had any questions, call him.
My 500 dollars was up.

Outside I walked the hard sidewalks
Of Fifth Avenue—bone against bone.
I allowed myself to limp.[9]

The Special Place of Hebrew Poetry

When I want to be at my most "midrashic"—to add to those other functions of poetry some Jewishly urgent language where we might experience the laden thoughts that spiritual language prompts, and to experience it all as coming from the overflow of Jewish idiom—I turn to the poets of Israel. Their very stanzas are embedded in a sense of eternal language with infinite meaning, and perhaps they even bear the pretentious notion that Hebrew is the language of creation—a natural ally of poetry. And, for Jewish readers, the community that reads the poetry shares a precious tradition—modern, secular variety. It is healing for many patients and caregivers to experience the tradition of Jewish culture along with the community of fellow sufferers—however virtual it may be. In the Kovner poem cited above, there is an added twist and an enriched portion to the theme that Marc Straus offers about the gigantic size of our medical institutions: the title of Kovner's book is *Sloan-Kettering*, written in large Hebrew-alphabet transliterations of the English, reiterated in fuller spelling in the title poem, "Memorial Sloan-Kettering Cancer Center." That full name, when written in Hebrew letters that look awkward when thinking of

America, is its own kind of "midrash" of alienation, suggesting the patient's distance from the vast medical apparatus that so characterizes America. In one of T. Carmi's poems, the Hebrew word for "terminal" turns into six variations of the word in Hebrew (*sofani*—the same root can mean everything from wind to gladiolas) so that the patient imagines that these homophones may really be what was intended, not the dreadful adjective that describes candidacy for the end of life.

Hope Struggles against Despair: A Midrash on Ecclesiastes and the Project of Reconciliation

It was Yehuda Amichai's good fortune, and ours, that the book of Ecclesiastes is so well-known; from a midrashic point of view, it is also good fortune that its meanings have been challenged in almost every generation. It was one of the books that Amichai most loved pondering and that most engaged him as he reflected on the senior years of life. Ecclesiastes has been exposed to numerous midrashic exercises, many of them within the framework of the midrash and still more within other mediums—and especially in modern Hebrew poetry. The scroll (which we call *Kohelet* in Hebrew) is one of those foundational texts against which one can multiply meanings.

Ecclesiastes provides a text that responds to a fundamental human experience: the anxiety about life's brevity and sometimes seemingly redundant paths. Some of the thoughts in Ecclesiastes that have stayed with the Western soul are the following: no matter how great our achievements, they are small indeed compared to the scope of the universe; a person does not leave much of a real memorial for his deeds; things go around and around in an endless cycle—"What was will surely be, and what will occur surely has already happened; thus, there is nothing new under the sun" (Ecclesiastes 1:9)—the rivers go around in their courses and return to the sea, only to wind up as rain that goes into rivers and out to the sea again; and "there is a [fixed] time for everything under the heavens" (Ecclesiastes 3:1), which renders human agency futile. No wonder Jews read this book especially in the autumn. For then, the seasonal heat turns cool and sometimes to a chill that enhances our sense of vulnerability when we dine or sleep in the frail booths we call sukkot. It is that ambivalence of the shelter that is not a full shelter that is its own "midrash" on the human condition as it faces a healing prospect. Sukkot is the October allegory of our finitude, and Ecclesiastes is its bible! Amichai's "Ecclesiastes" is a rebellious twin to the book of that season.

"A man in his life," Amichai wrote in a fairly early poem in his career, "doesn't have time for everything, Ecclesiastes was wrong when he said that." But the presumed poet of Ecclesiastes didn't really say that there was "time for everything." He said that there was *a* time for everything, and he also seemed to be saying that he didn't like that state of affairs because it meant that human agency was superfluous. Often when Amichai starts a poem by disagreeing with a well-known thought or turn of phrase, we are about to experience a new thought, or at least a different way of looking at an old thought, and sometimes we know that he is going to distort the original thought beyond what its author might have intended. So we may receive a "double midrash":

> *A man in his life has no time to have*
> *Time for everything.*
> *He has no room to have room*
> *For every desire. Ecclesiastes was wrong to claim that.*
>
> *A man has to hate and love all at once,*
> *With the same eyes to cry and to laugh*
> *With the same hands to throw stones*
> *And to gather them,*
> *Make love in war and war in love.*
>
> *And hate and forgive and remember and forget*
> *And order and confuse and eat and digest*
> *What long history does*
> *In so many years.*
>
> *A man in his life has no time.*
> *When he loses he seeks*
> *When he finds he forgets*
> *When he forgets he loves*
> *When he loves he begins forgetting.*

And his soul is knowing
And very professional,
Only his body remains an amateur
Always. It tries and fumbles.
He doesn't learn and gets confused,
Drunk and blind in his pleasures and pains.

In autumn, he will die like a fig,
Shriveled, sweet, full of himself.
The leaves dry out on the ground,
And the naked branches point
To the place where there is time for everything.[10]

I have read this poem at countless funerals. And whether the deceased person has been thirty or ninety-five, the congregation nods, because they recognize their own feelings that "we don't have enough time." But they also nod because they know the Ecclesiastes verses—at least as interpreted by the Byrds—and they love seeing the humor in Amichai's playful deceit—one of the strategies of midrash, as so many authors in this volume suggest. The poem of regret about the short life of one mortal is also a reflection on the shared destiny of the living. We will consider further the other things the Israeli laureate said about "the man who doesn't have time," that is, the proof that he didn't have time, or the implications of the idea that a person doesn't have time, but for now, just the beginning causes us to "sit up and take notice," as Norman Cohen urges. In Rabbinic study, we have been taught to use a phrase whose root is embedded in the word "midrash": *darsheni*—comment on this; something is standing out and it needs another look. Ecclesiastes, it seems, always needs another look.

It can take a moment to realize that Amichai was stretching the meaning of Ecclesiastes' sense of time—there is a time for everything under the sun in the sense of a fixed or proper time of life or of the year—to time as an issue of the clock and length of life. The shift in the meaning of "time" gives the reader a free range in which to think: and what is the consequence of "not having time for everything under the sun"? Well, we have to do a lot of things at the same time, and we are bound by the limits of time, and only now at our death will we find the infinite field of time (and space—see Dan Pagis, below) that is hinted at for us when we begin our lives. No amount of sunshine provided by optimistic and hopeful essays can take away that fact, and we must seek out the bright side of the human condition with more realistic consolations. The consolation for any particular discouraged individual may be to know that the entire human family has the same experience. (See Richard Address's essay in this volume, and the foreword by Michele Prince.)

The Amichai poem has about the same "tragic" dimension as the book of Ecclesiastes itself, but around a different condition, a different problem with time. In either case we must make peace with the reality that is dealt us from life's deck of cards, and we may find that midrashic ways of encountering experience help us to get over it. And the stunning last line of the poem invites even the most atheistic reader to pause and reflect on infinity.

But—and this is part of the glory of the poetic project—Amichai's distortion of the meaning of "time" from "a time" to "time" is precisely what poetry makes us do—to look at words that rhyme, at sounds that are alike, at puns and oxymorons, and to ask ourselves: How can these new experiences, new ways of seeing, enrich my understanding of the human condition? How are they alike and yet different from the traditional meaning? The poet takes us from mechanical experience of the human encounter to the playful, imaginative, and possibly healing strength of the human encounter as his words stretch us. It is part of the metaphoric universe that Simkha Y. Weintraub describes in our opening essay, and the wicked playfulness with which Stuart Schoffman delights us: no afterlife, perhaps, but bring a change of underwear just in case. In one poem that is a favorite of mine, "Recipe for *Bikkur Cholim*," poet Malka Shaked reminds visitors to engage in magic (which she rhymes by making a Hebrew verb out of "hocus-pocus") and to don a Purim-like mask even when it is not Purim. In one of Zelda's most stunning brief poems, we are made to realize how a strange intimacy can spring up in the fragile environment of the hospital, where in Israel especially, class distinctions are paradoxical because (after all) everyone is Jewish:

> *When the brown-faced woman—*
> *who was, at that moment,*
> *polishing the floor—*
> *heard the doctor's words,*
> *she said to me,*
> *"I will pray for you."*
> *A sudden, new friend*
> *said to me, "I will pray for you."*[11]

Ecclesiastes wasn't Amichai's exclusive property. Many Israeli poets have taken advantage of *Kohelet*'s poetic tropes, played with them, looked at the texts, and applied them to the deeply personal condition in which they find themselves. T. Carmi, as he neared his death, pronounced on the fact that his time has come, and there is a time for everything, like "a time to imagine the taste of good coffee."[12] This is, perhaps, the deepest thought one can have when life is so fragile—what the late American scholar Henry Samuel Levinson called the hope you can hope at the end because it has a chance to be fulfilled.[13] Even the dying patient can legitimately hope for a cup of coffee. And, finally, the less well-known but dazzling poet Meron Isaacson has devoted an entire collection of short poems to considering aspects of "A time for …"—all of which address the meaning of illness. In "A Time to Give Birth" Isaacson proposes this enigma:

> *Your mother's body was once only a delight*
> *until you took your place within her,*
> *to be either a limb or a life.*[14]

Dan Pagis and Intertextual Play

So now let's look at the image of infinity in each of two poets who were colleagues and who held a deep respect for each other. Dan Pagis, on the beginning of life, sees the infant's world as an expanse of floor on which it is "impossible to go wrong."[15] Yehuda Amichai's mortal experiences an even greater infinity at death:

In autumn, he will die like a fig,
Shriveled, sweet, full of himself.
The leaves dry out on the ground,
And the naked branches point
To the place where there is time for everything.

I have just complicated another midrashic strategy—what the fancier postmodern critics call "intertextuality"—a sort of free play across different pieces of literature so that they shed light on each other. In that play between texts we may realize the relationship between infancy and old age, themes that other writers like the Talmudic Rabbis and Shakespeare have phrased in different ways. It needn't be as bleak as Jaques's utterance about the world and the stage:

... and his big manly voice,
Turning again toward childish treble, pipes
And whistles in his sound. Last scene of all
That ends this strange eventful history
Is second childishness and mere oblivion
Sans teeth, sans eyes, sans taste, sans everything.[16]

It may, in fact, be the consciousness of a kind of infinity on either side of our lives.

Such "intertextual play" defies the kind of logic that is necessary for figuring out how things work, how markets produce results, or how testimony is given at a trial. It also defies the logic of the medical clinic where doctors desperately try to cure disease. But it invites rumination and a reorganizing of the way we can go about the day to day, and it promotes looking beyond empirical fact and clinical logic. In the busy life of doctors, the clinical logic often limits us to experiencing the mechanical data of a case; but the midrashic play, carried on with awareness of its limitations, expands the mind into a kind of give-and-take and captures the way in which the creative mind puts the world of meaning together. Infants and old people share a sense of space. My patient actually wants to be like me: she is dying and I am taking care of her! The office building I enter every day is actually hostile to my patient. Doctor, I know I have to undergo all these tests and take those medicines, but at the same time I have to love and plant and sow ... so forgive me if I don't want to take all my medicines or go to all my appointments, and forgive me if I just need to cry (as Ruhama Weiss's rabbis had to cry, in her essay in this volume). And, let us never forget that word order, rhymes, rhythms, assonances and dissonances, and the beloved oxymoron enrich the imagination that can be so important in the encounter between doctor and patient.

But I want to return to Ecclesiastes, which became a favorite source text for many poets and thinkers in modern Jewish life. In Amichai's final work of genius, *Open Closed Open,* the poet uses ideas and specific phrases from the book of *Kohelet* no less than seventy times.[17] He does so with such alacrity and such subtlety that it takes several readings to realize that when he jokingly says that he has tried all of the positions for making love, he is actually quoting Ecclesiastes: "what was will be." And when he does that, Kohelet the preacher's melancholy turns to fun—an important part of any experience in a doctor's office—if we can bring it off! The doctor's office: another place I've been before! (Or, as Ecclesiastes the preacher said, what was will surely be again.)

The Musical Midrashic Advantage

It has been one of the pleasures of my recent work in midrashic readings through modern poems to work with the eponymous Debbie Friedman, whose melodies when set to these words urge upon the listener yet another layer, another set of the mirror and the lamp for thinking about the meaning of an original text.[18] When we take the double and triple meanings found in the play between many ancient texts and new ideas, we can add a musical layer that shapes the reading of that text. The way in which we breathe when we sing, the things we hear when we listen carefully to music, the changes in rhythm and level of sound, and indeed the beauty of the melody itself invite us to hear the words in a new way. And perhaps most exciting, there are times when simply singing the same words with different cadences and in different keys can give a second "midrashic" meaning. So Debbie and I have begun a kind of modern musical midrash with well-known psalms like "Those who sow in tears will reap in joy"

(Psalm 126:5) or prophetic texts like "My beloved son, Ephraim" (from Jeremiah 31). We can see if there is a different way to "turn turn turn" some well-known phrases from Ecclesiastes. We move from classic text to song based on that text, to a modern poem that builds on that text, and back to song. Our work goes one step beyond "making the words and music go together," as they must in one way or another. One meaning can redeem another, and one art can turn another toward new tropes, as Sheldon Marder demonstrates in his essay here.

I have used the poems of the Hebrew literary renaissance in my own emergence into spiritual maturity and in my work with patients and their families. Like Rabbi Marder, my mentor in these matters, I have used modern Hebrew poems as a personal companion and as a midrashic goad to communicate issues to patients, families, and health professionals, and I have—more importantly—used these materials to urge those same people to design their own meanings from these poems. The points of recognition that have come from this technique have enriched my life quite amazingly, and I have enjoyed as well trying to translate many of these poems with both a midrashic eye and the scholarly eye of accuracy, or perhaps better said, intellectual propriety. A text cannot mean "everything," after all, and there are some limits to my freedom when I interpret a text. Every game has its rules. T. Carmi was a mighty poet of the generation after the Israeli War of Independence, and in the final ten poems of his life—written in response to his terminal cancer—he notes that many words of death may sound like something different when you are in the doctor's office; that there is even a time for the taste of good coffee; that—in the cancer context—"It ['he' and 'it' are the same in Hebrew] will probably return" does not refer to the Messiah, and a host of other mordant puns and metaphoric plays on words. In remission, Carmi noted, "My body is like a hotel—empty for the moment, but waiting for its guests to occupy it fully. Shall I turn on the light outside so that they can find the place?"[19] Equally sarcastic was Abba Kovner's reflection at the time of Yom Kippur that the prayer to "be humble" before God (the entreaty of the worship leader at Yom Kippur) is easily achieved when one is a patient at Memorial Sloan-Kettering Cancer Center.[20] Easy to be humble, when one can barely reach for the call button—so please, don't ask me to utter the prayer about the importance of humility. Both Kovner and Carmi wrote of their illnesses with exceptional personal reference and tied their personal reference to the rich textual tradition of Bible, liturgy, and Rabbinic literature, thus making their personal experience into a universal appreciation.

A Journey into Aging

Nothing could be more personal for me, at an age above three score and ten, than to read the following two poems by Lea Goldberg and Haim Gouri:

THE OLD POET
Many no longer remember my name
And few—very few—
Know that I have written one more
Verse for them.
I sit in the shade of a tree
And little flecks of sun
Fall upon my brow
From among the graying leaves.
I know, that tomorrow
It will be quiet. And only my heart will hear that divine sound
Of my thunderous youth.
God once listened to
My prayer sounds
But now He has to listen to so many
Of the voices of others.
A choir of lofty voices
Breaking through the clouds
Tossed at Him like a stone
That breaks a window pane.
But for one hour this year
He lends His ear to me
And gracious, says to me,
Old man—son of my old age
Is your voice still young?

Is your voice still filled with dew?
In the book of the Generations
I keep with me still
A dry rose petal
That had once fallen in your garden.[21]

EIVAL

And those things that are lacking, and the extra quiet,
And you, what are you going to do with the rest of your life
     between the memories and the pills
Like that legendary Talmud student, forgive the comparison,
you are bent over your desk for hours.
I'm sorry to say that I fear that you won't be able to finish all
     the work,
neither you nor the dybbuk that refuses to exit your body.
And it will remain "the great unfinished." Crazed and quiet,
     the accused wanders around, seeking its future
in the darkening streets.
So, if the main thing is already well-known, why are you
     doing all this? Why?[22]

The source "texts" in either of these poems may not be entirely clear to all English readers. "One more verse" in Goldberg's poem clearly echoes Chaim Nachman Bialik's legendary poem "After My Death." "Eival," the title of Gouri's poem, is about the mountain in the book of Deuteronomy whence curses emanate: "I have set before you today the blessing and the curse" (Deuteronomy 11:26). The Talmud student reference echoes Bialik's poems "HaMatmid" (The Talmud Student), about the lonely student bent over his books while most of his world is disappearing, and "Levadi" (Alone), about the student who toils for nothing all night long.

There are actually four or five different qualities that constitute what we might call "midrashic" method. For some people, the term simply means taking an event or a piece of written material and then describing its added meaning or elaborating on its relevance for different audiences. For others, the term is more technical—what professionals call "a term of art," which—in order to be used properly—has to fit certain qualifications. Furthermore, some modern poetic texts shed so much light on the original biblical or Talmudic texts that a new meaning emerges in the original. Midrashic method also has some other characteristics including a measure of consolation, a surprise association of ideas from the Bible that usually remain unconnected, and an explicit sense of alternate readings through the phrase "And another way of looking at this experience is...." Each of these dimensions has been introduced in one or another of the essays in this book. And the poet Malka Shaked notes that a wandering mind also performs midrash. If you let your mind wander while saying the *Shema*, you might think that you are misinterpreting it—rejecting the idea that Israel ought to hear, in favor of the notion that Israel should hear God: "Listen O Israel [to] God...."

So our midrash-poems offer us some or all of the following experiences: suggestions about new ways of looking at old experiences; an opportunity to be in the moment and focus strongly on the experience; the new possibilities of meanings through the relationships of words to each other; healing through words, as the patient can share in the community of meaning making; an antidote to the cultural trends that we face today—the busy schedule, the short attention span, the urgency of being somewhere else at the same time; and the opportunity to turn a dark meaning into light even as we see the reality behind our efforts to make light of the serious. So, the psychiatrist poet Robert Carroll writes about the death of his own father:

> *Later, Daniel, who is three now,*
> *asked his mother why we threw dirt on Papa Joe?*
> *Then he asked his father why are we sad?*
> *Then he asked Joshua*
> *why we laugh when we're sad?*
> *So we told him, "When you love*
> *you feel it all,"*
> *and we showed him*
> *the world*
> *on our backs.*[23]

Midrash and poetry, music and words, words and words, and all the time free of the important immediate and practical task at hand so that one may reach for the infinity of the task beyond the task at hand, and feel the world on our backs. The task at hand in the doctor's office is to achieve a cure that makes the patient feel well; but another task awaits the other hand: the healing that comes from empathy, support, the opportunity to speak, the invitation to be morbid, the giving of the hand, and a shared weeping over our common destinies. All the world on the doctor's back, and on the patient's. As Yehuda Amichai summed up his ruminations about pain and pleasure, "I learned to speak from my pains."[24]

Rabbi Sheldon Marder is rabbi of the Jewish Home of San Francisco, where he specializes in spiritual care for people with dementia, the pastoral use of sacred texts and poetry, creativity in old age, and end-of-life care. He is a coeditor of the new Reform High Holy Day *machzor*. "Psalms, Songs & Stories" was honored by the Society for the Arts in Healthcare for "using the arts to improve the quality of the healing experience."

"Psalms, Songs & Stories"
Midrash and Music at the Jewish Home of San Francisco

Rabbi Sheldon Marder

> *For Frances Mallin Marder, of blessed memory,*
> *singer and songwriter.*

A collaborative project called "Psalms, Songs & Stories" empowers elders of the Jewish Home of San Francisco to become students and interpreters of biblical poetry, encourages reflection on their spiritual beliefs, and gives them tools to transform their shared reflections into songs that are imaginative, melodic, and hopeful.[1] The goal is an encounter between self and God in the fertile ground of sacred text, nurtured by a creative process that is musical and midrashic, spiritual and intellectual. The elders are guided in this work by a musician/songwriter and a rabbi.[2]

"Psalms, Songs & Stories" was developed in the context of skilled nursing/long-term care; its participants are among the frailest of the aged population, seventy-five to one hundred years old.

The Jewish Home of San Francisco is a nursing home. There is sickness that cannot be cured and pain that persists, despite the best efforts of doctors and nurses. Matters of life and death are always near and palpable. Ambulances and gurneys come and go. Beloved friends grow weak from their illnesses and die. Memorial services happen often in the Jewish Home's synagogue. Palliative care, comfort care, end-of-life care—these terms are ubiquitous in the everyday life of the Home.

In a certain sense, "Psalms, Songs & Stories" is a palliative. Like the medical palliatives brought to bear at the end of life, we find that our focus on music, memory, and spirituality sometimes eases suffering and sometimes offers peace of mind when the violence of disease is apt to take over a person's life.

Why Psalms?

The Hasidic master Nachman of Breslov taught, "Every person, according to his or her nature, is able to find him- or herself within the book of Psalms and earn repentance through reading the psalms" (adapted).

Urging us to immerse ourselves in the psalms, Nachman offers both a purpose and a promise: the purpose is self-discovery, self-understanding; in short, finding oneself. The surprising promise—or reward—is *teshuvah*, usually translated as "repentance" and described by Adin Steinsaltz as "one of the ultimate spiritual realities of Jewish faith." Steinsaltz teaches that *teshuvah* can mean "a return" to God or to the Jewish faith, or "turning" in the sense of adopting a new orientation or direction, and it can also mean "response."[3] All three meanings of *teshuvah* are relevant to the subject at hand.

"Psalms, Songs & Stories" owes a great deal to Professor Dennis Sylva's observation that Hebrew Bible "traditions do not systematize or uncover the past for its own sake; rather, they explore the traditions of the past in the light of God's activity in the present. Their function is to help people participate in the God-filled present."[4]

Kathleen Norris provides ample justification for the use of psalms in spiritual care: "The psalms make us uncomfortable because they don't allow us to deny either the depth of our pain or the possibility of its transformation into praise.... If the psalm doesn't offer an answer," she writes, "it allows us to dwell on the question."[5]

Why Songs?

Music is a universal source of pleasure. It stirs the emotions and, for many people, it conveys meaning. (Of course, music accompanied by words almost always aims to convey a meaningful idea.) In their original use, the psalms themselves were intended for musical accompaniment.

The pleasure we derive from music has many sources, and the study of how music "works" vis-à-vis human perception is a complex subject. For our purposes, one fundamental pattern is helpful: expectation, suspense, and resolution. Referring mainly to Western classical music, Leonard B. Meyer states, "The greater the buildup of suspense, of tension, the greater the emotional release upon resolution."[6]

The simplicity of this pattern is deceptive. Professor Meyer's research has also found that the more complex the music, the greater our engagement with it. "Works in which the audience's every expectation was met were found to be ultimately unsatisfying. So, too, were works in which no expectations were met."[7]

Most relevant to our understanding of "Psalms, Songs & Stories" is Professor Meyer's insight that the experience of musical suspense is similar to what we experience in real life:

> Musical suspense seems to have direct analogies in experience in general; it makes us feel something of the insignificance and powerlessness of man in the face of the inscrutable workings of destiny.... The low foreboding rumble of distant thunder on an oppressive summer afternoon, its growing intensity as it approaches, the crescendo of the gradually rising wind, the ominous darkening of the sky, all give rise to an emotional experience in which expectation is fraught with powerful uncertainty—the primordial and poignant uncertainty of human existence in the face of the inexorable forces of nature. With mixed feelings of hope and apprehension ... we anxiously await the breaking of the storm, the discovery of what unrelenting fate has decreed.[8]

The psalms defy easy characterization, but many follow a pattern that leads from expectation (of God) to suspense and tension (when God is hidden or life looks dark and hopeless), and ends in a resolution (renewed hope and faith). As it follows this pattern, the psalm engages us in questions about the meaning of human existence and the emotions that accompany all of human experience. For instance, we may find ourselves on a journey from "the valley of the shadow of death" to "the goodness and mercy" that "will follow me all the days of my life" (Psalm 23). Or on a journey that begins, "When You hid Your face I was terrified," and finds resolution when "You turned my lament into dancing" (Psalm 30). The more complex the psalm—the more intense, ominous, and fraught—the more emotionally gratifying it is.

Although the fabric of life for many chronically ill people in nursing homes is woven from sorrow, disappointment, and uncertainty, it is rich with longings for hope, faith, and inner strength. That is why psalm study with residents of a nursing home is a meaningful spiritual activity: the psalms are models for finding inner strength in the face of life's storms. "Psalms, Songs & Stories" teaches us something more: when we add the dimension of music (for example, the group's argument and decision regarding the use of a major or minor key; a heated give-and-take about harmony; choices involving consonance and dissonance, texture and tone), the emotions already stirred by the psalm come alive.

Most important is the group process in which participants articulate their personal movement from (1) expectation to (2) suspense to (3) resolution (for example, [1] God is present; God is good. [2] Where is God? Why is there suffering? How could God allow the Holocaust? [3] We believe; we know; we hope). Some songs follow this pattern; others do not. What then constitutes success in this project? We know that we have succeeded when a combination of elements—psalm study, self-reflection, metaphor making, and musical composition—encourages the elders to write a song that expresses life experience as mediated by faith.

"Music responds to illness," writes William Cutter, "more naturally than speech—any speech, even the speech of prayer. Perhaps it requires non-cognitive expression to capture the infinities of sorrow and hope."[9] And when those who are ill compose their own music to respond to their sorrows and hopes—how much the more so.

Why Stories?

Dew descends from the mountain
And brings life to the land
As fine oil warms and comforts us

So we can understand
What is life all about?
What is life all about?...[10]

Weeks of reflection on Psalm 133 (*Hineh mah tov*—"Behold how good") led one group of Jewish Home elders to write a song that responds to three questions: What is goodness all about? What is kindness all about? What is life all about? The melody they composed has a plaintive quality that expresses the urgency of responding to important human concerns as we approach the end of life. Here we see one aspect of Rabbi Nachman's promise: *teshuvah* as "response."

Jenny Rose, a resident of the Jewish Home, died at the age of 105—but not before spending her last years as a participant in "Psalms, Songs & Stories."[11] When conversation about Psalm 133 turned to the philosophical question "What is life all about?" Jenny began to reminisce. Nothing in life had given her greater satisfaction, she said, than baking. She loved her kitchen: the fragrance of fresh ingredients, the warmth of the oven, but most of all, the inner warmth she felt when sharing her baked goods with loved ones, friends, and neighbors.

Listening to Jenny, I remembered a line from a poem by Nissim Ezekiel: "Memories, / add up to meanings."[12] In her reminiscence of the kitchen, Jenny's meanings were adding up like the layers of a cake. We learned about her passion for the physicality of baking: rolling the dough, shaping a crust, crushing almonds. And we got to know something about Jenny's generous spirit and openheartedness.

The creative process had brought forth important memories, but when we turned back to our lyrics, we realized that words like "cookies" and "pie" sound trivial in response to the question "What is life all about?" Fortunately, one of us thought to say, "Jenny, tell us more about the cookies." Jenny replied, "They were sweet."

What is life all about?
What is life all about?
To give devotion to all around us
Bestow sweetness on all who surround us
To enjoy each other's bounty

And love everlasting
In peace and harmony
In this big, wide world

The story of Jenny's kitchen shows us the "recipe" of "Psalms, Songs & Stories." (1) Cultivate an awareness of the creativity in everyday life, for example, baking. (2) Take time to appreciate one person's memory: dispensing homemade cookies far and wide. (3) Transform the essence of that memory into a line of poetry: "Bestow sweetness on all who surround us." (4) Slowly, over time, add this line to the poeticized memories and stories of other participants. (5) Ask questions: What is our song about? What exactly do we want to say? How is the song connected to the psalm and to our beliefs? (6) Listen deeply inside yourself for a melody, which often begins with just a single note or a simple musical phrase, and give voice to it. The memories do, indeed, add up to meanings. The richness of those meanings can inspire music.

When Jenny recalled sharing her baked goods with loved ones and friends, she was engaging in a process that anthropologist Barbara Myerhoff calls "re-membering." Re-membering, she writes, calls "attention to the reaggregation of members, the figures who belong to one's life story, one's own prior selves, as well as significant others who are a part of the story. Re-membering, then, is a purposive, significant unification...." The result of this unification is sense and order: "A life is given a shape that extends back in the past and forward into the future."[13]

As a form of late-life integration, re-membering has been called "self-narrative":

Some gerontologists have observed and studied the autobiographical impulse among the elderly, an impulse described as a seeking of integrity or internal harmony. There does appear to be a need among many older persons to sustain a sense of continuity of the self with the past, which was one of the elements Erikson included in both his ego-identity and ego-integrity concepts. There is little doubt that a cohesive life story, or the integration of a series of story lines ... can provide some sense of continuity.[14]

"Psalms, Songs & Stories" can help elders create a meaningful autobiography in a social setting that rewards creativity. This would seem to be a valuable element in what Erikson sees as the struggle of integrity to defeat despair in old age and thereby attain wisdom. As wisdom-seeking elders engage in re-membering, and fight to overcome despair, there is another related outcome: Nachman's promise of *teshuvah* as "turning"—adopting a new orientation or direction.

Encountering the Biblical Text: Authenticity and Values

> *Interpretation never exists in a vacuum and it is up to us to decide whether we wish to try to be aware of what we bring to our own reading of a text.... A price is paid for this approach because we lose the security of knowing that "this and only this" is what the Psalm means. But Jewish tradition has always preferred the greater security that comes from knowing that ... a Psalm is open to continual rediscovery, that it can speak in ever new ways as our own personal circumstances change.*
>
> JONATHAN MAGONET[15]

> *Midrash [is] the act and process of interpretation.... Where there are questions that demand answers ... Midrash comes into play as a way of resolving crisis and reaffirming continuity with the traditions of the past.*
>
> BARRY W. HOLTZ[16]

One of the most positive new orientations that songwriting brings to Jewish Home elders is identified in a recent essay by Theresa A. Allison as the ability to "transcend institutional boundaries." Institutional boundaries in nursing homes grow out of residents' dependence on staff for help with daily activities, the routinization of life, and an institutional model that can be "more suitable to acute illness management than long-term care."[17]

Dr. Allison cites nursing-home ethnographers who find that nursing-home elders "resist submission through techniques that range from the use of irony (Vesperi 2003) to the refusal to eat intolerable food (Diamond 1992), to the use of shouting to obtain assistance (Kayser-Jones 1981)."[18] We learn from the research Dr. Allison conducted at the Jewish Home that there are other, more positive paths that an institution can encourage: "Through physical products, concerts, memories, and moments of sacred transformation, [Jewish Home songwriters] continue to grow and expand in ways quite unexpected in an institutional setting."[19]

As one example of "transcending institutional boundaries," Dr. Allison describes the process of composing a song, based on Psalm 126, by "11 women and 3 men, one of whom could not see, several of whom were hard of hearing, and none of whom remembered anything from the past three sessions." She remarks on the group's excitement when the rabbi recommended using what is called a "chiastic structure"—a common feature of biblical poetics—to resolve an argument within the group over the order of the lines.[20] The main lesson of the group's sudden enthusiasm for chiasm—in this case, a reversal of two lines—is this: the authority of the Bible always carries great weight when there is disagreement, because the Bible (as interpreted by the rabbi) anchors the elders' songwriting in a timeless tradition. This is analogous to the Bible's authoritative role in Rabbinic midrash.

This is not songwriting for its own sake; for the elders, their song's connection to a biblical psalm imbues it with religious purpose and, most important, gives it authenticity. An appeal to authenticity is sometimes the only way to reach consensus. Here we see yet another aspect of Rabbi Nachman's promise: *teshuvah* as a "return"—a return to God or the Jewish faith.[21]

The four-month process of creating the song included the use of multiple interpretations by poets and scholars, as well as relevant artwork—including a colorful 1988 painting on the apartment door of refusenik-dissidents in Leningrad (former Soviet Union).[22] The painting depicts the verse "We were as dreamers" (Psalm 126:1). The door's actual handle, dead-bolt lock, and hinges are strange elements in the painting and add to its dreamlike quality. Moreover, these real-world elements embedded within the painting remind the elders that they, like the refusenik artist, are engaged in a midrashic process—a process that entails an interpretation of experience that melds reality and hope, the creation of a personal narrative, and meaning making that draws on diverse sources. This work of art suggests an analogy between dissident artist and nursing-home songwriter: each uses creativity to resist or transcend limitations.

These are the words of the song composed by fourteen Jewish Home elders with dementia:

> *Tears, dreamers, songs of joy*
> *Fill our mouths with laughter,* freylach *and good health*
>
> *Tears, dreamers, songs of joy*
> *Restore our fortunes, happiness is wealth*
>
> *Tears, dreamers, songs of joy*
> *Restore our fortunes, happiness is wealth*
>
> *Tears, dreamers, songs of joy*
> *Fill our mouths with laughter,* freylach *and good health*[23]

Dr. Allison concludes:

> They had chosen to start and end the song with the line about health in order to make it explicit that wealth in this context served as a metaphor for happiness and good health. The use of the psalm enabled the songwriters to create something sacred, an offering of thanks. Both dreaming and the restoration of fortune, which were discussed in agricultural metaphors of the psalm, were reinterpreted in the context of health and happiness by this group of elders.... They temporarily transcended both the limitations of their own cognitive impairments and the financial and physical limitations of the institutional setting in order to establish a different value system in which laughter and health are markers of true fortune.[24]

The Power of Prosody in the Interpretation of Psalms through Song

Rhyme: Capturing the Relationship with God

> *When a rhyme surprises and extends the fixed relations between words, that in itself protests against necessity. When language does more than enough, as it does in all achieved poetry, it opts for the condition of overlife, and rebels at limit.*
>
> SEAMUS HEANEY[25]

What Heaney says about rhyme applies equally to parallelism, the defining feature of biblical poetry (described below). Rhyme and parallelism are keys to understanding the elders' experience of "Psalms, Songs & Stories"—an experience in which they stretch themselves intellectually, spiritually, and musically. In their rebellion against the limits of loss, pain, and disease, the elders use language to achieve startling moments of transcendence or what Heaney calls "overlife."

We will look first at rhyme, then at parallelism. The song based on Psalm 126 is a good starting point. The rhyming of "health" and "wealth" establishes the relationship between these two elements of a person's status, and this particular rhyme, as Dr. Allison points out in her analysis, enables the elders to express an important value: health is a marker of true fortune. The chiastic reversal of lines also draws attention to the equation of health and wealth and even suggests an allusion to the idea of "reversal of fortune." It is a telling theme for these elders: all suffer from health problems; almost 90 percent of them lack the financial resources to pay for the Jewish Home's skilled nursing care.[26]

The elders enjoy learning about the tools of their trade—for example, different kinds of rhyme: end rhyme, internal rhyme, exact and approximate (slant) rhyme, male (one-syllable) and female (two-syllable) rhyme. For most of them, this is new information from which they take visible pleasure. Edward Hirsch helps us understand why rhyming is a very satisfying experience:

It creates a partnership between words, lines of poetry, feelings, ideas.... It is as if the poet had called up the inner yearning of words to find each other.... There is a pleasure in the sound of words coming together.... Rhyme helps to define and individuate a line of poetry even as it links it to another line or lines. Rhyme creates ... a sense of interaction between words and lines.[27]

The elders' use of rhyme goes beyond the mastery of a technique. The rhymes they choose often underscore what is important in their lived environment and reflect their concerns and beliefs. In a song based on Psalms 117 and 134, we hear how the elders experience their partnership and interaction with God:

> *In our minds and hearts God is with us all*
> *In our minds and hearts to catch us if we fall*
> *God will always hear our call....*

What does it mean to say that "God is with us" in a nursing home? This cluster of three rhymes responds to that question with precision: In a place where falls are an ever-present danger, God will catch us. In a place where not being heard is an all too common experience, God will hear us. With their carefully chosen rhymes, the songwriters translate the technical language of "fall prevention" and "active listening" into personal theology.

Parallelism: A Framework for Spiritual Exploration

The opening words of Psalm 42 are among the most beautiful in the book of Psalms, an image Robert Alter calls "utterly arresting":

> *As a deer yearns for streams of water,*
> *so I yearn for You, O God.*
> *My whole being thirsts for God,*
> *for the living God.*
>
> PSALM 42:2–3[28]

The significance of biblical parallelism is hotly debated by scholars, but, in essence, the term refers to the dynamic relationship between the two (or sometimes three) parts of a verse. Robert Alter sees the parallel relationships in biblical poetry as a movement of meaning, which can manifest itself in a number of ways: intensification (or heightening), focusing, specification, concretization, and dramatization.[29]

Using Psalm 42 as an example (where "yearns" is parallel to "thirsts" and "God" is parallel to "the living God"), we can see how Alter's theory helps us understand the way the poetry works. "Yearns" is a powerful word, but a vague one compared to the more specific and concrete word "thirsts." And "thirsts" also carries more dramatic weight. The movement from "yearns" to "thirsts" dramatizes and concretizes what the poet experiences when he longs for God. When "God" becomes "the living God," we sense a heightening of the spiritual experience that shows the intensity of the poet's feelings about God and what God means to the poet.

A song based on Psalm 128 shows how the Jewish Home songwriters have incorporated the principles of parallelism. The main body of the song is as follows:

> *You shall enjoy the fruit of your labors*
> *Collecting memories from year to year*
> *Live to see your children's children*
> *With much joy and few tears*
> *May you see the beauty of their growing*
> *Like saplings into trees*
> *As we look ahead to the future*
> *May we leave God's world in peace*

When we view the last four lines through the lens of temporality, we see forward movement that builds in drama and intensity. A younger generation grows in beauty; an older generation looks ahead toward the most dramatic life change a person experiences. Saplings become trees; elders (the "old growth") pray for a peaceful departure from this world. There is a movement of meaning from "trees" to "peace": the elders experience a feeling of wholeness (peace of mind) when they see their grandchildren's maturation. The literary technique of parallelism provides a framework for the elders' exploration of the most important relationship in their lives.

James Kugel has invented a clever phrase to describe the kind of movement he sees between clauses in a psalm (or other parts of the Bible). He calls it a "what's more" relationship.[30] Let's return to the opening of Psalm 42 to see how it works:

> ... *I yearn for You, O God.*
> And what's more,
> *my whole being thirsts for God.*
> And what's more,
> *[my whole being thirsts] for the living God.*

By inserting the phrase "and what's more" between parallel parts of a line, we see more easily the relationships between words and the connections between ideas. That is why "what's more" has become an indispensable tool for the Jewish Home songwriters: it encourages them to think in terms of relationships and connections.

The scholarship of Professors Kugel and Alter has contributed greatly to the "Psalms, Songs & Stories" project, as has the work of Adele Berlin, who sees parallelism as a larger, dynamic phenomenon that can unfold throughout an entire psalm, and Walter Brueggemann, whose division of psalms into three related types—psalms of orientation, disorientation, and new orientation—is an important tool for those engaged in pastoral care.[31] Such scholarship is important to the goal of intellectual stimulation.

During one of our sessions, the elders were fascinated by S. Mowinckel's imaginative definition of parallelism as "thought rhyme."[32] The notion of thoughts that rhyme calls our attention to the common ground of rhyme and parallelism. The pervasiveness of either of these elements leads to poetry and song in which relationship and connection are the primary ingredients, just as they are in our lives within a family or community. In "Psalms, Songs & Stories," the poetry and music reflect a purpose that soars above the songs themselves to the elders' relationships with one another, with their loved ones, and with God.

Gapping: The Pastoral Significance of Formal Structure

Yet another technique that the elders enthusiastically adopted is called gapping. The same section of Psalm 42 provides a good example:

> My *whole being thirsts for God,*
> *for the living God.*

In the second clause, the phrase "my whole being thirsts" is missing. The missing words (the gap) are unspoken but are clearly understood by the reader. In this verse, gapping intensifies the psalmist's experience of God by creating a feeling of breathless movement from the first phrase to the second.

Poetic devices can have spiritual significance in the songwriting process. One result of gapping is that it may draw attention to the gap itself, thereby emphasizing the missing words. In one of the songwriting groups, a few elders picked up on that idea and realized that gapping is analogous to their experience of old age. How so? Having suffered the loss of many loved ones and friends, they said, they are more aware, at times, of what (or who) is absent than what is physically present. Gapping drew a group of elders into a profound conversation about the loss of relationships and the feeling of absence in their lives.

Conclusion: Enjoying the Fruit of Our Labors

> *What is meant by "runneth over"* [revayah]? *"Full to*
> *overflowing," as in the words "abundantly watering*
> [ravveh] *her ridges" (Psalm 65:11).*
> FROM A MIDRASH ON PSALM 23:5[33]

On June 13, 2007, the Jewish Home's new synagogue was dedicated in the presence of residents, board members, major donors, staff members, and community supporters. Three residents of the Home accompanied three lay leaders in a dramatic Torah procession and first-time placement of the Torah scrolls in the *aron kodesh* (holy ark). Prayers of gratitude were offered; reflections on the meaning of the synagogue in Jewish history were shared; several speeches were made. Most remarkable was the selection of six original songs based on Psalms 1, 23, 29, 128, 133, and 117/134.

The synagogue's dedication was a climax of the five years of "Psalms, Songs & Stories" to that point, because it brought the elders' deeply religious songs to the widest community yet, thereby expanding their circle of relationships and enlarging their world during the stage of life when a person's world diminishes in many ways.

Dr. Allison has described how, over the course of a grueling two-week period of rehearsals, the songwriters "pushed themselves to their intellectual and physical limits to participate.... Despite breathing difficulties and mobility limitations, some residents came almost two city blocks to get to rehearsals.... They sang, and worried, and sang their hearts out."[34] In their rooms they practiced from a CD of the songs made by their beloved teacher, Judith-Kate Friedman, who taught them the art of "freeing the voice within."[35]

When the Torah scrolls had been given their new home in the ark, eleven elders sang "Kosi Revayah," a song with a lilting beat inspired by the twenty-third psalm: "My cup overflows with a heart full of dreams." And with that affirmation of hopefulness and abundance in the later years of life, a room made of stone, wood, and steel took on the glow of sacred space.

4

God in the Doctor's Office
Some Midrashic Elaborations

Rabbi William Cutter, PhD, is emeritus professor of Hebrew literature and human relations at Hebrew Union College–Jewish Institute of Religion, with which he has been affiliated for over fifty years, as student, faculty member, and developer of programs in Jewish studies, education, museum education, and pastoral training. He is the editor of *Healing and the Jewish Imagination: Spiritual and Practical Perspectives on Judaism and Health* (Jewish Lights).

Talking to Physicians about Talking about God
A Midrashic Invitation

Rabbi William Cutter, PhD

*Dedicated to the memory of Henry Samuel Levinson—
wise teacher and loyal friend.*

When I was in rabbinical seminary, we studied Hebrew short stories of the late nineteenth century, a time when Jewish tradition was taking a hit from the emerging modern era with its nationalism and its freedom from religious orthodoxy—new patterns that took place amidst the promise of technology and industrial-economic expansion. The authors we studied had all emerged from the Orthodox Jewish world of Eastern Europe and without exception had left that world for the lights and breezes of the secular West. The father of modern Hebrew poetry, Chaim Nachman Bialik, gave poetic expression to this tension in his melancholy lyric of 1902: "The wind has carried them all away; the light has swept them up; a new song has enlivened the morning of their lives."[1]

Our professor, a pleasant but perhaps stodgy gentleman who didn't share much imagination with us, would begin every lecture in Hebrew by quoting some "positivist" scholars who flourished in the early twentieth century—the generation just after the beginning of this literary renaissance. Some of these scholars tried to explain how the purely aesthetic literary form emerged from such a constricted religious environment. Often we would hear such descriptions of the writer's artistic motivation as "From his father he inherited a scholastic rigor and learned the intricacies of Jewish law and ritual, and from his mother he inherited (either) his romantic tendencies (or) his love of nature, (or) a Hasidic appreciation for God's spirit." (Sometimes the gender was reversed. My memory is approximate.) Presumably this combination of qualities is what created the great generation of Hebrew authors and poets who knew traditional Judaism but longed to combat it with their art, even as their art included constant reference to the abandoned world of religion. What really animated these writers, it seemed to me, was a rebellion against rigidity, a loss of faith in old norms, and an appreciation of the new world, filled with the promises of freedom, and the opportunity to experience new worlds. Odessa and Warsaw, and surely Berlin, and sometimes points even farther west lured these former "believers" into contact with the arts of the Occident. The breeze and the spirit that Bialik's talmud student longed for, and eros as well! Towering geniuses like Tolstoy and Nietzsche and proto-existentialists like Dostoevsky became part of the Jewish menu. An enlarging world of intellectuals embraced philosophical skepticism to foster a kind of creative atheism among learned Jews who were deeply attached to the remarkable Jewish culture, but resistant to its theological promptings and its rigorous rules. The result for many of these people (men and women, but mostly men) was dislocation.

That resistance continues to pester religious Judaism while it promises increasing freedom to those of us who embrace the scientific approach to health and healing. Medicine, by embracing that science, can actually "cure" many illnesses today in a way only dimly imagined at the turn of the twentieth century. The progress we enjoy from clinical medicine is largely a result of the very technological progress that lured young men away from Orthodoxy over one hundred years ago. Spiritual matters seem to decline with the inclines of science (both directions related to the word "clinic," it would seem). My essay argues that there is a price for progress and that the newly emerging healing communities and their related activities are compensating for what has come to be missing in contemporary medical practice.

In my professor's understanding, it was the combination of some kind of spiritual delicacy and scholarly precision that made up the genius of the writers whom I later came to study more fully. It was as if there were two separate brains. Such a simple two-sidedness to one's brain function has probably been discredited from a purely scientific point of view, and yet it remains a way to look at much of the human condition. And perhaps it is a way to understand the main issue that this essay addresses. Which part of the curing/healing process depends on the scientific rigor of the laboratory, the research bench, and the diagnostic setting, and which part has to do with less tangible elements like spirituality, imagination, and the companionship that fosters human community? Our book is part of a growing effort to bridge the apparent gaps, and yet—before the bridge—we have to look at the ground on either side of the divide. A lot of popular physicians have written about this: Groopman, Nuland, Gupta, Gawande, Siegel, and Charon, to name just a few, and there are many more people interested in narratives of medicine and healing.[2] But this narrative reporting, heralded though it has been, is still part of a way of thinking that is counter to what really goes on in the day to day. Even the taking of medical history is only a part of the narrative process for busy clinicians. American health practice is, I suggest, a vivid instance of the divide, the abyss, and the bridge between the two worlds that are involved in the treatment of patients and the engagement of their families.

I thought of my old professor while I was enjoying an article by Jerome Groopman, physician, spiritual booster, and humanist, and one of America's serious writers on health, humanism, and spirituality. Dr. Groopman offers a unique view of the abyss and the bridge in a stunning *New Yorker* essay of about ten years ago: "God on the Brain."[3] "My Jewish heritage," he wrote, "is mixed, the tight scholastic rationalism of Vilna, in Lithuania, on my father's side, and the ecstatic Hasidic mysticism of Hungary's Carpathian Mountains, on my mother's." So there we have that old paradigm, only this time in a twenty-first-century framework, and in autobiography—not the ruminations of an old professor about someone else. What is the strength of this distinction, and how can it help us to understand the full human being? Dr. Groopman surprises us at his morning prayers:

While praying, I try to touch both traditions. Sometimes I will think about the root of a particular word in an attempt to delve deeper into the message of the text. Other times, I recite the ancient Hebrew words in a rapid monotone until they flood over me, submerging distinct thought.

What doctor, I wondered, wants to "submerge distinct thought"? And what patient wants his doctor to submerge that thought? I reflect on my own medical condition, as I am visited each year by nearly a dozen physicians, from whom we will hear later, specialists and excellent clinicians—each of them—but people without the time to think about the things that I am thinking about in this essay. "No doctor, I hope, and probably no patient," I answer myself, hopefully, as I ready myself for another visit to address a distinct problem or concern prompted by my cancer and my heart disease. I am actually grateful that my doctors engage in distinct thought, which analyzes my cardiac output, my PSA, the strength of my bones, the size of my tumor, the output of my adrenal gland, and a host of other clinical manifestations that seem too obvious and too physical for the elegant aspirations of my book.

Yes, I am grateful for the "distinct thought" but after dealing with the clinical stuff, where am I getting the sense of spiritual support, and where is the communication among my doctors that assures me that my entire body is being dealt with as a unit? Is my doctor catching my personal signals? Are my anxieties being considered? Have I been touched? Is there some opening for "discourse" between us so that some of the really important nonphysical matters in my life can be addressed? And how much time is there for the opportunity to find out something slightly unpredictable or invisible about my health? What might—in my wildest fantasy—be the consequences of all my doctors talking with each other—about me, and at the same time in the same room? (This latter can be summarized in the word "co-location," which I have heard only a few times.) On the "distinct thought" side of this ledger, by the way, even narrower and more specific clinical manifestations are sometimes missed by the persistently fragmented nature of my treatment in the hands of specialists. I must note at this early point in my essay that the practice of psychotherapy has to be excepted from some of this discussion, although it merits its own consideration and suffers from its own restricted relationships. (That consideration is provided by this volume in the essays of Philip Cushman and Lewis Barth.) Furthermore, as Dr. Ronald Andiman points out, there are several treatment environments in which "co-location" is common practice—further argument for my case, as I believe we shall see.

I seek to join the "physicians of the empirical" with healers who are urgent to narrow the divide between faith and science and eager to find a bond between human experience and the experience of cells, organs, and muscles. If a positive outlook is helpful at all, and if a meditative way of relating to the world can be salutary, what can my physicians do to help build that environment? Would it help my healing for the doctor to know that a building with no place to sit and slow elevators makes me dread a visit to her office—especially if my sciatic nerve is sore? Can the sweats and depression that seem to result from androgen-blocking hormones be addressed in some meaningful way besides by tranquilizers or by a casual referral for acupuncture? Can I talk about trying some of my more intrusive therapies intermittently? Would I feel better if my cardiologist and my oncologist spoke of my condition and treatment while seated in the same room so that my fears of drug interactions could be addressed? But most important, can my physician contribute to my understanding that a good healing includes learning to accept the tentative and temporary nature of cure? What can the "curing" doctor contribute to my ability to integrate my clinical situation with my spiritual aspirations? And might my doctor's own work be more satisfying if we shared aspects of our professional and dependent journeys?

An increasing number of recent articles in the *New York Times* and even in the *New England Journal of Medicine* and discussions with many doctors over the years suggest to me that part of the answer lies in a slow and ambient communication for which few physicians have time anymore. So this essay is a pitch for more conversation, more communication, and more discourse between patient and doctor and among doctors. Where that is not possible, many patients have opted for at least one half of that experience by seeking discourse in other places: healing groups, synagogues, shared reading in the humanistically oriented periodical literature. There's nothing new in that; but it may be novel to consider that pitch within a theological frame and to include physicians in that frame.

Speech: The Key to Communication, and the Possibilities of Midrash

Jewish tradition has struggled for more than two centuries with the importance of speech. And the subject of words and speech seems to be increasingly important for those who cure and for those who heal.

First, about words in the Jewish tradition: the subject appears prominently if not systematically, and each time, the texts in which the subject is embedded hold a strange power over the reader. The idea that comes to mind immediately might be the famous notion in Genesis that the world was created with a word. But I want to begin with one of the places that most folks don't know about but that religious Jews see frequently—the morning prayer for the Sabbath, called "The Soul of all the living...." (*Nishmat*), where the prayer claims that speech is inadequate to capture the power of the divine enterprise: "Were our mouths as full of song as the sea, we would still be unable to utter even a thousandth part of the majesty of God." In a moment we are going to see that an enormous paradox resides in this suggestion, because I believe that this passage—about the inadequacy of speech—is the greatest argument for speech and for much of the communication that results from speech. But it does insist that God is part of the important discussions about speech.

Speech is indeed powerless to capture the magnificence of the experience of God. I am reminded of the exaggerations and flights of John Donne in one of his meditations from the seventeenth century:

> My God, my God, thou art a direct God, may I not say a literal God ... but thou art also a figurative, a metaphorical God too; a God in whose words there is such a height of figures, such voyages, such peregrinations to fetch remote and precious metaphors, such extensions, such spreadings, such curtains of allegories, such third heavens of hyperboles, so harmonious elocutions, so retired and so reserved expressions, so commanding persuasions, so persuading commandments, such sinews even in thy milk and such things in thy words.... Oh, what words but thine can express the inexpressive texture and composition of thy word.[4]

In Donne's hyperbole, only the words of God can express the nature of God. We are, in fact, speechless. And yet we reach for God through speech—or, in more secular terms, we reach for higher understandings through speech.

Yet another interesting trouble spot is the notion of "Creation with a word" that is the foundation point and very beginning of the Hebrew Bible, and its having been carried forth in the psalm's affirmation "By the word of God were the heavens created" (Psalm 33:6). Everyone knows that God said, "Let there be light and there was light" (Genesis 1:3); the only problem is that the modern techno-world we live in suggests that saying "Let there be light" is like a command to someone to turn on a switch, rather than the idea that it is the act of speech that "turns on" the light.

And then, of course, we have also inherited the famous fable of the Tower of Babel—probably not meant to suggest babble, even though it sounds mighty like it, since the story is about the cacophony of voices that resulted from the efforts of people to create a unified world. Humans from that time on were "spread abroad" (presumably because of their arrogance in building a tower), with different speech for each nation, and we have spent the rest of history trying to understand each other's language. People, no less than nations, have to keep translating from the private language of each, as the contemporary writer Jhumpa Lahiri suggests in her wonderful book of short stories *The Interpreter of Maladies*.

Finally there is the dicey notion (for Jews, in any event) that God's word (or The Word) can become flesh or that it did at one critical time in history. This embodiment of word into flesh, which Jews always seem to have rejected, is actually not so foreign to Jews—and it is not at all foreign to thinkers for whom theories of writing include an effort to explain how we make an idea into a thing (as in the elegant nobility of the doctor's task into a simple curing by medicine or surgery, or in the equally intriguing task of taking the material act of curing and elevating it to a realm more filled with spirit and imagination).

In one way or another, speech creates, and these ancient expressions of the importance of speech are elaborate ways of saying what we all experience. At every level of our being, speech creates—either through the illusion of reality that is common to advertising and fictional literature or through the more physical fact that something doesn't (seem, at least, to) exist unless its existence can be uttered in speech. And we surely create the new out of communication with each other about the old—which is the practice of midrash. I am going to stay with the theology of the notion, which—as I note above—may not please every physician.

Theology: The Specialty for Which There Is No Residency

In a letter that I wrote recently to a bunch of my doctors (twelve in all, specialists every one, with the suffix "-ology" attached to the name of their specialties), I suggested that what people like me needed was a little moderation of cardiology, urology, endocrinology, neurology, and oncology and a little more theology. Medical specialties are the best expressions of Groopman's "distinct thought," after all, and have created a powerful and curative medical environment. I myself have been "cured" or certainly made alive by the distinct practices and thoughts involved in radiation, cardiac surgery, and a ton of pills. "Theology for many of you doctors," I wrote, "will seem irrelevant in the busy ins and outs and ups and downs of your workday, but I ask you only for a bit of an audience just now. My idea is that patients and doctors need to talk more with each other in order to arrive at the wholeness that might be the goal of our healing impulses."

I realized after I wrote that letter that I was writing in the spirit of an address Abraham Joshua Heschel had delivered to the American Medical Association in 1964. Heschel urged the doctors not to flee from the notion that they are God's partners. (See the reference to this speech in the essay by Richard Address in this volume.) But since that powerful nineteenth-century split that separated Jews into two camps, religiously speaking, the idea of God divides rather than unifies; it offends people of science rather than drawing them near. In the kabbalistic tradition of Judaism, beginning in about the thirteenth century, the question of speech and words begins to take on the strongest metaphysical and theological status it ever occupied in the history of Jewish thought. I risk introducing the relationship between speech and light into this discussion.

My thinking begins with the notion that God as Infinite Light occupied all of the universe and that all speech was summarized by a kind of soundlessness. In that imagined myth, God had to diminish or restrict his light in order for there to be room for the world, for creation of things, and surely, even for words. The process by which this myth-narrative took place is divine contraction (known as *tzimtzum*). That contraction, which takes place to the sides of an infinite circular image, leaves a space in the middle in which finite products and elements may appear that would not otherwise have been able to appear because of the dominance of the Infinite Light. And so, in the middle, there is a kind of tragedy accompanying the paradox that Creation requires God's absence. But there is speech there, and it could only be there if finite elements had room to establish themselves. Those who speak must keep talking in order to reach out across the abyss, and this is not a matter of the speech of one person, but of a community of speakers; and as the individuals within that community come to an understanding, their communication is less fragmented. It is that community of speakers that is missing between a battalion of doctors and their patients. And it is that move toward unity that can bring all the specialists together to create light.

According to Rabbi Nachman of Breslov, the late-eighteenth-century Hasidic master,

> You must realize that discourse is an aspect of Creation. For the essence of the act of Creation is the empty space that was formed when God contracted Himself from within. Otherwise everything would have been Infinity (and infinite light), and there would have been no room for the creation of mundane things. So, just as in the act of Creation, the essence of God being divine light, there was originally no room for the creation of any of the finite things—and especially speech—that we associate with the very being in the world, there is not only room, but there is the invitation to shared speech in order to return some of the light to the center.[5]

Recently, in the *New York Times*, Dr. Nell Burger Kirst wrote that words are paramount in the business of medicine. Diagnoses are illuminated by the patients' own accounts of their illnesses. Treatment options are discussed using conditional verbs, plans described in the future tense. And in the end everything is documented. Making the case for the importance of attention to the nonverbal hints and dispositions of patients, Dr. Kirst nonetheless winds up making the serious case for discourse as a divine act.[6]

And the truth is that both verbal speech and nonverbal cues are necessary in the relationship of patient to doctor, and both the nonverbal cues and the speech that uses words are part of the necessary baggage of the physician; and both partake of the metaphysics of the Breslover rabbi who wrote the popular version of the notion about speech that we read just a few paragraphs above. For without some differentiation there would be nothing to say, yet because of differentiation we often do not understand each other. Co-location (and collocation) is necessary in one form or another to help the patient feel "communicated with." Dr. Groopman seems to experience both sides of this pattern while at his morning devotions, and John Donne seems to capture an exaggerated notion of it in his attraction to the literal and metaphoric sides of speech.

Wholeness Is a Hope

So it seems that in discourse we move toward a fullness that is both unachievable and yet necessary to the human ambition, as we all—patients and physicians, clients and social workers—strive to reach the fullness that is a hint of God. In mystical terms, there is more light when there is more communication. In practical terms, doctors ought—at the least—to imagine themselves in the same room when working together regarding a shared patient. In social terms, patients may now create communities to compensate for that lack of discourse—in both clinical specificity and in narrative desire.[7]

A Humorous Note about God

Aside from playing God sometimes, what do physicians think I mean by the word "God"? Are they victims of the endless attention to TV evangelists whose rhetorical ballets reinforce the smell of snake oil?

Are they bombarded, as many of us are, by images of God as healer that make us see God in a surgical gown? It is surely not their fault that God images default to a kind of "old man in the sky." After all, the prayer book insists on this, and the public press can't seem to put it away. But behind it all resides the possibility of mystery and all those unknowns that seem to prompt everything from the intensities of nature to the confounding unfairness of early and undeserved disease, unwarranted accidents and failures that often afflict the innocent. And when it comes to prayer, the hucksters and fundamentalists speak of a god who listens to billions of prayers a day and somehow decides day by day whose prayers will be answered.

But there is an alternative vision of God that resides within Jewish tradition. It is a vision of a God who cannot be seen and to whom access can be achieved only through elaborate behavior or interpretive midrashic practice here on earth. My argument has been that one of those practices is speech and communication. In most of the key generations of Jewish history, the religious leaders and thinkers have either struggled mightily with the philosophical problems presented by the notion of having a God at all, or they have embellished their search with a lush verbal machinery that makes the concept of God into a master mystery. Sometimes they have struggled through the paradoxes of presence and absence that are features of profound mystical longings or secrets built upon secrets so that truth is refracted through multiple prisms. And for sure, the tradition of midrash and commentary has tried over time to diminish literalness and anthropomorphism. "O God," said John Donne, "thou art a metaphoric God even if you are not only a metaphoric God."

It is for that reason that I am surprised at the simple atheisms that renounce the existence of a God who cannot exist in the first place. I seek a more complex relationship to a God who prompts awe, mystery, and an indeterminate or even tragic relationship to the universe in which we live.

You may or may not believe that God answers prayer, and you may believe that notions of some spirit pulling the physician upward is romantic nonsense. But we cannot dismiss the needs of people to be touched, to see meaning in their health experience, and to rely on their doctors, who are ultimately the source and object of medical communication. And we can imagine the richness of a dialogue among physicians as they stand in one room at the same time speaking about their specialties in regard to one patient. There's a lot of Lithuania in our modern life, and perhaps to the scientifically oriented busy physician, a lot of the Carpathian mumbo jumbo. Yet talking about a patient is hardly about mumbo jumbo, but about the distinct words that reflect distinct thought but that—when shared—can wind up influencing the romantic and even deeply spiritual needs of the fragile person we serve. What we need are more Groopmans, contemplating prayer and its words and talking to other physicians while keeping God on the brain. And when there is no impulse for that difficult aspect of healing practice, we surely need communities that provide what is missing. They may even be communities for whom midrash and "the Midrash" may become companions.

Ronald M. Andiman, MD, is a partner of the Kalsman Institute and a founding member of the doctors' study group Assaf. He is clinical chief of the Department of Neurology at Cedars-Sinai Medical Center in Los Angeles and clinical professor of neurology at the Keck School of Medicine of the University of Southern California. He is a committed synagogue member and practices general neurology with a special interest in headache management.

A Physician's Response to the Midrashic Invitation

Ronald M. Andiman, MD

In my fantasy about how I would like to practice neurology, the scene opens upon an office similar to the introductory minutes of *Masterpiece Theatre* where, before Alistair Cook prefaces the drama soon to unfold, the camera roams a large room with old and eclectic furnishings, tables strewn with items suggestive of a wide-ranging intellect—old scientific instruments, objets d'art, and personal bric-a-brac reflective of wide travel and varied interests. My office would be similarly decorated. There I would enter at 9 a.m., after having arisen at a respectably early hour for exercise after a nutritious breakfast. My first patient of the day would be ushered in, and we would sit in my idiosyncratically decorated office, patient in a comfortable armchair and I in a suitably positioned armchair. Our discussion would deal with the medical issues that brought the patient to my office but would be wide-ranging and comprehensive. We would spend one and a half hours together. The patient's many questions and concerns would be covered in detail, I would be able to glimpse the patient's personality and emotional needs, and there would be enough interaction that the patient would have time to develop a trusting relationship with me. We would formulate a plan of investigation and treatment, and the patient would leave with a sense of having been heard and perhaps with a sense of relief. After she leaves, I would dictate a detailed report after researching the latest as well as the classic literature; the report would be cogent yet literary, as much an essay as a clinical document. And then I would go to lunch. I would read some poetry for dessert, and at 2 p.m. I would return to the office for another clinical encounter.

I present this description as a satire on what Rabbi Cutter seems to be proposing in an ideal world. And, while I understand that his essay tries to set forth a theological model for patient and doctor, a way of making God and spirit a part of the doctor-patient discourse, I believe it holds limited promise.

Patients have their own expectations of a doctor, and many patients would actually be impatient with an extended process of communication; they value efficiency over breadth or depth, especially if they don't think of their problem as complex. Sometimes even if the problem is complex, some patients, because of a heavily defended psyche or because of their value system, merely want to get a brief "answer"; they get their emotional support elsewhere or perhaps not at all. The point is, one size (of verbal discourse) doesn't fit all.

Perhaps at the very least, though, the clinician should know his patient well enough to decide how much emotional, psychological, or spiritual support is optimal. It would, in fact, be a valid ideal to work toward a satisfactory discourse in its own right, one that increases the likelihood of learning more about the patient, to better fulfill his needs. I like to think I achieve some of this in my practice, but I confess that I haven't conceived of this practice in religious terms.

There is another issue. What exactly is spiritual support, and in what form is the clinician supposed to offer this? Is it the same or different from emotional or psychological support? Doctors are not spiritual healers—that is not what we were trained to do, and most of us don't even know what "skill set" might reasonably be acquired to obtain it. Getting too involved with matters of the spirit might be considered by some patients as inappropriate or intrusive. I remember very well patients complaining to me about an endocrinologist I had referred them to because he had discussed religious matters with them that they felt were not salient to the clinical situation. I know that the "religion" that Rabbi Cutter is proposing is more complex than what that endocrinologist was promoting, but the danger of misaligning the patient's needs and the doctor's perception of them must be avoided.

When Dr. Groopman is held out as a champion of humanism and spirituality in health care, the example given has to do with his own personal process, not his process in a one-on-one situation with a patient. In some way his personal devotions may influence the way he approaches his patients, but it doesn't seem clear exactly how that works or whether that process would work for everyone.

You ask, "Is my doctor catching my personal signals?" Maybe the doctor is tired or busy and his antennae are blunted. Maybe he is psychologically unsophisticated or just obtuse. There may be time constraints in an office follow-up appointment of just fifteen minutes to deal with the important issues Rabbi Cutter would like to discuss. Now more than ever, with the ratcheting down of reimbursements, doctors are less able out of economic constraints, if not out of mere ineptitude or disinclination, to deal with less concrete issues in the context of a routine appointment. As Cutter pointed out in his essay, words have creative force. If you feel your signals are not being heard, then is it not incumbent upon you as a patient to use words to express your needs and see what kind of creative response such words engender?

In making these remarks I do not wish to act as an apologist for mediocre doctoring but rather to point out quotidian realities. I have no argument with the idea that a good physician might help with "learning to accept the tentative and temporary nature of cure." But I doubt he is the sole source of this insight, which is likely to involve the patient's own soul-searching, the support of friends and family, and one or another form of psychotherapy. I cannot argue with the need for "more communication and discourse between patient and physician," though there may be practical limitations as noted above. It is only toward the end of Cutter's essay that he acknowledges that there may be a nonverbal component to the communication that occurs in the relationship between the patient and his doctor, though I wouldn't characterize it as "necessary baggage." Rather, words may pale in importance to certain actions taken by the doctor on behalf of the patient, most of which are not compensated: the seeking out and review of voluminous old medical records; reviewing the images of old diagnostic scans rather than relying solely on the previous reports; filling out insurance forms and disability forms in a timely way; responding to the inquiries of relatives and friends; appealing adverse insurance decisions regarding reimbursement for services or medication. In addition to words, these actions show that you care. I agree with Dr. Les Zendle, who said at the first Kalsman conference, "Patients don't care how much you know until they know that you care."

The physician in this country at this time feels assailed by forces he can't control and that seem to consider him an expensive and expendable (and certainly ignorable) cog that clogs the smooth flow of inexpensive health care to Americans. My somewhat peevish response is in part colored by the economic and political atmosphere in which medicine is practiced. The thrust for health-care reform, though much needed, will result in a big chunk taken out of the doctor's hide. Reimbursements will be predicated on conformity to certain formats of care, which will have to be documented. There will be less room for creative relationships. Physicians will be paid for what can be measured, and the likelihood of a measure for the ineffable (the "spiritual" if you wish) in the doctor-patient relationship is small. Doctors who do a very good job relating to their patients and caring for the psyche/soul as well as for the body, which often translates into more time spent with patients, will not be rewarded any more than their colleagues who do not. The system is geared to reward complex technical procedures above relationships. Procedures are measurable; relationships are not.

My tone is engendered by this contemporary aberration in the politics and economics of medicine. I would not wish this to cloud my response to the more universal theme of Cutter's discourse. He argues for the pluripotentiality of the Word and I threw back at him nuts and bolts; now I toss more (mere) words.

This book nominally addresses the role of midrash in and its relationship to the practice of medicine. The term *midrash* is being used metaphorically as a shorthand way of combining such cognitive and interpersonal elements of the physician's own experience and the doctor-patient relationship as communication (dialogue in particular), reflection, interpretation, poetic insight, self-examination, and dealing with issues of the spirit.

The philosophical underpinning that allows me to cope with clinical practice doesn't so much parallel Donne's attitude or that of the *Nishmat* prayer (although I am sympathetic to both). Rather, I take as my mantra the morning prayer:

Blessed are you, O Lord our God, Sovereign of the Universe, who has formed humankind in wisdom and has created in humans many orifices and vessels. It is revealed and known before the throne of your glory that if one of these be opened or one of these be closed, it would be impossible to exist and stand before you. Blessed are you O Lord, who heals all flesh and does so wondrously.[1]

My attitudes are fundamentally based on notions of the vastness, complexity, intricacy, and beauty of the physical world, as well as the personal and psychological complexity of human beings. My meditation on these matters, which occurs in the small interstices between other activities of a busy professional and personal life, is based on readings of natural history and the other sciences. Some poetry helps to dress up the thought process. Thinking about nature and the nature of the world leads to humility in the face of the vastness and beauty of the universe, in which we are, in all of our complexity, the merest speck.

The elusiveness of knowledge is another theme one may derive from reading science. When God pulled up the skirt of light to give a little room for the vortex-spot that exhaled itself into our universe, it became a universe that keeps unfolding itself and expanding itself into larger and more complex forms, like a reverse set of Chinese nested boxes. Oscar Wilde said, "The true mystery of the world is the visible." I am in awe enough when thinking about the physical world. The spiritual completely eludes me. That there is any wisdom in the world at all is miracle enough.

On the one hand, there is the concept of the material world evolving people and people evolving speech, enabling us to express the intangible. On the other hand (in classic midrashic form) there is the intangible Word creating the tangible world, the Word being the creative medium through which new ideas, concepts, and new material objects (the wheel, the lightbulb, the computer) come into existence.

My internal midrashic dialogue involves the struggle to attain a level of virtue that I can live with. I worry about the comforting word I might have said but didn't think of in time to assist the patient. I fret over my delay in sending a letter required to allow the performance of a diagnostic study denied by the insurance company. There is too much to do and too little time in which to do it. There is no choice but to carry on and try to do better next time. This is the wisdom of my fitness instructor who advises us not to get caught up with trespasses of the day, but to go on and show greater discipline at the next meal.

Rabbi Cutter expands on this idea rather narrowly, arguing that what the world needs now is "that patients and doctors need to talk more with each other in order to arrive at ... wholeness ... healing." I would argue instead that, as the song says, "What the world needs now is love, sweet love." Doctors and patients need to communicate better, and that communication takes place on a number of planes, only one of which involves speaking. Earlier I alluded to the mundane role of following through with phone calls and reports; there is also the act of hugging, of holding hands, of the well-timed nod acknowledging pain, of attentiveness (active listening, listening with the third ear) to what the patient is saying and not saying.

My own theological perspective doesn't allow me the presumption of considering myself God's partner. I really can't begin to identify with that concept. Rather, my sources of instruction come from, and my dialogue is with, the sages of my tradition: "Say little and do much," said Shammai (*Pirkei Avot* I.15). "It is not thy duty to complete the work, but neither art thou free to desist from it," taught Rabbi Tarfon (*Pirkei Avot* II.20).[2]

Another notion that animates my professional work is the idea of bringing greater peace to the world. In Hebrew, "wholeness" and "peace" derive from the same root—they are different aspects of each other. This etymological truth embodies a certain cultural way of looking at the world, which is my heritage. I see my goal as having the patient leave my office feeling better than when she arrives. When making rounds in the hospital, I see myself as part of the hospital experience, fraught with all sorts of discomforts, indignities, and stresses, and I therefore seek to allay some of those agonies.

I take issue with the implications of the phrase "the scientifically oriented busy physician." It implies that doctors are insensitive to emotional (or, in other terms, spiritual) needs of their patients. Doctors' strengths and weaknesses probably run the same gamut as rabbis'—some of whom work in concrete ways and some of whom deal well with nuance and metaphor. Many of my colleagues are broadly educated—they have studied philosophy, literature, and psychology; some write creatively; some are practicing artists; others are students of history. And even those who don't do any of these things are rarely insensitive dolts. There is a spectrum of behavior, even among surgeons.

Cutter argues forcibly not only for doctors to talk to patients but to talk among themselves *about* patients. This, of course, does occur all the time. I receive and make calls several times a day to try to solve clinical issues (some of which are emotional) that don't lend themselves to rote solutions. There are even times when groups of doctors meet to solve a problem, or meet with patients' families and close friends to reach a decision about changing a course of management. In my experience, many of these meetings are called to reach end-of-life decisions. They are deep, respectful, and multidisciplinary (not only the patient's doctors but a social worker and a bioethicist also attend). So, Rabbi Cutter, be careful what you wish for!

I value the power of words. When I worked as the medical director of an inpatient rehabilitation unit I was often appalled at the disparaging language staff members used at weekly staff conferences to describe the behavior of difficult patients. I reasoned that direct criticism of such language would make staff discussion more guarded but would not change attitudes. I decided to inject within the mechanical discussion of gait, balance, transfers, toileting, and bathing skills a brief hiatus of poetry (a five-minute interlude of reading and discussing a poem together) to move the mind-set of the group to another plane and see if this would suffuse the tenor of discourse in the conference. It was a noble idea and perhaps it had some value in elevating the tone of the group discussion.

I myself read poetry every day—and I understand the power of words to incite action, to change mood, to console, to enhance understanding, to express love. But words also have their limitations. Silence is also powerful. Silence is also pregnant with meaning. There are interactions between patient and doctor for which only silence is the proper response, for which words would never match the power of the patient's revelation; sometimes only silence is capable of communicating awe.

The lesson I take from my daily work, from living my life, is that ultimate reality is not tactile and can't be measured easily. I learn this not only from reading poetry and traditional religious texts but also from reading books about physics. The world is mostly empty space, not only in the intergalactic universe but also within the world of the atom. Even the ultimate particles are not hard but composed of tiny diaphanous loops beating out the rhythms of mystery. With such metaphysical musings it is perhaps only a short leap to characterize elevated relationships as having, in Cutter's terms, a spiritual dimension.

I think *caring* is the salient issue, though, not words. What makes a good doctor is his or her capacity for *empathy*, which includes but is not limited to skill at or time expended in verbal communication. It is in being empathic that the relationship between a patient and a physician becomes elevated out of the mundane. Whether the expression of kindness is in the form of words or in physical contact, in the doing of good deeds for the patient or in being present, it all counts. The reward to "good" doctors may await them in the world to come, but *this* is the world that really matters. Rabbi Nachman said, "People believe there are two worlds, this world and the world to come, but in truth this world does not exist." However, somehow we have to believe this world matters. If faith plays a role, then this, at least, is my faith.

5

Contexts of Suffering,
Contexts of Hope

Ruhama Weiss, PhD, is director of the Blaustein Center for Pastoral Counseling and lecturer in Talmud at Hebrew Union College–Jewish Institute of Religion in Jerusalem. She is a poet and the author of *Mithayevet B'Nafshi* (Committing My Soul) and *Okhlim LaDat* (The Meal in the World of the Sages). She is a fellow of the Kalsman Institute on Judaism and Health.

Neither Suffering nor Its Rewards
A Story about Intimacy and Dealing with Suffering and with Death

Ruhama Weiss, PhD

At the heart of this chapter we will deal with three stories that consider the meaning of suffering and death.[1] Each of the stories describes a sage (*chacham*) who becomes ill and whose friend visits him and helps him to free himself from the trials of the disease and his suffering. In the final story there is a dialogue that proposes a personal, painful encounter about the meaning of death.

> Rabbi Chiyya bar Abba became ill.
> Rabbi Yochanan came to see him. He said to him: Is your suffering pleasing to you?
> He said to him: Neither it nor its reward.
> He said to him: Give me your hand.
> He gave him his hand, and he lifted him up.

> Rabbi Yochanan became ill.
> Rabbi Chanina came to see him. He said to him: Is your suffering pleasing to you?
> He said to him: Neither it nor its reward.
> He said to him: Give me your hand.
> He gave him his hand and he lifted him up.

Why? So that Rabbi Yochanan should lift himself up?

It is said: "The prisoner cannot free himself from prison."

Rabbi Elazar became sick.

Rabbi Yochanan came to see him.

He saw that he was lying in a dark place. Rabbi Yochanan uncovered his arm and light fell from it.

He saw that Rabbi Elazar was crying.

He said to him: Why are you crying? If you are crying because you did not accomplish enough Torah, surely we have learned: it makes no difference whether you accomplish a great deal of Torah or a small amount, as long as your heart is directed toward heaven.

Or if it is because you had little money to sustain yourself—not every man earns two tables.

If it is because you didn't have a lot of children or any in fact, see, here is the bone of my tenth son.

He said to him: I am crying on account of this beauty that will waste in the dust.

He said to him: Surely that is what you are crying for.

So the two of them cried.

Either way he said to him: Is your suffering pleasing to you?

He said to him: Neither it nor its reward.

He said to him: Give me your hand.

He gave him his hand, and he lifted him up.

BABYLONIAN TALMUD, *BERAKHOT* 5B

The Underground That Didn't Believe in Suffering

We have here three stories of nearly identical narrative framework that deal with the recovery of sick people. I imagine that the three protagonists are members of a small group, nearly secret, known as the "Underground against Suffering." Let us imagine that this group has a secret code, a slogan by which the members can identify each other: "Is your suffering pleasing to you?" One member of the group would ask this question, and if someone wanted to demonstrate that he was "inside" or wanted to become a member of the group, he would say, "Neither it nor its reward"—an answer that would merit the invitation to extend his hand, and the reciprocal tendering of the hand whereby he would be saved from the bonds of suffering.

Rabbi Yochanan, the Leader of the Underground against Suffering

Four figures are featured in the three stories, and in each story, a pair appears: one who is ill and one who invites him to offer his hand, receives the offered hand, and returns the ill person to the kingdom of the living. The only one of the sages who is featured in all the stories is Rabbi Yochanan.

In the first story, Rabbi Yochanan is the healer, and Rabbi Chiyya bar Abba is the ill person. In the second story, Rabbi Yochanan himself is ill, and Rabbi Chanina is the one who heals. And in the third story, the longest and most developed of the three, Rabbi Yochanan resumes his task as the healer, and this time Rabbi Elazar is the ill person.

The three sages who appear in these stories alongside Rabbi Yochanan are connected to his life: Rabbi Chanina was a sage who was born in Babylon and migrated to Eretz Yisrael, where he became Rabbi Yochanan's teacher; Rabbi Chiyya bar Abba and Rabbi Elazar were two sages who left the Babylonian community for Eretz Yisrael. Both became students of Rabbi Yochanan.

Rabbi Yochanan is the link between the generations. Even at this early stage of our journey, I learn that Rabbi Yochanan is the leader of this group. (I imagine that perhaps Rabbi Chanina, Rabbi Yochanan's teacher, who was also his "doctor," transmitted the "secret of healing" to Rabbi Yochanan, the chief sage of Eretz Yisrael.) The story of Yochanan's life is the key to understanding the unique worldview of the Underground against Suffering.

Rabbi Yochanan Was a Handsome Man

Rabbi Yochanan was the head of the Tiberias yeshiva and the greatest *Amora* in Eretz Yisrael (he lived in the second generation of the Talmudic Sages, the *Amoraim*, and died in old age at the end of the third century CE). The two Talmuds, the Babylonian and the Jerusalem, are replete with his teaching. Rabbi Yochanan was not only a major sage, but also a very handsome one. In the Babylonian Talmud this rare description of his beauty appears:

> Whoever wishes to see the beauty of Rabbi Yochanan should bring a silver goblet directly from the artisan's shop, fill it with red pomegranate seeds, and surround the brim with a wreath of red roses, and place the goblet between sun and shade. The glow you will see is like Rabbi Yochanan's beauty.
>
> BABYLONIAN TALMUD, *BAVA METZIA* 84A
> (ADAPTED FROM THE SONCINO TRANSLATION)

Rabbi Yochanan was aware of his beauty and he took pleasure in it. He said of himself that he used to sit at the doorway of the *mikvehs*, so that the women who came to immerse themselves after their menstruation (so that they could return to resume sexual relations with their husbands) would see him, and they would think of him during lovemaking. As a consequence they would give birth to children as handsome as he was.

In the same *sugya* (major unit that addresses a particular problem) of the Talmud, there is an important story that describes the moving and complicated relationship between the two great sages of the Land of Israel, Rabbi Yochanan and Resh Lakish. Their friendship begins with the wonder experienced by Resh Lakish at the beauty of Yochanan, who was bathing in the Jordan. Resh Lakish was not, at that time, among the Sages, and following that episode he began a life of study in the *beit midrash*.

Rabbi Yochanan loved beauty, and beauty loved Rabbi Yochanan. When we study the story about Rabbi Yochanan and Rabbi Elazar crying for the beauty that will languish in the earth, we ought to recall and understand how deep and important was Rabbi Yochanan's attachment to this beauty.

Rabbi Yochanan Was Acquainted with Suffering

According to one tradition, Rabbi Yochanan was born into orphanhood. His father died when his mother became pregnant, and when he was born, his mother died (Babylonian Talmud, *Kiddushin* 31b). Our *aggadah* from the beginning of this chapter preserves the tradition according to which Rabbi Yochanan lost all ten of his children. We do not know the facts of the story, but in the commentary of Rabbenu Nissim of Girondei (fourteenth-century Spain), Rabbi Yochanan's tragic words "Here is the bone of my tenth son" suggest the shocking story that Nissim heard from his teachers about the death of Yochanan's children, and especially the death of his tenth (and final) son: "Rabbi Yochanan buried ten male sons, and the tenth among them fell into a large boiling pit [of water] so that his flesh melted and wasted away. Rabbi Yochanan took the bone of his little finger, wrapped it in a kerchief, and with that he would comfort others."

An orphan without mother or father from his very first day of life and utterly alone, Rabbi Yochanan kept this finger in his pocket as evidence that he visited the sick with special depth. I imagine the possibility that Rabbi Yochanan, who was beautiful and loved life, was the leader of the Underground against Suffering. He knew that those who suffered would claim that he didn't understand, that he slighted their feelings and even made light of their mourning. The bone in his pocket was a way of defending himself against those who mocked him, for with a bone like this in his pocket, no one would be able to accuse him of not knowing what pain was about. Rabbi Yochanan lived with extreme and almost incomprehensible tension. He was smitten with pain and suffering, but he never let them dominate his life. In a paradoxical way, it seems that the permanent presence of this bone enabled him to be free from his suffering and to liberate him. It is even possible that he felt that from his perspective, choosing life represented an entirely authentic choice.

I am most interested in his choice to carry a bone. He carried neither a spiritual reminder nor a symbolic treasure nor a picture, but the very bone, a piece of dead body that would accompany him wherever he went. In this tradition and in other traditions, Rabbi Yochanan is understood as a man whose love for life was directly connected to the material side of life. He did not interpret the body as only an external shell, a lodging for the soul. He found the body to be the very essence of life.

Beauty, learning, and community standing will be the background to my understanding of the meaning of Rabbi Yochanan's struggle with suffering and love of life.

"Is Your Suffering Pleasing to You?"

This may seem to be a strange question, for how many people would ever answer this question in the affirmative? We are accustomed to telling ourselves that we love being healthy and hate being sick. We live within a culture that waves the flag in its war against death and suffering. The most casual examination of the medicine shelves in a Western pharmacy demonstrates how much money and effort we spend in the battle against suffering. What is pleasing are pain relievers, tranquilizers, antidepressants. Suffering? Neither suffering nor its rewards. In the interest of full disclosure I want to acknowledge that I am a faithful friend who is active in the community that leads the way in diminishing pain. I am thankful to God and my doctors for special loving-kindness, for the opportunity granted me and my generation to withstand trials of heart and body through chemical means. I therefore seek to call attention to our initial reaction of amazement at the very question "Is your suffering pleasing to you?" And consistent with that reaction, it is also difficult to understand what could possibly be positive in response to "Neither it nor its reward." For who loves suffering? And who desires or believes in its reward?

And yet, at second reading, this isn't so easy a matter: "Neither it [suffering] nor its reward." Psychology has devoted a great deal of attention to the complex connections between people, the suffering they endure, and the relief from it. With suffering, with disease and the burdens that take up residence within the body and soul, we have a fully developed commerce. Suffering becomes a compelling playground for our bodies and our souls, and we gladly accept the ample defense and forgiveness that our suffering supplies. Our suffering provides an explanation for our lack of gratification, for underperformance, for helpless failures, and for our neglect of body and soul. It enables us to postpone life, and to justify ourselves to those around us: "When I get better I ..." and in the meantime, we don't actualize our dreams. Suffering enables us to occupy ourselves and the surroundings with the miasma of diseases, to call attention to our wounds, and to ignore our desires, quality of life, and our self-actualization. Yes, my sufferings are (sometimes) pleasing, more than I often want to acknowledge.

Thinking about suffering in the secular arena is more natural to me. Leora Elias Bar-Levav, my friend—with whom I have built my special study partnership—turned at first reading to the religious meaning of suffering and reminded me how much courage a religious person must exert in order to reject suffering. The assumption that God, the Master of the universe, brings about everything invites the religious person to submit, to accept the world, and to bless both evil and good, or at least to accept both. The epigram "Neither it nor its reward" protests not only suffering, but above all the Sovereign of the sufferings. Suffering is a component of a fully developed religious language, and it is part of a system of reward. The members of our "group," the Underground against Suffering, know that there are rewards to suffering from a religious point of view, and out of that knowledge, they complain about the pious form of commerce in suffering. They do not deny the existence of reward, but they do complain before the Lord of suffering, "No, thank you. Neither the honey nor the sting" (citing the well-known figure of speech for appreciating both the good and the bad). We delight in life. "Neither suffering nor its reward."

And that is why I call this group by the name "Underground"— this is a small collection of people, and as I have tried to demonstrate, their standing would not be very high within either the religious or the secular world. Jewish culture was never characterized by a focused religious effort to bring about suffering.[2] In spite of this, I ask myself how many people in the world would have the courage or the strength to turn around and utter, "Neither it nor its reward"? How many people in the world are capable of uttering a long and persistent rejection of suffering or its reward with the same pleasure that characterized Rabbi Yochanan's relationship to life?

The stories that we are considering here emerged from the *beit midrash* of a small collection of people who studied the secret of the love of life. Did their faith and unremitting effort give them the strength to free each other from the depths of suffering and to embrace life every time they were challenged anew?

The Talmudic Context of the Stories: A Consideration of the Religious Meaning of Suffering

Our three stories come from Tractate *Berakhot* in the Babylonian Talmud as a consideration of the religious meaning of suffering. I propose a partial and brief examination of this complex *sugya* and the overall problem with which the *sugya* deals:

> They were divided over this question and Rabbi Yaakov bar Idi and Rabbi Acha bar Chanina spoke. One said, "These must be the sufferings of love—in which there is no abdication of Torah study."… And one said, "These are the chastisements of love— those in which there is no abdication of prayer obligation."
>
> Rabbi Abba, the son of Rabbi Chiyya bar Abba, said, "Thus did Rabbi Chiyya bar Abba say that Rabbi Yochanan said: 'Each represents chastisements [or sufferings] that come from [God's] love, as it says: "God reproves those whom He loves...."'" *Yissurim* [chastisements] wipe away people's sins.
>
> Rabbi Shimon ben Yochai said, "Three magnificent gifts has the Holy One, Blessed be He, given to Israel, and He gave each of them by way of suffering, and they are: Torah, Eretz Yisrael, and the world to come."
>
> The first opinion [*Tanna Kamah*, the anonymous, but official, opening comment] taught Rabbi Yochanan: "Whoever occupies himself with Torah and deeds of loving-kindness and buries his [own] children—is forgiven for his sins...." Rabbi Yochanan said, "Wounds and children are not chastisements of love."… And so Rabbi Yochanan said, "This is the bone of my tenth child."
>
> BABYLONIAN TALMUD, *BERAKHOT* 5A–B

From this text we learn several important things about the religious meaning of suffering:

1. It is difficult to give full expression to ourselves when we are suffering from pain and disease of soul or body. Prayer, study, artistic creation, caring for children—in regard to any of these, too great a portion of suffering is likely to harm the ability to produce, and therefore a worldview that sees suffering as a religious ideal presents a con-

trast to the religious worldview that sees the purpose of the religious life as the activity of people within the physical (or real) world. Prayer and study are not only replacements for the world of chastisements, but also two different religious ways to come to grips with suffering and to reject it.

2. "Chastisements of love": This is an expression that comes from Rabbi Yochanan, the hero of our stories, in which he is presented as the leader in the struggle against acceptance of suffering. According to this worldview, suffering is the best proof of God's love. Is the purpose of suffering to express love only, or do we see in suffering the basis for cleansing, whose purpose is to merit God's love in the fullest way in the world to come? These possibilities are not proved one way or another by Yochanan's words. From my perspective, it is sad to believe in the religious possibility of chastisements of love. It is sad to see the many expressions of this worldview even in the secular world—so many of the conditions of suffering ("Prove to me that you love me ..."; "Give up something for me ..."; "If you loved me you would ...") occur within loving relationships.

3. Cleansing through suffering: This concept is one way of understanding the concept of "chastisements of love." According to this worldview, the divine chastisements of love (*yissurim shel ahavah*) are designed for the purpose of cleansing a person for the world to come.

4. Good gifts are given along with chastisements: According to this perspective, there is a connection between suffering and achievement, and it is painfully known to me: "our way is not easy"; whoever works hard succeeds. Success is proof of hard work. Torah, Eretz Yisrael, and the world to come are achieved through suffering (or chastisements). I try to teach myself and my children that good things are achieved with pleasure, by paying attention to yourself, and by responding to desires (mine and others') with generosity. Nonetheless, in opposition to this desire of mine, occasionally something awakens in me that is a demon of suffering (or chastisements): even if you are happy, act as if you are suffering.

5. The continuation of the *sugya* deals with the complexity of Rabbi Yochanan's relationship to suffering (or chastisements). In the preceding segment, Rabbi Yochanan speaks of the chastisements of love, but now he stops the Mishnah editor abruptly in his *beit midrash*

and complains about the source that the editor has introduced: "Wounds and children are not chastisements of love." As we have seen, Rabbi Yochanan does not oppose the religious understanding of chastisements of love as such, but he believes that there has to be a limit: bodily wounds and the loss of his children are such awful disasters that chastisements of love cannot be applied to those events. The Talmudic discourse about the life of Rabbi Yochanan and his worldview continues, and the Talmud now recalls the painful story about Yochanan's tenth son. Rabbi Yochanan, as the bereft father, is not prepared to accept the reward for the loss of his children and he asserts, "Neither suffering nor its reward." He offers his hand to all bereft parents and to all wounded people who are part of his community and frees them from their prison of suffering and its reward.

Rabbi Yochanan is the hero of our stories, the principle figure in the fellowship that struggled with suffering, a man experienced in suffering, for he had and lost his sons. With these words, our discourse about the meaning of suffering ends and our own chain of stories begins.

"The Prisoner Cannot Free Himself from Prison"

Here the word *yissurim* moves back once again to mean something closer to "suffering."

Yet another hint that Rabbi Yochanan may be the leader of this group is found in the question that appears in the second story. After the descriptions of Rabbi Yochanan's cure, the question arises as to why Rabbi Yochanan, the prominent doctor, needs a doctor when he is ill, and from this question we learn that Rabbi Yochanan, the well-known doctor, is also the leader of the fellowship.

The story of Rabbi Yochanan's illness is an important addition to our understanding of the need for fellowship and assistance when we are in difficulty. It is possible that Yochanan's difficult illness was the crisis that came upon him when his sons died, and perhaps especially the death of his tenth son. Rabbi Yochanan is suffering from terrible sorrow. He, the very one who invented the method for battling the power of suffering, cannot free himself from these troubles. Rabbi Yochanan needs someone else, a good friend who will understand that he can carry on no longer, who will say the very things to him that he has said to others, someone who will remind him of the law of life that he himself has developed.

"The prisoner cannot free himself from prison"—how very much humility is required of the person who has developed an effective treatment when he himself needs help! How much courage, openness, and loving-kindness is required to understand that the one who is usually a supporter and healer seeks a guiding and loving hand? Both sides of this interaction require a rare kind of flexibility to permit this cure to take place. It seems to me that this sentence summarizes the entire Torah and the meaning of human community at times of crisis: "The prisoner cannot free himself."

The Group by the Name
"Pleasing Is Suffering" Is Established

The close of the sentence "Is your suffering pleasing to you?" with a question mark, and—of course—the response "Neither it nor its reward" aroused a double interest and wonderment in the presence of sages who utilized that very sentence precisely with an exclamation mark at the end. Rabbi Yehudah HaNasi, the editor of the Mishnah and Rabbi Chanina's teacher (Chanina from our original story), established the "pleasing are your sufferings" principle, and he functioned according to that formula. He decreed for himself thirteen years of difficult illnesses and accepted them. (See the story in Babylonian Talmud, *Bava Metzia* 85a.) The one who established the concept—sufferings are pleasing—will surely find the power to create and bring suffering upon himself, and he who established "Neither it nor its reward" will find the strength to cast off from body and soul all the illnesses that took up residence in him in a weak moment.

The story of Rabbi Akiva is also well-known. Akiva, one of the important Mishnaic sages, accepted in love the torments inflicted on him by the Romans during the Bar Kokhba rebellion (132–135 CE). It is told of Rabbi Akiva that when he came to Rabbi Elazar's sickbed along with a group of sages, the sages attempted to comfort and encourage their dying rabbi's spirit with all kinds of compliments and praise for the good work he did in his life and the merit he had earned in the world to come. Rabbi Akiva, in contrast, spread out for the dying man his simple and straightforward summary of a worldview, and announced, "Your sufferings are pleasing" (Babylonian Talmud, *Sanhedrin* 101b and elsewhere).

Rabbi Yehudah HaNasi proposed the most extreme approach—an active step to bring about sufferings; whereas Rabbi Akiva proposed a more moderate way—he would not bring about suffering intentionally. The members of our fellowship continued to raise up the ill from their beds and to protest the human condition in which divine sufferings are meted out.

"He Came to See Him": Visiting the Sick Is Not an Easy Matter

While I was writing this chapter, I discovered that the Aramaic phrase for "coming to see him" (to visit the sick, in other words), *al legabeih*, occurs in the Babylonian Talmud almost exclusively in *aggadot* about visiting the sick. These stories have a definite structure: an ill rabbi is visited by one or two others, and *al legabeih* is used to mean they came to see him.

The picture we get here about the *mitzvah* of *bikkur cholim* is not fully balanced. The sick person is weakened and finds himself lying down: a physical situation that is lower than that of the visitor. For that reason it seems to me that the linguistic form *al legabeih* for the beginning of the description of the visit is chosen intentionally. It would have been possible to say he "sat by his side" or he "lingered with him," whereas the word that is chosen in fact is *al* (meaning "entered") and it recalls also the Hebrew sense of the word, the superior position of the visitor; but the principal importance of this word is its indication of action or movement. The word reminds us of the superior position of the visitor: he moves. He was outside and then entered inside to the world of the sick person, and he will conclude the visit, go outside, and return to the world of the healthy. One of the compelling questions in all the stories about visiting the sick is where the participants in the narrative will lead the story of the ill person after this opening, in light of the fact that the categories "strong" and "weak" seem so clear.

Some Thoughts about the Compelling Desire to Make Ill People Healthy

I have not been able to move from the framework of the first two stories to the contents of the third, more detailed, version. The formula that concludes each of the stories, "and he lifted him up," does not permit me to continue with my analysis of the *aggadot*. I am thinking of my good friend Leora, my partner in this chapter, who has cancer. My thoughts about her, about our relationship, and about illnesses that are not yet conquered interrupt my analysis. Is the most important task of visitors to the sick to save their friends? To be the redeemers, to provide answers and cures? Is it our task as human beings to "conquer" illness? Is the desire for equality between the visitor and the ill person not an example of hubris about our ability to accept reality?

The question and the answer "Is your suffering pleasing to you? Neither it nor its reward" sharpens the difficulty I have in reading the *aggadah*. Many people claim these days that there is a connection between our personalities and the specific nature of the diseases we may acquire. I am in no way protesting the psychophysical connection that does exist in many diseases. I myself have experienced that connection in an extended and complex way, and for a long period of time I suffered from symptoms of a widespread disease that has not yet been adequately studied called "chronic fatigue syndrome" (which, as its name implies, is chronic, and its symptoms never completely disappear and continue to recur during difficult times). I can't speak for others who suffer from this disease, but my personal experience has taught me that the disease breaks out during difficult spiritual times and that physical rehabilitation has been connected with my coming to grips with unsolved spiritual issues.

Nevertheless, claims about the connection between one's spiritual situation and a physical disease can sometimes be cruel. It seems to me that the common effort to find a spiritual reason behind every illness is a version of defense and denial on the part of healthy people: if every disease is the consequence of a troubled spirit, and if we can find out the nature of the spiritual problem that leads to disease, then we can deceive ourselves into thinking that we can save ourselves from disease. Furthermore, according to this theory, if we are physically healthy, we can say that our spiritual condition is better than that of people who are ill. So we learn from this that a sick person bears a kind of double responsibility, for he bears the stigma of social guilt that hovers like an ill wind over his illness. All diseases then are likely to become like *tzara'at* (the biblical disease that used to be understood as "leprosy")—if you are sick that means that your soul is weak and even damaged.

Place Your Hand in Mine, I Am Yours and You Are Mine

The hand is a metaphor for our actions. Offering the hand is the deciding feature of every act in the stories. In the third story, there is also another action: the uncovering of Rabbi Yochanan's arm, which casts light into Rabbi Elazar's darkened house, beginning the process of the cure. His hand is the principal instrument of both giving and receiving. I have dealt with this metaphor along with the mixing of fluids and other acts of intimacy in other essays.[3]

The eyes, ears, and mouth (by way of speech) are the limbs that first expose us to the world and that expose the world to us. The connection created through sexual organs and the mouth (through spit) expresses the height of this connection, and the hand is a kind of intermediary that touches, taking and giving, while retaining the boundary of the physical body and not unifying or mixing liquids.

Our hands may symbolize giving help or withholding help: "Do not restrain your hand from your needy brother, but rather open your hand to him" (Deuteronomy 15:7–8). The hand may express concern for another: "Arise and lift up the boy and strengthen his hand" (Genesis 21:18). In contrast, the hand may also express our cruel deeds: "He will be a wild man with his hand against everything and the hand of everyone against him" (Genesis 16:12). The hand that holds the magical staff and makes its owner into an omnipotent being symbolizes the omnipotent fantasy: "And Aaron put forth his hand over the waters of Egypt, and frogs emerged and covered the land of Egypt" (Exodus 8:2); "And *Adonai* said to Moses: 'Stretch out your hand to the heavens so that there will be hail in all the land of Egypt over people and animals and on every grass of the field" (Exodus 9:22). And so forth and so on.

I ask myself, which are the hands that the sages receive and which do they offer in order to free their colleagues? What sort of human connection do they express, and what do they want to tell about God's place in the world and God's control?

In the third story of the *bikkur cholim* series, when Rabbi Yochanan wants to illuminate the darkened house of Rabbi Elazar, he uncovers his arm, and light "falls" into the house. This description reminds us of the Talmudic story of Choma, Rabbi Abaye's widow, who comes to the court of Rabbah and wants him to require that she be provided with wine from the provisions made available through the orphan's funds. Rabbah refuses with the claim "I know that Abaye did not drink wine." Choma, angry but clever, reacts to Rabbah's denial as follows:

> She said to him, "By your life, dear sir, Abaye used to give me a goblet about this size." As she showed [it] to him, her arm was uncovered, and light was shed into the *beit din*. Rabbah got up, went into his house, and requested sexual relations of his wife [the daughter of Rav Chisda].
>
> BABYLONIAN TALMUD, KETUBOT 65A

This story occurs in the Talmud within the framework of the discussion about distributing wine to women as part of their sustenance. The discussion about women drinking wine is in fact a discussion about control and the right to give up control. Are women entitled to the liberating graces of wine? Are men willing to allow them to have it? Will they seek control and hold back this freedom from women? Rabbah tries to keep wine from Choma. Choma complains before him, arouses him with her naked arm, and enhances his excitement through a competition over whose is bigger, his or her dead husband, Abaye's: "He would have me drink from a goblet of this size." Rabbah doesn't resist the temptation and runs home to "water" his wife. In the battle of the sexes, Choma succeeds in demonstrating who is really light-headed (although that won't guarantee that she will achieve what she wants). Rabbah experiences what he imagined would have happened to Choma if she drank wine, without his even imbibing one drop.

And as for our subject, the theme of the arm that reveals light appears in the same form in two stories. From the story about Choma we learn that the light that is shed by the arm represents sexual arousal. As I have already mentioned, Rabbi Yochanan was very handsome indeed. Rabbi Yochanan's good looks are the first thing experienced by Resh Lakish. This connects the two men in the fellowship of life and death of Rabbi Yochanan. In this story Yochanan's beauty is the key to the connection, the connection that will return Rabbi Elazar from the world of the dead to the world of the living. I plan to continue to read the interaction between Rabbi Elazar and Rabbi Yochanan in terms of sexual arousal.

What Is Worth Crying For?

In each of the three stories we get a template for the stages of illness and cure: he became sick, someone came to see him, he asked, someone responded, offered a hand, and helped him stand up. The third story presents an intimate examination of one setting by way of one conversation that takes place between a sick person and a visitor, and at the end of that story the visitor offers the sick person his hand and helps him to stand up.

I imagine that the condition of Rabbi Elazar, lying in his darkened house, was especially precarious. He was in such a heavy depression that he didn't even want to get better, and in this third story only at the end can he say, "Neither suffering nor its reward."

Rabbi Yochanan "saw that he was crying," but didn't hear. Rabbi Elazar cried quietly, so quietly in fact that even Rabbi Yochanan, his teacher and friend, did not hear him, and he only saw that Elazar was crying when he had shed light in the house. On second thought, it could be that the shedding of light was the thing that aroused Rabbi Elazar's crying, which was the first sign of a connection between the two men and the possibility of coming out of his depression.

"Why are you crying?" What is the question? He is crying because he is ill. He is crying because he thinks that he is about to die. Rabbi Yochanan does not accept the idea that the crying is about the illness or about impending death as a self-evident matter, and he wants to propose other reasons. All the reasons that he can propose are explained simply and straightforwardly by the knowledge that Rabbi Elazar's life is soon to end, and it is for this apparent reason that Rabbi Elazar is having difficulty separating himself from this world: he hadn't studied a great deal of Torah, he lived in poverty, and it's possible that he didn't have children. For every problem, Rabbi Yochanan hastens to propose a solution that will lighten the burden Rabbi Elazar is experiencing. With regard to his financial condition, Yochanan hastens to remind Rabbi Elazar, who is deathly ill, that "not every man earns two tables [or the wealth of two tables]" but that he does merit the second table—that is, the table for the righteous (*tzaddikim*) in the world to come. As the leader of the Underground against Suffering, Rabbi Yochanan carries around with him the little finger of his youngest son, the tenth one whom he lost, wrapped in a kerchief. He presents it to any desolate, bereft person he meets.

I ask myself what Rabbi Yochanan wants to say by presenting the bone to Rabbi Elazar. It's difficult for me to believe that he wants to claim to his friend that "my sufferings are greater than yours," for surely this would not be very consoling. I prefer to think that he presents the bone as an indication of partnership in the lot of his friend, and as the most personal kind of proof that it is possible to continue in life, that one must continue in life (and in life complete with pleasure and libido, as in the case of Rabbi Yochanan).

Rabbi Yochanan Feared Paying Attention to a Dying Man

But in spite of all of this I believe that Rabbi Yochanan errs. He gets himself into the customary pit that his friends and his many colleagues who take care of people who are about to die also fall into—he is afraid to pay attention. In Rabbi Yochanan's string of questions and answers, I can identify the anxiety he feels in the conversation with someone who is about to die. Rabbi Yochanan is strong enough to speak openly with Rabbi Elazar about death and its meaning, but he doesn't yet have enough strength to pay attention to Rabbi Elazar and to let him cry. He prefers to propose immediately reasons and solutions for the crying. He instructs in questions and responses. He suggests problems that, it seems to him, are given to simple solutions. He wants to subdue Rabbi Elazar's fear of death and, most of all, his own fear of death. He does not propose conversation, and he does not propose paying attention. He lectures.

Rabbi Elazar Doesn't Give Up

Rabbi Elazar could have become discouraged by his encounter with Rabbi Yochanan and might have accepted his teacher's inability to conduct an authentic conversation about his advancing death. But he does not give up. I assume that he wasn't able to carry on a lengthy conversation or to render speeches as lengthy as Yochanan's had been. Rabbi Elazar lays out his pain with brevity and courage: "I am crying on account of this beauty that will waste in the dust."

In his reason for crying about his impending death, Rabbi Elazar passes on to Rabbi Yochanan several important processes. He forces him to pay attention to the ill person, brings him into touch with the fact that there are irresolvable tribulations, and forces Rabbi Yochanan to be with him "where he is"—not to resolve, not to correct, and not to save. Just to be. Rabbi Yochanan learns his lesson and agrees just to be. Afterwards he identifies with Rabbi Elazar and joins in his tears.

To Be with Someone "Where He Is"

In my description of the change that Rabbi Yochanan undergoes in relation to Rabbi Elazar, I have employed the expression "where he is," an important expression in the discourse that has been established in the world of those who are spiritual companions and who give spiritual support to people in their time of need. The source of this expression has to do with the saving of Hagar and Ishmael when they are driven out to the desert:

> And God heard the voice of the boy, and an angel of God called out to Hagar from heaven and said to her, "What is it, Hagar? Do not fear, because God has heard the voice of the lad where he is

[at, or to be found]. Arise and lift up the child and take his hand, for I will make him a great nation.

GENESIS 21:17–18

"Where he is"—a phrase suitable to the ill person herself more than anything.

"Where he is"—Rabbi Simon says: "The Ministering Angels hastened to contend against Ishmael, and they said to God, 'Master of the worlds, a man who is destined to kill your children through starvation, you are providing a well.' He said to them, 'What is he now?' They said to Him, 'A *tzaddik*.' He said to them, 'I judge people as they are when they are being judged.'"

BEREISHIT RABBAH 53[4]

"Where he is": To understand the prayer of the ill person and his needs. To see the "other" in the situation in which she finds herself at that very moment. To see ourselves wherever we are at each moment. To live the present in the present and not by way of the distorted perspective of future generations. One should judge people from the perspective of the time in which they acted.

"I Am Crying for This Beauty That Will Waste in the Dust"

Rabbi Elazar surprises me, and perhaps he surprises Rabbi Yochanan. He is crying not for Talmud, not for Torah, not for material success, and not even for the generation of the future. Rabbi Elazar cries because of the beauty that will waste in the dust. For death itself. For the loss that cannot be retrieved and for which the world to come won't be adequate consolation. This beauty: the skin, the flesh, the eyes, the hair. These things belong only to the world of the living. These will be lost in death. Rabbi Elazar suggests a clear and forthright examination of the pain of death, the fear of death, and the loss of the world that is known to us. It is possible that a table is prepared for righteous people in the world to come, and it is possible that there is a spiritual or religious meaning to all that we accomplish in this world. It is possible to explain many things, and it is possible to suggest many mollifying responses for many difficult matters. But no amount of effort at connecting everything can overcome one fundamental and simple painful fact: at the moment of death, the world that we know ends. The eyes, the hands, the tears, human contact—these will be no longer, and only because of that does Rabbi Elazar cry.

In my study with Leora, we thought that it is Rabbi Yochanan who examines Rabbi Elazar. Had Rabbi Elazar been satisfied with the first of Rabbi Yochanan's answers (that the sadness about death is connected to study, children, or desire for money), he would not have merited the outstretched hand. You only understand the secret of the Underground against Suffering and thus earn the offering of the hand if you understand the sole reason for crying as the disappearance of beauty into the earth. And so I, with my own wonderment over the suggestions of Rabbi Yochanan, have failed the test.

The Conversation between Christianity and Judaism

The story about Rabbi Elazar's crying enabled me to understand in a new way why we study Jewish sources for spiritual and inner processes. We should study Jewish sources as a way of getting at our spirits and our spiritual lives. In the area of spiritual support it is very common—and appropriate, to my way of thinking—that we should learn from all possible spiritual approaches and sources about the life of the spirit. Furthermore, in the very nature of that field, it is quite common for someone from one religious community to respond to the needs of people from other communities. The need for spiritual guidance leads many people in distress to a rare religious pluralism.

Yet, religion is also a complex of particular qualities—faith and hope, norms and behaviors—and religions are different from each other in regard to the responses they give to the meaning of existence. I myself deal primarily with the Talmud. Because of this I find myself seeking particular utterances of the Talmudic culture about the meaning of life and death. The conversation between Rabbi Elazar and Rabbi Yochanan strikes me in its difference and particularity in regard to ideas about death in the Christian world. While thinking about Rabbi Elazar's words, I recalled the books of Elisabeth Kübler-Ross, a doctor who was born in Switzerland and died some years ago in the United States, "the high priestess of care for the dying." Kübler-Ross struggled throughout her lifetime to convince people not to be taken aback by death or fear of dying, to speak about death, to live our lives out of a permanent consciousness of death; to accept the notion of life after death, and to understand the unique function of death for understanding life. And even though I very often find myself resisting the confidence reflected in Christian writings, I must render a profound thanks for its courage, which has helped me think about issues that I might have avoided.

Kübler-Ross was within the Christian culture and very much a part of it. When she writes of death, she often employs the comparison of the butterfly (the soul) that leaves its cocoon (the body).[5] For her the distinction between soul and body is clear, and the soul's privilege over the body is equally clear.

Each of us, born from the Source that is God, is the recipient of a divine aspect. That is to say, in simplest terms, we each have within us a portion of that very Source, and this bequeaths to us a sense of immortality. Many people begin to understand that the physical body is only the house or the sanctuary or, as we might call it, the cocoon that we wrap ourselves in for some months or years until we cross the threshold we call death. At the time of death we cast off this shell and we become free as butterflies.

When Leora and I read Rabbi Elazar's words and think about his crying with Rabbi Yochanan, we realize that we have arrived at one of the most moving moments in our culture and that the Jewish Talmudic culture proposes an entirely different idea than the Christian. The sanctified distinction between soul and body and the superiority of the soul are not evident in the story before us. What is present here is actually the lack of distinction between body and soul.

For Sexuality That Is Aroused and Quenched I Cry

At the beginning of their encounter, the handsome Rabbi Yochanan reveals his arm in the darkened house of Rabbi Elazar, and the house lights up. At the end of the conversation, Rabbi Elazar determines that "I am crying on account of the beauty that will waste in the dust," and I think of the illuminating arm of Rabbi Yochanan and about the spot of light that it presents when the lust for life is aroused once again. Lust, sexuality, seduction, suggestions of connection, human contact. The experience that returned the light to Rabbi Elazar's life is also what caused him to cry. I am almost certain that Rabbi Elazar began to cry only when Rabbi Yochanan uncovered his arm. The crying began with the light, with the reminder of sexuality and life. Rabbi Elazar, like Rabbi Yochanan, knows about the solution of the world to come, the reward that is promised to righteous people, but when he suddenly notices Yochanan's beautiful hand, he recalls the precious thing that will indeed be concluded with death: life.

"Surely that is what you are crying for"—that is how Rashi understands the verse. Rabbi Yochanan was a good, attentive friend and a man who loved life. From the depth of the suffering he experienced in his lifetime, he knew how to love life—not only the life of the spirit but also the life of the flesh. I do not even know how much of a distinction he made between those two worlds. In the moment of truth, Rabbi Yochanan doesn't need more than one sentence to understand precisely what Rabbi Elazar intended and how right he may have been. In a rare moment of kinship, just a moment before this connection would terminate in the eternity of death, the two friends sit and cry together.

Out of Rabbi Yochanan's ability to understand—to understand Rabbi Elazar in truth and to be present with him where he is—he succeeds in releasing Elazar from the darkened house. He succeeds in offering him his hand—which just a moment before had shed light in his house, wakened him to life and to tears—and returns him to the world of those who protest against suffering. And finally, Rabbi Elazar says, "Neither it [suffering] nor its reward."

I Am Not Certain That I Like the End of the Story

All along I have been arguing with myself about my own relationship to the Underground against Suffering. I am grateful to Rabbi Elazar for the simplicity with which he formulates the meaning of the fear of death: "For this beauty that will waste in the dust." I am not certain that I want to believe that an understanding of fear and the heavy price it extracts promises redemption.[6]

Rabbi Aryeh Cohen, PhD, is associate professor of Rabbinic literature at the Ziegler School for Rabbinic Studies of American Jewish University. He is the author of *Rereading Talmud: Gender, Law, and the Poetics of* Sugyot and *Beginning/Again: Toward a Hermeneutics of Jewish Texts.*

The Experience of Suffering
A Response to Ruhama Weiss

Rabbi Aryeh Cohen, PhD

> *Do not mistakenly understand that the conversation is speech.*
>
> HAVA PINCHAS COHEN (FROM THE COVER ART
> BY NEHAMA GOLAN FOR RUHAMA WEISS'S
> BOOK *COMMITTING MY SOUL*)

I am struck by a seemingly innocuous detail in this lustrous chapter. In describing the group of sages whom Weiss categorizes as those who go by the name "Pleasing Is Suffering" she includes Rabbi Akiva. Weiss identifies Rabbi Akiva by saying that he "accepted in love the torments inflicted on him by the Romans during the Bar Kokhba rebellion (132–135 CE)." This parenthetical claim stops me. What rhetorical function is served by this interpolation of the historical dating of the Bar Kokhba rebellion? While the rebellion is a historical fact of one sort or another, both its attribution to Bar Kokhba and especially Rabbi Akiva's participation in it are facts only of a literary nature.[1] Ascribing Rabbi Akiva's literary martyrdom to a specific three-year period does not seem to grant it any more power than it already has living in the Babylonian Talmud. What is gained by the insertion of this "fact"? Roland Barthes, the French literary theorist, in his book *S/Z* describes what he calls the "effect of the real."[2] This is when a novelist introduces real events into her story in order to make the fictions feel more factual. It is not, however, the facticity of the Akiva stories that are at stake in Weiss's essay. It is possible that this is merely the reflexive nod to the gods of history that is required of the academic guild. I would like to posit that this is not the case, however.

Abraham Joshua Heschel in his magnum opus *Torah min Hashamayim*, or *Heavenly Torah*, deals with this material.[3] Heschel's basic insight is that there were two philosophical approaches to or understandings of Judaism from Rabbinic times to the present.[4] These two schools are attributed by Heschel to the great Rabbinic sages Rabbi Akiva and Rabbi Yishmael. Rabbi Akiva's approach was prophetic, and his theology was mystical. He broke the boundaries between heaven and earth, his God was immanent, his hermeneutics were fantastic, and his theology was intimate and, at times, wildly anthropomorphic. Rabbi Yishmael, on the other hand, was a rationalist. His hermeneutics were philologically based and logical. His God was radically transcendent, omniscient, and omnipotent.

According to Heschel, these two sages and their schools held dialectically opposed positions on every topic. On the issue of suffering, Akiva held that there was suffering without cause. More to the point of the material under discussion, Akiva held that there were *yissurim shel ahavah*—sufferings brought on by God out of love. Rabbi Yishmael held that there was no suffering without sin, that the relation between sin and punishment was rational, because God was rational. Both sides had to make painful tradeoffs. The Akivan school, in order to retain the notion of a merciful God, had to tolerate and justify unwarranted suffering. The Yishmaelian school, in order to retain a rational God, had to find a sin (that is, a cause) for every affliction.

Weiss personifies the disputants and puts flesh and blood on their bones. The two camps are, on the one side, those who are in favor of suffering, those who think that suffering is good and the reward for suffering is good. These are the folks who bring afflictions upon themselves, who chastise themselves in the name of piety. On the other side is the group led (according to Weiss) by Rabbi Yochanan, the Underground against Suffering. This group rejects both suffering and its rewards in this world and the next. By personifying these choices, by personalizing these choices, Weiss evades the pitfalls of the theologians. The questions here are direct and concrete questions. Is physical suffering good or bad, helpful or hurtful spiritually? This is a question that individuals must ask and answer. It is not, according to Weiss's reading, only a question for theologians. She states in the Hebrew text of her book:

> The conclusion of the *sugya* is a compelling example of the infinite capability of Talmudic discourse to turn personal suffering into a halakhic issue. It can be a hermeneutic locus in which those who have studied the *sugya* throughout history find a place from which to consider their own personal sufferings.

Weiss's major claim as a Talmudist in this essay is that reading the text of the Talmud without considering one's own personal feelings is falling short of the hermeneutic possibilities of any *sugya*. This is an interesting and complicated claim. To analyze this claim we should retrace some of Weiss's steps—especially her first move.

In the three stories that are the heart of this chapter, Weiss notes some interesting phenomena. First, Rabbi Yochanan appears in all the stories. Second, the stories involve Rabbi Yochanan, his teacher, and his student. Finally, there is an exchange that is repeated in each and every story. This exchange catches Weiss's eye and opens up the text. In each story the sick person is asked, "Is your suffering pleasing to you?" In each story the reply is "Neither it [suffering] nor its reward." This is followed by the caregiver miraculously healing the sick person of his affliction and raising him out of his bed. Weiss, focusing on the almost ritualistic nature of these exchanges, draws out of these stories the "Underground against Suffering." The members are distinguished by their declaration that they want neither suffering nor its reward.

This fanciful notion acquires flesh and blood only in the presence of actual sick people. Ruhama Weiss and Leora Elias Bar-Levav are the real "Underground against Suffering." In this move out of the page and into the lived reality of people who study this text in and through their own illnesses the petulant notion of an "Underground against Suffering" becomes the organizational principle for a noble and courageous path.

Studying texts about suffering, dying, and miraculous healing with someone who is suffering and dying without miraculous healing is itself a painful, perhaps impossible undertaking. It is not for comfort or reassurance that the *chavrutot* lean their heads close to each other over these hoary words. This is perhaps the ultimate expression of what, in *Committing My Soul*, Weiss calls *kriyot mehuyyavot*, an expression that can be translated as "committed readings" or "necessary readings." This reading practice can only come from a feeling of necessity. I read these texts because I cannot not read these texts.

This reading practice is something like a hermeneutic of the real. It moves in an opposite direction from Barthes's "effect of the real." When a realistic element is added to a novel, the fiction is given a more robust "reality." A hermeneutic of the real places the text as a frame to a reality, a lexical filter to enable a discourse. The real animates the text, and the text supplies a conceptual vocabulary for the reality to which the text points.

When I first read Ruhama Weiss's essay and wrote the first two parts of this response, I was struck by those things that I am usually struck by as someone who spends his life reading Talmudic texts. I was intrigued by the way that she picked up on the repetitive antiphonal chorus ("Is your suffering pleasing to you?... Neither it nor its reward") and deepened the narrative with the tale of the Underground against Suffering. I was also intrigued by some of the rhetorical twists of her essay. There seemed to be a persistent effort to historicize these stories—dates of birth and death, places, dates of the Bar Kokhba revolt. The stories were obviously highly crafted literature. It was somewhat reminiscent of those who try to pinpoint where Sherlock Holmes goes to school or to retrace the route that Balak, the dog in Agnon's *T'mol Shilshom*, followed through Meah She'arim in an important scene in the novel, or the tourists who visit the house that Carrie from *Sex in the City* "lived" in. Yet, at the same time, Weiss read the stories through the filter of real people who were suffering and dying.

However, upon a second or third reading, I realized that I was missing the point. Weiss's argument is somewhat similar to German existentialist philosopher Franz Rosenzweig's argument in the beginning of *The Star of Redemption*. Rosenzweig claims that philosophy constantly dupes people because it treats death as an illusion, as a passage to something else. The reason that it does this is that it is in denial about the terror of death that is the basic constitutive experience of all people. That fear of death has epistemological valence for Rosenzweig.

It is only in acknowledging the fact of death that one can start thinking in concrete terms about people of flesh and blood and not people as philosophical abstractions.

Weiss is making a similar claim.

I was making the mistake that the philosophers made. I was reading these texts about suffering and dying, and I was noticing their rhetorical nuances; I was interested in their theological statements. For Weiss these texts can only be made sense of when read in concert with the suffering that parallels, reflects, and intersects with that in the text. Weiss's *chavruta* in the study of these texts is not incidental, but essential to understanding them. Whereas Weiss claims (correctly) that the Rabbinic view is that there is no separation between body and soul, she is also claiming that there is no difference between living bodies and reading bodies, between suffering bodies and textual bodies. The texts might only make sense imbricated in the space between the dying partner and the accompanying partner.

6

Midrashic Renderings
of Age and Obligation

Thomas R. Cole, PhD, is director of the McGovern Center for Humanities and Ethics at the University of Texas Health Science Center at Houston. Among his publications are *The Journey of Life: A Cultural History of Aging in America* and *A Guide to Humanistic Studies in Aging*. His documentary films include *Stroke: Conversations and Explanations*.

After the Life Cycle
The Moral Challenges of Later Life

Thomas R. Cole, PhD

> *Men die because they cannot join the end to the beginning.*
>
> ALCEMEON OF GROTON

In more than thirty years of reading and writing about later life, my favorite book is still a slender volume by Catholic theologian Henri Nouwen and Walter Gaffney, entitled *Aging: The Fulfillment of Life* (1974).[1] As in many books on aging in the 1970s and 1980s, Nouwen strives against negative stereotypes and attitudes toward older people, offering images and ideals that emphasize solidarity based on our shared humanity. The book's central motif is a large wagon wheel leaning against a birch tree in the white snow, beautifully photographed by Ron P. Van Den Bosch. The photo invites each of us to think of ourselves as a spoke on the great wheel of life, part of the ongoing cycle of generations. It also implies that each of us has our own cycle to traverse, a moving up and a going down, moving forward, yet also somehow returning to the beginning. Nouwen's wagon wheel resembles the Christ-centered circular life cycle, which his medieval forebears rendered on stained-glass cathedral windows. Circles and repetitions have competed with straight lines as the central imagery in our life journey. (See Ecclesiastes 1:6 for a pessimistic apprehension of cycles.)

Medieval Christians considered earthly time as a mere shadow of eternity. Nouwen asserts that "we have only one life cycle to live, and that living it is the source of our greatest joy."[2] Modern Western culture since the Reformation has placed great emphasis on the affirmation of everyday life, on relief of suffering, and on respect for the dignity and rights of individuals.[3] As a modern, Nouwen sets the issue of a good life squarely in the province of ordinary living. Leaning heavily on developmental psychologist Erik Erikson's work, Nouwen writes that our "greatest vocation" is to "live carefully and gracefully." Aging, then, becomes the gradual fulfillment of the life cycle, "in which receiving matures in giving and living makes dying worthwhile."[4] With elegant simplicity, he describes the three-stage life cycle as it cogwheels with previous and future generations:

> The restful accomplishment of the old wheel tells us the story of life. Entering into the world we are what we are given, and for many years thereafter parents and grandparents, brothers and sisters, friends and lovers keep giving to us, some more, some less, some hesitantly, some generously. When we can finally stand on our own feet, speak our own words, and express our own unique self in work and love, we realize how much is given to us. But while reaching the height of our cycle, and saying with a great sense of confidence, "I really am," we sense that to fulfill our life we now are called to become parents and grandparents, brothers and sisters, teachers, friends, and lovers ourselves, and to give to others so that, when we leave this world, we can be what we have given.[5]

Such progressive descriptions share a certain pattern with other life outlines—one of which is the formula found near the end of *Pirkei Avot* (Ethics of the Fathers), in the great Rabbinic literature of the Mishnah, which—while it was apparently not meant as a scientific description—is among the paradigms that influenced a certain kind of thinking about aging. I will return to this and other Jewish perspectives below. They share a kind of patterning with Nouwen, but they do not share Nouwen's view.

I love the lyrical beauty of Nouwen's view that an individual's personal development naturally entails self-transcendence and moral responsibility in later life. As Nouwen puts it, "receiving matures in giving."

But contemporary American culture seems to emphasize individual development without a clear consensus—even a rich debate—about the meanings of later life and the responsibilities of older people to future generations. With the rise of ever-lengthening life expectancy, the roles, responsibilities, virtues, vices, and meanings of an extended old age take on new urgency in both private and public life. Strangely, there is little written on this subject. And this is why we in the Jewish community should applaud the work of such figures as Dayle Friedman and Richard Address, who have staked their careers on alerting the Jewish community to the subject of aging and have rewritten, in midrashic fashion, models for our thinking about aging. Dayle Friedman has, in addition, tried to shift the concern from caring for the elderly to the obligations of the elderly—one of the key points in my essay here.

There is a plethora of literature focusing (appropriately) on the ethics of caregiving, on private and public responsibilities to older people, and on the rights of older people. But there is too little discussion of the reciprocal responsibilities of older people. In the bioethics literature, older people (or their proxies) are viewed solely as bearers of rights, as individuals entitled to make their own choices regarding health care. And this in itself is a valid perspective. But there is precious little work on the content of those choices—or on the larger issues of accountability, responsibilities, virtues, and vices of older people. To contextualize this issue, I will first provide a brief interpretation of Nouwen and Erikson, focusing on the normative dimension of their views on aging and the life cycle. Next, I will offer a historical argument that we are living "after the life cycle" both normatively and structurally. Finally, I will provide a tentative sketch of the moral challenges of later life, both for healthy, active older people and for those who are frail, sick, and dependent.

Is the Life Cycle Naturally Normative?

Let me begin with a brief analysis of Nouwen's perspective and that of his more famous counterpart, Erik Erikson. Philosophically, Nouwen's view rests on an ancient doctrine shared by Greeks, Romans, and Christians alike—that the human life span constitutes a single natural order and that each stage possesses its own characteristics and moral norms. "Life's racecourse is fixed," wrote Cicero in *De Senectute*, "nature has only a single path and that path is run but once, and to each stage of existence has been allotted its appropriate quality."[6] With the rise of Christianity, this normative life cycle is folded into a divinely ordained natural order—and the Stoic ideal of rational self-mastery is replaced with a journey toward salvation. And while we don't know how "normative" the *Pirkei Avot* material is meant to be, there it is staring at us with its sense of inevitability—like Shakespeare's "The Seven Ages of Man."

While Nouwen writes as a Catholic, his view of the life cycle is couched mostly in secular psychological terms that echo Erik Erikson's famous psychoanalytic formulation of the "eight ages of man," each with its own psychosocial conflict and its corresponding virtue. First formulated in the mid-twentieth century, Erikson's version of the life cycle virtually dominated American academic thought and public imagination for over twenty-five years. Erikson's theory is actually a restatement of the Stoic ideal, supplemented by evolutionary and psychoanalytic theories. Like the Stoics, Erikson argued that the cycle of human life contained its own stages, each with its own moral norms. He saw the virtues not as "lofty ideals" formulated by theologians and moralists, but rather as essential qualities rooted in human evolution.[7]

According to Erikson, the central psychosocial conflict in old age is integrity versus despair; wisdom is the corresponding virtue arising from successful resolution of that conflict. Integrity for Erikson is "an experience which conveys some world order and spiritual sense. No matter how dearly paid for, it is the acceptance of one's one and only life cycle as something that had to be and that, by necessity, permitted no substitutions."[8] Wisdom is described as "detached concern with life itself, in the face of death itself."[9]

Erikson understood that the life cycle itself does not biologically generate the prescribed virtues, values, and behaviors associated with each stage. Rather every version of the normative life cycle is created by the forces of biology, culture, demography, history, social structure, and patterns of family life. Many of Erikson's followers, however, have treated the "eight ages of man" as if it were a universal paradigm of human development. In my view, the model described by Erikson and Nouwen should be understood as the culmination of the modern Western ideal life cycle, first imagined in early modern Europe and fully realized during the middle third of the twentieth century.[10] Ironically, modernization removed the traditional structural underpinnings of the normative life *cycle* and replaced it with the life *course*.

In both modern and postmodern society, old age emerges as a historically unprecedented, marginal, and culturally unstable phase of life. Herein lies the poignancy of our situation. We are living "after the life cycle."[11] In this context, Erikson's extensive life-cycle writings take on an almost numinous quality. They offer hope for an ideal of the life cycle we desperately want to believe in.[12] But however attractive, Erikson's ideal cannot accommodate the social, cultural, and demographic complexities of our era; we need a richer, pluralistic dialogue about how to live the ever-lengthening years of later life. But first, let me sketch the historical context of our uncertainty about the roles, responsibilities, purposes, and meanings of old age. I intend to show that Jewish living can accommodate this understanding and that Jewish tradition can be utilized as an inspirational source for enriching that understanding; that, while not scientifically meant to be our guide, the sources offer a particularly interesting opportunity for what Judaism has specialized in: commentary on an early text that adapts the broad outlines of that text to the new environment.

Modernization: From the Cycle of Life to the Course of Life

The modern life course began to take shape with the rise of urban, industrial society.

> Set free from older bonds of status, family, and locality, aspiring individuals increasingly came to view their lives as careers—as sequences of expected positions in school, at work, and in retirement. In the twentieth century, this pattern of expectations has become both statistically and ideologically normative, constituting what Martin Kohli aptly calls a "moral economy of the life

course." By the third quarter of the twentieth century, Western democracies had institutionalized this "moral economy" by providing age-homogenous schools for youthful preparation, jobs organized according to skills, experience, and seniority for middle-aged productivity, and publicly-funded retirement benefits for the aged who were considered too slow, too frail, or too old-fashioned to be productive.[13]

This stable sequence is sometimes referred to as the three boxes of life: education for youth, work for adulthood, and retirement for old age.[14] Old age was roughly divided into a period of active retirement supported by Social Security and pensions, and a period of frailty supported by Medicare, Medicaid, and private insurance.

During this transition to modernity, the cycle of life—lived organically from generation to generation in an agrarian culture—was effectively severed from the course of life, the model of an individual's life as a career. In premodern society, when generations of people lived on farms, in villages and small towns, local traditions of practice, belief, and behavior provided external moral norms as each generation visibly cycled into the next; the problem of identity did not arise. In Germany and Austria, for example, the burial plot of the older generation (even today) was often reused when their children died, just as houses, farms, and businesses were passed down. "The idea of the 'life cycle,'" writes Anthony Giddens, "makes very little sense once the connections between the individual life and the interchange of the generations have been broken."[15] In a modern, mobile society, stages of life are disembedded from place; the individual "is more and more freed from externalities associated with pre-established ties to" family, individuals, and groups.[16]

For many older people in an urban, mobile, and rapidly changing society, achieving a stable identity, knowing one's obligations, one's place in the cycle of generations and in a worldview of ultimate meanings—these things became problematic. At a practical level, some suggest that many skills that parents and grandparents knew are no longer useful in the information age, although emotional balance, love, and wisdom are still in short supply. Grandmothers have little need to tell granddaughters how to bake bread except as a story of the past. There is little utility in having a grandfather show his grandson how to sharpen a tool on a grindstone. And while, in one sense, attachment to tradition as "the story of the past" is to relegate that story to a casual folktale, for Jewish life, dependent as it is upon the encounter of tradition with contemporary life, that function is increasingly important to the maintenance of the Jewish people and its morals and various values. The elderly, in this scenario, are especially suited to fulfill an obligation to Jewish society.

Even as older people in the last half of the twentieth century experienced vastly improved medical and economic conditions, they encountered a culture with no clear consensus about the meanings and purposes of later life. People who retired often surprised themselves and the rest of us by living an additional twenty or thirty years. Continued increases in life expectancy have allowed four- and even five-generational families. What were we to do with this abundance of life?[17] The dominant social identities available to older people were narrowly confined to the roles of patients, pensioners, and consumers. Consumer culture, the leisure industry, the welfare state, and the medical establishment each had their own interest in shaping the culture of aging.

From some perspectives, it is in the very nature of religious tradition to have the culture of aging and the culture of the contemporary scene modify and inflect each other, and authors of this volume argue for a midrashic frame of mind as an antidote to separation. But the fact remains that for most of the twentieth century, the notion of progress relegates the elderly and pays less attention to their obligations than to their rights.

In the last quarter of the twentieth century, this relatively stable institutionalized life course began to unravel. The 1970s witnessed a powerful movement of older people and their advocates to overcome negative stereotypes of older people as frail and dependent. Mandatory retirement was challenged under the banner of age discrimination. The 1980s initiated a rebellion against the bureaucratized life course and against restrictive age norms. Writers and scholars called for an "age-irrelevant" society that allowed more flexibility for moving in and out of school and the workforce. At the same time, serious doubts about the proportion of the federal budget devoted to old people were voiced in the name of "generational equity," as were fears of an unsupportable public obligation to sick and dependent older people. Political support for the welfare state began to erode.

And finally, the transition to an "information economy"—spurred by the rise of computers and decline of industrial manufacturing—accelerated the pace of life and the speed of technological and social change. Amid a globalizing economy, declining corporate commitment to long-term employment, seniority, and defined pension benefits undercut expectations for income stability during retirement. Postmodern or late-modern society confirmed with a vengeance Marx's famous observation about capitalism: "All that is solid melts into air." Sociologist Zygmunt Bauman characterizes the resulting ontological insecurity in terms especially apt for older people: "The boundaries [that] tend to be simultaneously most strongly desired and most acutely missed are those of a rightful and secure place in society ... [a place where] the rules do not change overnight and without notice.... It is the widespread characteristic of men and women in our type of society that they live perpetually with the 'identity problem' unresolved. They suffer, one might say, from a chronic absence of resources with which they could build a truly solid and lasting identity, anchor it and stop it from drifting."[18] Identity is not a purely personal issue; it is crucial to the development of wisdom and to knowing one's responsibilities.

After the Life Cycle: The Moral Life of Older People

When we begin to think about the issues of identity and morality in later life, we immediately run into an obstacle articulated by Erikson in 1964: "Our civilization," he wrote, "does not really harbor a concept of the whole of life, as do the civilizations of the East.... As our world-image is a one-way street to never ending progress interrupted only by small and big catastrophes, our lives are to be one-way streets to success—and sudden oblivion."[19] The absence of a culturally viable image of the life cycle set within a larger frame of transcendent meaning makes it difficult for many people to grasp the possibilities of spiritual growth and moral purpose amidst physical decline.

In his seminal work *After Virtue*, moral philosopher Alasdair MacIntyre argues that we no longer possess a commonly shared moral language. MacIntyre claims that the only alternatives are Aristotle or

Nietzsche—that is, tradition or chaos.[20] By analogy, I think that we are living "after the life cycle"—after the collapse of widely shared images and socially cohesive experiences of the life cycle. But I do not think we are forced to choose between idealized tradition or exaggerated chaos. First of all, the lack of a scholarly literature or articulated norms does not imply that most older people are leading morally incoherent lives. And second, the very search for identity itself holds important moral promise. Here, while the notion that identity is related to morality is comfortable for most Jews, I am drawing on the work of Canadian philosopher Charles Taylor. Taylor argues that despite the moral limitations of liberal individualism, the biblical tradition lives on as a kind of background cultural inheritance. Jews, it seems to me, may be uniquely suited for the paradigm that Taylor proffers. But Taylor's approach is more purely ontological. For Taylor, selfhood or identity is inextricably bound up with some historically specific (and often unarticulated) moral framework or notion of "the good." The quest to become one's authentic self, therefore, need not degenerate into self-indulgence, emotivism, or moral relativism.

In Taylor's view, human life and identity are fundamentally dialogical.[21] We become full, self-aware, and responsible human persons by engaging with others. Self-definition is not possible in isolation, apart from social forms of expression and the expectations, needs, and values of others. Taylor acknowledges that the contemporary culture of authenticity often encourages a purely personal understanding of self-fulfillment. But he calls on us to retrieve the full moral potential of authenticity.

A person in search of identity always exists within a "horizon of important questions" that transcend the self. Attempts at self-definition and self-fulfillment that ignore questions and demands outside the self suppress the very conditions of meaning and purpose. As he writes, "Only if I exist in a world in which history, or the demands of nature, or the needs of my fellow human beings, or the duties of citizenship, or the call of God, or something else of this order matters crucially can I define an identity for myself that is not trivial."[22] And, once again, the perspective of the Jewish apodictic tradition is compatible with Taylor's view because of the moral status of "passing the tradition on."

We should not, in other words, view the search for identity in old age as a narrowly personal quest. Of course we are all familiar with examples of late-life narcissism. Yet the effort to live an authentic life is itself a moral ideal—an attempt to understand and fulfill the uniqueness of each human life. Older people trying to make sense of their past through various forms of life review, spiritual autobiography, reminiscence, storytelling, or life-story writing groups are often doing important moral and spiritual work with genuine implications for others. And those who are passionately involved in the arts, in public service, and in new forms of self-exploration exemplify models of elderhood. As Erikson puts it at the end of *Childhood and Society*, without elders who possess integrity, children will be unable to trust.[23]

Authenticity alone provides no reasons to restrain the person who authentically chooses selfishness or evil. It contains no intrinsic moral norms or prohibitions. For Jews this raises the question, What does it mean to be an authentic Jewish elder? One does not "retire" from the covenant, which provides a fundamental framework of obligation between God (however defined) and the Jewish people. Torah study, prayer, family, celebration of Shabbat and the holidays, performance of *mitzvot* … these are the elements that frame a Jewish life morally and spiritually at any age. And they may become even more meaningful as frailty sets in and death is no longer a distant destiny. But how does a person fulfill his unique identity in later life? And especially in the "later" life that is unfolding while a person is yet vigorous? By study and contemplation? Bringing meals to the homebound? In recent years, Rabbi Dayle Friedman, Rabbi Richard Address, and Rabbi Zalman Schachter-Shalomi have offered ideas and programs about the moral worlds of Jewish elders, and a body of literature is slowly emerging that will serve as a commentary on some of the earlier and— admittedly—schematic formulas of ancient Rabbinic literature. (I think of the chart of progression in *Pirkei Avot* as an example.) The years to come will require much more guidance from scholars and rabbis, and from rabbinical schools and congregations grappling with these issues in dialogue with their aging congregants.

The dominant ideal of late life today seems to be what the Austrian sociologist Leopold Rosenmayr calls *Die späte Freiheit*—or "the late freedom."[24] Free from social obligations, retirement—for those who possess good health and adequate income—is equated with leisure activities (visiting family or friends, golf, mah-jongg, bridge, travel, taking up new hobbies, attending classes at Elderhostel or Institutes for Learning in Retirement). The problem here is not that these activities are wrong or bad. Rather they are based on the concept of freedom *from*—that is, from the obligations of midlife—with little or no attention paid to what the freedom is *for*—that is, which principles or commitments should govern the choices being made. Today, senior marketing and advertising specialists have a primary influence on activities, programs, and products for seniors looking for ways to spend their free time. And maintaining one's health is a primary goal spurred on by the commodification of the body.

Services, products, and programs for healthy aging are perhaps the most lucrative segment of the senior market. Health is increasingly construed as physical functioning divorced from any reference to human meaning or purpose. The reduction of health to physical function fits hand in glove with the notion of freedom as unfettered free choice. In the 1970s, for example, the biologist Alex Comfort wrote two popular books: *The Joy of Sex* and *A Good Age*.[25] In both cases, Comfort celebrated technique, functioning, and achievement. In the early 1980s, I invited Comfort to participate in the conference "Aging and Meaning," where Bill May gave his prescient paper "The Virtues and Vices of Aging."[26] Comfort bluntly declined to participate on the grounds that he had no interest in "grannyology." His response reveals an obvious disdain for frail older women, a single-minded focus on control and functioning, and a (common but rarely expressed) discomfort or contempt for existential concerns that underlies most discussions of "successful aging." Instead, we need to reclaim the notion of health along the lines suggested by the Association of American Medical Colleges (AAMC): "Health is not just the absence of disease but a state of well-being that includes a sense that life has purpose and meaning."[27]

In today's consumer culture, drug companies, peddlers of over-the-counter products, and anti-aging hucksters make billions of dollars selling the false hope that aging is an option or a treatable disease. Before the twentieth century, health was understood as a means to an end—living a good life according to the standards embedded in religious traditions. After "the triumph of the therapeutic," health was transformed from a means to an end in itself. Rarely does one hear the question, What do we want to be healthy *for*? A medicalized consumer society crowds out the cultural space necessary for grappling with the most important questions of all: To whom am I accountable? What makes life worth living? What legacy am I passing on to my family? How can I prepare for my death in ways that minimize disruption and give hope to my children?

Given the limitations of authenticity, individual freedom, and health as adequate ideals, how should we begin to explore the moral challenges of aging? Ronald Blythe offers a penetrating, if harsh, starting point:

> Perhaps, with full-span lives the norm, people may need to learn how to be aged as they once had to learn to be adult.... Just as the old should be convinced that, whatever happens during senescence, they will never suffer exclusion, so they should understand that age does not exempt them from being despicable. To fall into purposelessness is to fall out of real consideration.[28]

Learning to grow old is indeed an important concern in our aging society—one that calls for human development policies that help people develop the strengths and skills to solve their own problems. As Harry R. Moody has pointed out, aging policy that responds only to problems intensifies "depreciation of the strengths and capacities of older people," and may inadvertently increase dependency rather than try to prevent it.[29] Falling into purposelessness is not only a matter of individual will and character but also a matter of culture and public policy. Older people—like all people—need to be needed.

In approaching the moral challenges of aging from the individual's point of view, I have always appreciated Rabbi Hillel's three ancient questions: "If I am not for myself, who will be for me? If I am only for myself, what am I? If not now, when?" I take each of these questions to stand for a phase of the life cycle, harkening back to Nouwen's formulation. As children and adolescents, there is a natural tendency to see the world as one's oyster. In midlife, we realize that to mature we must attend to the needs of others. And in later life, with time running out, we must learn how to balance our own needs and interests against the needs of others. Interestingly, whereas Nouwen speaks only of giving as we age, Hillel speaks of balancing competing needs and interests.

If we take Hillel's questions and apply them to later life today, we can begin to specify key questions that demand careful and balanced responses:

1. As citizens, what responsibilities do we have to our community and the larger society? To the poor and vulnerable? To our communities of faith? How do we balance these against our personal interests?

2. What are our responsibilities to our children, grandchildren? For caregiving, economic support? How do we balance these against our own needs and interests?

3. What responsibility do we have for older parents who may be in their eighties or nineties? How do we balance these against responsibilities to our children? To our own personal interests and well-being?

4. What responsibilities do we have to future generations to help safeguard the environment, to work for sustainable sources of energy?

5. What responsibility do we have for a spouse who is permanently disabled, perhaps by the later stages of dementia? Can we say, this isn't the person I married and I need to live my own life? Do we owe a degree of loyalty that includes daily visits and care?

6. What responsibilities do we have to shoulder, depending on circumstances, part of the burden of our economic support?

7. What responsibility do we have for our own health? How do we exercise prudence regarding our personal health-care responsibilities?

8. What responsibility do nursing-home residents have to assist each other?

9. What responsibility do we have to pursue a path of continued growth and spiritual development that aims at self-transcendence, compassion, commitment to others, acceptance of physical and mental decline, and preparation for death?

We need a great deal of social and behavioral study of what older people think about these issues as well as how they act. We need studies of the moral and spiritual lives of older people in various geographic, ethnic, racial, gender, and class situations. We need diverse religious reflections and their translation into practical programs in congregational life. We need philosophical inquiry and public conversation. And we need to listen carefully to the life stories of both ordinary and exemplary old people.

I do not think we can expect universally true, decontextualized norms and values to which all elders should be held accountable. In a pluralist society, we need to hear from various religious, ethnic, racial, and political groups. We need to hear, for example, from the AARP, which is perceived only as a powerful lobbying group for older people. I think we need new models and ideals. One example is the "spiritual eldering" project initiative by Rabbi Zalman Schachter-Shalomi, which sponsors a series of workshops around the country for older people who would like to become real elders.[30] Another is the "Civic Engagement" project currently under way in the Gerontological Society, or Marc Freedman's efforts to generate voluntary movements of older people offering their care and their skills to underprivileged urban youth.[31]

The complexity and nuance required to grapple with these moral questions were aptly described by John Cowper Powys in his book *The Art of Growing Old*: "If by the time we're sixty we haven't learnt what a knot of paradox and contradiction life is, and how exquisitely the good and the bad are mingled in every action we take, and what a compromising hostess Our Lady of Truth is, we haven't grown old to much purpose."[32] In a Jewish context one might say, "What a compromising emblem is *the seal of the Blessed Holy One*" (the Talmud's definition of "truth"; *Shabbat 55a*).

In other words, we need to strive for wisdom and spiritual development to help understand and respond to the moral challenges of aging. What are the paradoxes and contradictions we face on the way to wisdom? (We are always on the way, of course; we are never there.) One prominent paradox is that wise people know that they don't know; they can tolerate uncertainty because they understand the limits (especially their own) of any attempt to grasp the entire truth and the need for multiple points of view. As Florida Scott-Maxwell puts it, "I cannot speak the truth until I have contradicted myself."[33] Wise people cultivate habits of self-examination and self-awareness; they do not attempt to impose their will on the world but learn to observe and accept reality as it is, and acceptance changes the reality. Consider the paradox that loss is gain: failed expectations are a precondition for acquiring experience, which reflection may turn to growth. Or the paradox that unless we accept our own limited subjectivity and projections, we will be unable to work on transcending them. These paradoxes and contradictions are not solvable problems. They must be worked through by each individual in search of spiritual growth, but this does not happen without guidance and community. Our society, therefore, needs to support a variety of contemplative practices, including prayer, meditation, self-reflection, yoga, tai chi, and so on.

One of the most difficult and important paradoxes of life is the relationship of physical decline to spiritual growth. How can we learn to work hard maintaining our physical health while at the same time preparing for our own decline and death? How do we learn to hold on and let go at the same time? One of the central obstacles to wrestling with the challenges of old age lies in the intractable American hostility toward and denigration of physical decline, decay, and dependence. Rather than acknowledge these harsh realities, we pretend that we can master them, and we feel like failures when we don't. Let me turn next to the moral and spiritual aspects of dependency.

The Moral Contours of Dependence

Dependency raises a special range of moral challenges for older people. There are no guidelines about how to be a "good" dependent person, and I doubt that such guidelines would be a worthwhile goal. Hence we must first enter dependency's inner workings before we can understand its moral challenges. Imagine a life in which you cannot walk, cannot carry out your accustomed activities of daily living, are perhaps blind, demented, or incontinent—a world where you must wait for others to bathe you, take you to the grocery store or the doctor. Time stretches before you like a desert; shame and self-loathing lacerate you for the loss of your independence. You are tempted both to false displays of self-sufficiency and to letting yourself go, lapsing into pure passivity. Family relationships become strained, especially when givers and receivers of care are dutifully playing their proper roles, without acknowledging their own and each other's emotional turmoil.

When my grandmother became demented in 1986, I asked if she would consider going into an excellent Jewish home for the aged. "What do you think I am," she replied, "a no-goodnik?" This woman, who had postponed marriage to care for her own mother, lost her husband and her only son, had still managed to scrape together enough money to leave her grandchildren an inheritance. Stripped of an acceptable identity and the ability to be useful, she tried to jump off her twelfth-story balcony. Before slipping into deep dementia, she agonized as the money intended for her grandchildren was spent on her round-the-clock health care. What professor of social work Wendy Lustbader calls "the alchemy of successful frailty" depends on finding ways of turning "the 'nothing' of empty time into the 'something' of good days."[34] The possibilities of "successful frailty" depend on innumerable factors, not the least of which is reciprocity.

In her book *Counting on Kindness: The Dilemmas of Dependency*, Lustbader makes an unusual and controversial point about mercy. The word in old French, *merci*, originally meant compassion and forbearance toward a person in one's power. In Latin, *merces* signified payment or reward, referring to aspects of commerce. "Mercy," writes Lustbader, is based entirely on exchange. "Giving help eventually embitters us, unless we are compensated at least by appreciation; accepting help degrades us, unless we are convinced that our helpers are getting something in return. As much as we might prefer to reject this stark accounting, we discover in living through situations of dependence that good will is not enough. [There is] a delicate balance at the heart of mercy."[35]

We seem to lack language to acknowledge the difficulty of receiving. Hence the dependent person may feel doubly burdened—"disliking the help that cannot be repaid and feeling guilty for the dislike." Increasing frailty shrinks the opportunities to be useful, eliminating external obligations: "No one expects our presence and no one needs our efforts."[36] Finding ways to be useful requires imagination and willpower, for example, among nursing home patients who figure out ways to look after one another.

Wendy Lustbader spent many years going to the homes of frail elders who were ashamed of their needs and struggled to conceal them. Lustbader once visited a woman who allowed her in only because of a sudden illness. The woman's lightbulbs had burned out. She was reading by daylight and sitting alone in the dark. Having nothing to offer her neighbors in return, she decided not to ask them for help. The woman refused to allow Lustbader to stand on a stool to change her lightbulbs; Lustbader said she hated thinking of the woman unable to sleep, tossing fitfully in her bed, and unable to read. At last the woman's pride relented, and Lustbader changed the bulbs. "As I left, I thanked her for giving me the honor of helping her. She understood what I meant, for it was she who was carrying the burden of uselessness and I who was being granted satisfaction."[37]

Despite an extensive literature search in English, I have been able to find only two contemporary articles on the virtues and vices of dependent older people. One is by the theologian, culture critic, and ethicist William May, and the other is by the feminist, secular philosopher Sara Ruddick. Before I turn to the topic of virtue and age, I want to offer three words of caution: (1) although I'll be discussing ideals of virtue in a relatively decontextualized way, any full exploration must take into account differences in culture, gender, race, ethnicity, and social class; (2) contrary to Cicero's exclusive emphasis on character, exercising virtue is not simply a matter of individual will; virtues occur amid social conditions and relationships that foster or inhibit them; and (3) a given person's capacity for exercising virtues (especially more subtle and demanding virtues) also depends on her prior level of emotional and spiritual development.

In "The Virtues and Vices of Aging," ethicist William F. May contextualizes his discussion when he observes the power imbalance between older patients and health professionals. He observes that caregivers who unwittingly display their health and youth are "like a bustling cold front that moves in and stiffens the landscape." Hence they cannot see that their vocation depends on their patients, which compounds the power imbalance and obscures the moral significance of reciprocal dependency. Examining the specific adversities and virtues of aging, May argues, is central to exploring the moral status of the aged. Writing across the boundaries of psychology, ethics, and theology, he emphasizes that virtues do not emerge automatically with age; rather, they "grow only through resolution, struggle, perhaps prayer, and perseverance."[38] Sensitive to the confusion of infirmity with moral failure, May offers a cursory sketch of vices and temptations that oppose the virtues. He begins with a list of virtues appropriate to various ages. A person needs *courage* to rise to the occasion of loss and the certainty of death. Aquinas defined courage as "firmness of soul in the face of adversity."[39] The Hasidic master Nachman of Breslov observed, "All the world is a very narrow bridge, but the main thing is to have no fear."

Courage requires "keeping one's fears, one's dislikes, one's laziness under control for the sake of *the* good as well as one's own good."[40] Public virtue requires older people (as well as others) to temper pursuit of self-interest with the sake of the common good.

Caregivers and care receivers alike need the virtue of *humility.* Humility restrains the arrogance of caregivers' power, even as it removes the sting of humiliation from those assaulted by disease and disability. Like humility, *patience* is a desirable response to anger, frustration, and bitterness; but patience, on May's account, is not a form of passivity or detached Stoic endurance. "Patience is purposive waiting, receiving, willing; it demands a most intense sort of activity." For May, the moral is never very far from the spiritual: "Precisely when all else goes out of control, when panic would send us sprawling in all directions ... [patience] requires us once again to become centered in the deepest levels of our lives as purposive beings."[41]

Drawing from the Benedictine tradition, May lists the virtues of *simplicity, benevolence,* and *integrity.* The aged pilgrim learns to travel light, to cast off the extraneous and embrace the path to God. "Benevolence opposes the tightfistedness of avarice, not with the empty-handedness of death but with the open-handedness of love."[42] According to May, integrity requires a re-collection of the self that is not fragmented or dispersed. Creating a unity of inner and outer, word and deed, depends upon the spiritual work of autobiography. In Augustinian terms, a person can commune with God only after the disciplined work that yields integrity, which itself rests on conviction of forgiveness for sin. Israel Salanter, founder of the Musar (moral self-scrutiny) movement, noted that a person can live with himself for seventy years and still not know himself. May also believes that integrity in old age requires that a person's death be framed in a context of transcendent meaning or ultimate concerns. These, however, are not mere abstractions but rather patterns of ritual and behavior woven into the fabric of everyday life.

To Erikson's rather vague definition of wisdom, May adds additional virtues originating in medieval Christianity. Integrity and wisdom are made possible by prudence, which consists of the temporal virtues of *memoria, docilitas,* and *solertia.* A person who resists nostalgia and regret—as well as the temptation to airbrush her past—earns the virtue of *memoria.* Interestingly, many contemporary approaches to psychotherapy, life review, and life-story work are not so much interested in the historical truth as in the narrative truth that may enable a person to achieve a healing that comes from new meanings of old events. *Docilitas* does not connote the meanings of docility; rather it "signifies a capacity to be silent," to be alert, attentive to the present moment. *Solertia* is a characteristic of those who "learn to sit loose to life"; it signifies openness to the future, readiness for the unexpected.

The Stoic grounds wisdom on rational self-mastery and detachment. The biblical tradition, on the other hand, grounds wisdom "through a primordial attachment ... to the divine love [that] sustains, but also orders and limits all other attachments and fears. In the Christian tradition, attachment to God makes possible the virtues of *nonchalance* and *courtesy.* Nonchalance signifies the capacity to take life's gifts and assaults in stride; courtesy is the capacity to "deal honorably with all that is urgent, jarring, and rancorous."[43] The evils and tragedies of life are understood to be "*real* but not *ultimate.*" Love rather than death has the last word. *Hilaritas* is *the* final virtue handed down by the Benedictine monks. Or in common parlance, humor is a "saving grace," allowed by the capacity to see life's experience from a more spacious perspective. In Jewish terms, humor is a *nechemta,* "consolation," the kind of upbeat nuance that one typically finds at the end of a midrash.

May aptly criticizes academic ethicists who focus chiefly on moral dilemmas and provide critical guidelines to professionals. It has been over twenty years since he observed that ethics "does not offer much help to patients facing the ordeal of fading powers. [The aged] need guidelines for action, to be sure, but more than that they need strength of character in the face of ordeals."[44]

I have been able to find only one significant essay that takes up this challenge. In her essay "Virtues and Age," Sara Ruddick argues that there are indeed virtues especially salient in the lives of people "situated between a lengthening, unalterable past and short future, where loss is predictable, but its timing and form is not."[45] Ruddick writes as a secular, feminist philosopher who is quite wary of articulating ideals that become burdensome to those who are meant to be governed by them. She states, quite convincingly, that the elderly, like people at any age, "struggle to maintain conceptions of themselves as good people. Many also try both to preserve relationships and to do well by the people to whom they are importantly related. These efforts of virtue are intrinsically rewarding for the elderly themselves, confirming their sense of agency, accountability, and moral standing." These efforts also benefit "the people they care for and who care for them."[46]

Ruddick's account of virtue focuses particularly on the vulnerable, needy elderly and those who care for them. She draws not only on philosophical reasoning but also on her experience of caregiving and witnessing in nursing homes. Ruddick acknowledges that being virtuous is sometimes beyond the control of demented elders, but she insists that mental deterioration, which occurs slowly, allows time for adaptation and rarely makes efforts of virtue impossible. She lists a set of five virtues especially appropriate for those in their seventies and older, people "whose future is dwindling, and who will likely experience multiple losses and decline." These include curiosity; a capacity for pleasure and delight; concern for near and distant others; capacities to forgive and let go, to accept, adjust, and appreciate; and "wise independence," which is the ability to plan and control one's life as well as the ability "to acknowledge one's limitations and accept help in ways that are gratifying to the helper." Wise independence also includes "the ability to manage pain, to mourn and integrate the loss of people dear to them, to handle, without bitterness, their increasing disabilities, and to prepare for death and its effect on those they care about."[47]

Ruddick criticizes theories that characterize virtue primarily as a characteristic of individuals, a charge that may be leveled against May. Such theories, she argues, show little tolerance for "outlaw emotions" such as righteous anger, and they are conceptually unable to guide the moral challenges facing receivers and givers of care. Ruddick is also wary of the stereotypical vices that shadow any list of virtues. She therefore speaks of "ongoing efforts of virtues" (rather than achieved dispositions or traits) that individuals strive to acquire and maintain. Reversing traditional theological arguments, Ruddick argues that "being virtuous is something one *sometimes* does, not something one is." She not only focuses on process rather than achievement, she also believes that virtue is created between and among people.[48]

Ruddick takes pains to avoid creating an unrealistically burdensome account of virtues that requires continuous and unremitting effort, which she criticizes as another form of the masculine Protestant work ethic—perhaps another challenge to May. She reformulates her definitions this way: "So being virtuous is something people *sometimes* do together.... There are days when one isn't up to creating virtue alone or with others. Hours, days, even weeks of sadness, sloth, and apathy are an integral part rather than an interruption of ongoing efforts to be virtuous. They do not mark a person as bad; processes of doing virtue are marked by vicissitude, not failure. Over a period of time, a virtuous person may do more rather than less.... But no one needs to be counting or judging."[49]

Ruddick, then, presents a secular, feminist account that is close to experience. She emphasizes process over achievement, relationships over individual virtue, behavior over character. May, on the other hand, offers both secular and theological theories of virtue, emphasizes individual character, and does not shrink from light-handed and contextually sensitive moral judgment.

What can we expect from this kind of analysis of character and action among the frail elderly? What is missing from these accounts? Can we educate caregivers on the importance of acknowledging reciprocity and fostering relationships that allow their patients to be useful? What would relationships look like if moral language and reciprocity between dependent patients were introduced in nursing homes or home care? How can we educate clergy, both in the pulpit and at the bedside, in the moral challenges of aging? Seminaries have only recently begun to provide some gerontological education to their students, focusing entirely on the needs of older people. What should be added to revitalize religious understanding of older people as moral agents? Finally, with the proliferation of lifelong learning through Elderhostel and Institutes for Learning in Retirement, could older people be engaged in seminars and workshops about moral issues in their lives? (I am skeptical about this last idea, since older people notoriously avoid classes on aging. But the use of biblical material, films, fiction, and theater might slip behind their defenses and open up their own moral and spiritual horizons. Think of the old King Saul or King David, *King Lear*, *Oedipus at Colonus*, *Driving Miss Daisy*, *Cocoon*, or *The Trip to Bountiful* approached through the lenses of ethics and the human spirit.) Think of what it would be like if our Jewish institutions could honestly get hold of the vision and of the sense of obligation that would drive the elderly to a sure sense of fulfilling a life's mission.

Concluding Thoughts

Where do these thoughts about life-cycle norms, mass longevity, post-modernity, moral obligations, spiritual development, and vices and virtues leave us? Personally, I feel a sense of awe and amazement at the sheer abundance of life made possible by the gift of mass longevity. But what is the price of that gift? Perhaps, as Theodore Roszak argues in *America the Wise*, the wisdom of a maturing population promises to be our richest resource.[50] Or perhaps, as a voice from the Talmud suggests, a man who is a fool in his youth is also a fool in his old age, while a man who is wise in his youth is also wise in his old age. I suspect that the truth will depend on how well we learn to identify, support, and accomplish the moral and spiritual work of aging in our era. As Plato understood, one of the best ways to learn is by listening to those who have traveled this road ahead of us. Let me close by listening again to one of my favorite elders, Florida Scott-Maxwell. Writing in her eighties as a Jungian analyst, she encourages us to learn "that life is a tragic mystery. We are pierced and driven by laws we only half understand, we find that the lesson we learn again and again is that of heroic helplessness. Some uncomprehended law holds us at a point of contradiction where we have no choice, where we do not like that which we love, where good and bad are inseparable partners to tell apart, and where we—heart-broken and ecstatic—can only resolve the conflict by blindly taking it into our hearts. This used to be called being in the hands of God. Has anyone any better words to describe it?"[51]

Rabbi Dayle A. Friedman, MSW, MAJCS, BCC, works to develop spiritual resources for later life through spiritual direction, pastoral care, and scholarship. She is the founding director of Hiddur: The Center for Aging and Judaism of the Reconstructionist Rabbinical College. Her publications include *Jewish Visions for Aging: A Professional Guide for Fostering Wholeness* and *Jewish Pastoral Care: A Practical Handbook from Traditional & Contemporary Sources* (both Jewish Lights).

The Journey of Later Life
Moses as Our Guide

Rabbi Dayle A. Friedman, MSW, MAJCS, BCC

Longevity: Blessing or Curse?

We who are now adults can expect to live longer than any generation in history. We may be "old" for a quarter century or more, facing unprecedented blessings and vicissitudes. We may have expansive opportunities for adventure, reinvention, and discovery. But there is also the likelihood of prolonged illness and dependency.

The challenges of longevity are personal *and* communal. Jewry will be transformed by an ever greater proportion of elders. In 2000 only 12 percent of the U.S. population was over sixty-five, but over 20 percent of the Jewish community had crossed that threshold. Because the first baby boomers have since begun turning sixty-five, the numbers of elders will only skyrocket. Political and social commentators have signaled panic about the age wave and its consequences for medical care, housing, and pensions. Witness the alarm of David Walker, then U.S. comptroller general: "We face a demographic tsunami [that] will never recede."[1]

Most of us would do anything to disavow our aging. When my husband turned sixty, I planned an elaborate party with many of his friends and relatives. Still, I was stunned a couple of months later when it hit me: "David is sixty! That's the same sixty I refer to in my teaching as the beginning of later life!"

I had failed to absorb the implications of this milestone. Of course, this sixty is not our parents' or grandparents' sixty. David is a parent of school-age children and the child of an aging mother, and he intends to work in the career he loves for the foreseeable future. Yet that future will certainly include change and difficulty.

How are we to build purpose and connection on a path toward loss, limits, vulnerability, and mortality? How can we understand ourselves when we are no longer as we were? We will not find the answers in contemporary popular culture, which seeks to deny, evade, ridicule, or conquer old age. But Jewish tradition offers us resources to address these questions. Our biblical ancestors are credited with extraordinarily long lives. These heroes and heroines find productivity of all kinds, even miraculous parenthood, well into old age. Their experience might be less factual than legendary, but it offers us a pairing of aging and possibility.

A richer understanding of later life's promise and value is opened up by Rabbinic literature, such as the biblically inspired legends called midrash. Through midrashic inquiry we place our experience in a larger frame; we draw on the text and the dialogue of the centuries to shed light on our chaotic experience. We bring our own imagination and questions and build on the tradition we've inherited. This endeavor helps us to make sense out of the inchoate mess of our lives.

The Rabbis found dignity in the aging of our heroes, especially Moses. We, too, can receive guidance in later life from the Moses depicted in Scripture and explicated in midrash. This greatest prophet and leader in the Torah is already eighty when he begins his mission to confront the power of the day, liberate the Israelites, receive and transmit revelation, and provide for his people on their wilderness trek. Even if the specific number may be the hyperbolic age of a mythic hero, the tradition's images of Moses over his later years demonstrate a meaningful grappling with both beauty and hardship.

Resisting the Conventional View

Our dread of aging is informed by two misleading pictures of senescence. Television commercials give us a glimpse of both. In a spot for an investment firm, a leather-clad, ponytailed man rides his Harley toward the horizon as the voice-over talks about doing retirement "your way." Nike ads feature bungee-jumping elders exhorted to "just do it." These vignettes hint that you can grow older without losing fitness, energy, or engagement. Maybe this can go on for decades, or forever!

On the other hand, we are barraged by images of aging as inevitable decline. We see commercials for adult diapers and for a button to press if we have "fallen and can't get up." Mysteriously, then, there are two kinds of aging, glorious and terrible: who's to say which one awaits us?

We have been fed a false dichotomy: defy age by remaining physically and in every other way vital, the so-called positive aging, *or* face illness or incapacity and languish in what philosopher and activist Ronald Manheimer has called "the vortex of nothingness."[2]

Philosopher George Santayana suggested that religion's vistas and mysteries can offer us "another world to live in"—a perspective unavailable in our mundane reality.[3] In Judaism, this alternative plane is provided by midrash, the record of how the Rabbis interpreted and reimagined biblical narratives. Our sacred text and our encounter with it provide a model for approaching and holding the *whole* of later life, the complexity and paradox within it.

Moses in Later Life

Moses has lately resurfaced in our popular literature. Bruce Feiler's *America's Prophet: Moses and the American Story* reminds us who has been the favorite biblical figure of our patriots and visionaries. Among his other virtues, Moshe Rabbenu might be a guide to changes in later life. In the Torah, most of Moses's achievements came after middle age. His younger years were tranquil when he was working as a shepherd for his father-in-law in Midian. Then, at eighty, he received the call at the burning bush, followed by forty years of accomplishment, disappointment, loss, limits, and mortality. Examining Moses's biography with the lens of midrash can provide a map for our own sojourn through later life.

The Brink of Change

> Now Moshe was shepherding the flock of Yitro his father-in-law,
> priest of Midyan.[4]
>
> EXODUS 3:1

Moses's life at midpoint, as described in the Bible, was continuous
with what had come before. He was still living in Midian, working as
a shepherd for his father-in-law, Jethro. Perhaps Moses believed he
would simply remain in the familiar roles and surroundings.

But the reader is aware that Moses is on the threshold of transformation. The midrash asks the question, what prepared Moses for the
call he was about to receive? What was happening during this period
of continuity, before everything changed?

> "Now Moshe was shepherding the flock" (Exodus 3:1). The Holy
> One tested Moses by means of the flock, as our masters explained:
> When Moses our teacher was shepherding Jethro's flock in the
> wilderness, a lamb scampered off, and Moses followed it until it
> approached a shelter under a rock. As the lamb reached the shel-
> ter, it came upon a pool of water and stopped to drink. When
> Moses caught up with it, he said, "I did not know that you ran
> away because you were thirsty. Now you must be tired." So he
> hoisted the lamb on his shoulder and started walking back with it.
> The Holy One then said, "Because you showed such compassion
> in shepherding the flock of a mortal, as you live, you shall become
> shepherd of Israel, the flock that is Mine."
>
> *EXODUS RABBAH* 2:2

The midrash envisions a different Moses than the Bible describes. He is
concerned about the errant lamb and willing to endure discomfort and
inconvenience for its sake. He is humble and able to admit his errors—
he tells the lamb that he hadn't initially sensed its real need. He recognizes that the heart of his job is to be mindful, to be aware of and
responsive to the needs of those in his care. The midrash shows us
Moses honing qualities of being, *middot*, that would serve him when
the call came.

This reading of Moses at midlife is not only more interesting than the biblical account, but also offers a chance to expand our sense of who we are. We generally expect things to stay as they are now. At the same time, we know that change awaits us. A job can be downsized; our children will leave home to start their lives; our parents are fading or dying. Perhaps we feel restless in the job or career that we have held for some time.

Midrash is a technique of disclosure. It brings to light what is implicit in the biblical text. Just as important, it brings to light what is implicit in our human experience, in our daily tasks and struggles, in our hopes and fears and fantasies. Moses the shepherd is a mirror reflecting the quiet evolution of whoever wrote this midrash and whoever reads it. The midrash suggests that we are preparing for the next stage even in the apparent homeostasis of the status quo. The skills, values, sensibilities, and character traits we have nurtured to this point will sustain us on the journey of later life.

The Call

Moses was eighty years old when everything changed (Exodus 7:7).

Now Moshe was shepherding the flock of Yitro his father-in-law, priest of Midyan. He led the flock behind the wilderness—and he came to the mountain of God, to Horev. And YHWH's messenger was seen by him, in the flame of a fire out of the midst of a bush. He saw: here, the bush is burning with fire, and the bush is not consumed!

Moshe said: "Now let me turn aside that I might see this great sight—why the bush does not burn up!"

When YHWH saw that he had turned aside to see, God called to him out of the midst of the bush, he said: "Moshe! Moshe!" He said: "Here I am."

EXODUS 3:1–4

Moses's call was subtle. He was walking along minding his business and his flock when he passed a bush that burned without being consumed. What made Moses notice this remarkable phenomenon? The attentiveness he nurtured as a shepherd served him well. Instead of walking on by, Moses said, "Now let me turn aside that I might see this great sight—why the bush does not burn up!" Moses's alertness was matched by patience. He must have watched the bush for some time to ascertain that it was not being consumed.

Moses was willing for his assumptions about nature and purpose to be challenged.[5] Perhaps he was even looking for a change, wishing that something different lay ahead. Maybe he wondered, Is this all there is?

Sara Lawrence-Lightfoot writes, "We must develop a compelling vision of later life, one that does not assume a trajectory of decline after 50 but recognizes this as a time of potential change, growth and new learning, a time when 'our courage gives us hope.'"[6] Perhaps Moses hoped things would be shaken up when "he led the flock behind the wilderness—and he came to the mountain of God, to Horev." The call at the burning bush may have come not as a shock, but as the fulfillment of a time of seeking and yearning.

When Moses said *hineini*, "Here I am," he said yes to a demanding and absorbing new mission. A story I once heard claimed that until this moment, Moses was an average old man. He was a bit creaky, more than a little kvetchy, and then, when his life took on new purpose, he was restored to youthful vigor, which would last until his death. The description of Moses as having undimmed vision and unabated vigor in his old age (Deuteronomy 34:7) could be a denial of aging. Clearly, though, finding meaning enhances physical and emotional health.

As a nursing-home chaplain, I met Mr. Fairstein, a distinguished but deflated individual at age ninety. He had several advanced degrees and had run a successful business. He had cared for his second wife for years of descent into dementia, even as his own health declined. Mr. Fairstein was confined to his room for nine months, but he was hardly idle. By chance his new roommate was Dr. Rose, a retired Jewish studies professor. Always fascinated by Jewish history, Mr. Fairstein asked Dr. Rose to give him a tutorial. Thus began a daily study session, filled with discourse, debate, good humor, and mutual respect. Dr. Rose said of Mr. Fairstein, "He is my best pupil." Mr. Fairstein said, "Ours is a true intellectual peership." Mr. Fairstein found a compelling calling when he might have thought his life was over.

The Mission

Moses commenced a new mission late in life. His concerns broadened from the small flock in Midian to the entire Israelite people and its liberation. He would stretch beyond discomfort, developing new strengths to compensate for his weaknesses. He would teach, nurture, and contend with humans and God as he led the Israelites out of Egypt, to Sinai and the Promised Land.

Moses brought all he had learned and experienced to this later life path. We will examine three dimensions of Moses's mission: his relationship with God; the juxtaposition of blessings and curses; and his struggle to accept finitude and mortality.

God's Intimate

Moses is depicted as having a uniquely intimate relationship with God. This has sweet and positive manifestations, as in this midrash:

> Rabbi Yehoshua ben Levi also said: When Moses ascended on high, he found the Holy One of blessing tying crowns on the letters [of the Torah, and Moses remained respectfully silent]. Finally God asked, "Moses, where you come from, were you not taught to extend greetings?" Moses replied, "May a servant presume to greet his master?" "Nevertheless," said God, "you should have encouraged Me [by saying something]." Presently [during a later ascent] Moses cried out [without being reminded], "May the power of the Lord increase!" [Then he added], "Is this not what You told me to do?"[7]
>
> BABYLONIAN TALMUD, *SHABBAT* 89A

God wants to be greeted by Moses, to be treated as a companion, a friend. Perhaps this is because God is also aging, according to the midrash. We are taught that God was a young warrior at the Red Sea and an old man at Mount Sinai and beyond. The book of Daniel calls

God *Atik Yomaya*, "the Ancient of Days."[8] What a poignant image: the aging God and the aging prophet, who have been through so much together.

Moses's tender relationship with God models possibility in later life. God has enough time to receive greetings and pleasantries from every one of us. As we grow older, our capacity for spiritual intimacy deepens. We grow beyond earlier struggles, and our hearts may open to God in new ways. We may become conscious of a shared history with God, who has been with us from the beginning. We can even remind God of commonalities between the divine experience and our own. If we have sometimes felt neglected or misunderstood, God has also been neglected and misunderstood; if we are lonely, God has also been lonely.

I learned this from the elders I accompanied as a nursing home chaplain. Many had abandoned Jewish practice once they had left their childhood homes and shuls. They had lost faith or lacked the time for faith and observance amid the tasks of daily life. Now, in the nursing home, as they coped with chronic illness and continual loss, spiritual questions were at the heart of their concerns. Just as their body fat had fallen away with aging, so the trivial concerns of midlife striving had eroded down to the bone. They were preoccupied with the meaning of their lives, the cause of suffering, and what might be awaiting them beyond this life. In the corridors of the home I heard profound remarks uttered quite casually: "Tell me what happens when we die? My husband has been gone ten years—not a letter, not a phone call, nothing!" "Why won't God take me?" "I am so glad to be alive."

Reb Zalman Schachter-Shalomi, after a full career as the founder of the Jewish Renewal philosophy, now embodies the spiritual elder-ing movement.[9] In his eighties, he is consciously living the December of his life and facing limits on his health and energy. He practices dying each night by saying the *Shema* with a particular breath pat-tern, in the hope that he will have this prayer on his lips when he breathes his last. He focuses on projects that will sustain his legacy when he is gone. He told me that he is comforted by traditional prayer—*davenen*—more than ever, and that certain words and phrases resonate strongly. Praying to the *Ribbono shel olam* (Master of the universe) now feels like sitting and schmoozing with an old friend on a park bench.

Spiritual intimacy has another side for Moses, as well. He is so close to God that he feels entitled to challenge the Holy One when he believes divine actions are unjust.

> "And now let Me be" (Exodus 32:10). Rabbi Abbahu said: Were Torah not so explicit, it would have been impossible to say such a thing. For the verse implies that, like a man who grabs hold of his fellow by his garment, Moses, if one dare say it, grabbed hold of the Holy One and brazenly said to God, "Master of the universe, I will not release You until You pardon and forgive Israel."
>
> BABYLONIAN TALMUD, *BERAKHOT* 32A

According to this midrash, Moses grabs the Holy One by the lapels, as it were, and refuses to let go until he gets his way. Like the older Abraham, Moses calls the Judge of all the earth to account. This audacity is part of later life's spiritual intimacy. The late Maggie Kuhn, founder of the Gray Panthers, said upon reaching eighty, "Old age is an excellent time for outrage. My goal is to say or do at least one outrageous thing every week."[10] Maggie Kuhn took political action with humor and force. She wrote to then-president Ronald Reagan to criticize his approval of funding for MX missiles: "We need Amtrak, not MX,"[11] an oft-cited quip.

What if someone doesn't think of himself as spiritual or religious? These labels belie the psychic depths that can be plumbed in later life. My uncle Sidney, a beloved family friend, survived an unimaginable accident when he was seventy-eight. After a dump truck fell off of a highway overpass onto his car, he lay unconscious in the ICU for several weeks. Uncle Sidney awoke from the coma, survived months of rehabilitation, and returned home to his wife. He is more upbeat than before the accident, when he was embittered by constant pain from chronic illness. He has begun work on a novel. He says, "My survival was *not* a miracle.... If it were, why wouldn't God have saved the hundreds of thousands of people who died in the tsunami?" What meaning does he find in life now? "I'm overwhelmed at how loved I am.... I feel I am supposed to tell the story of my recovery to others who are in rehab ... to inspire them with the sheer will it takes to get through." Although Uncle Sidney remains a skeptic, he is feeling spiritual intimacy!

Gifts amid Curses

Moses's calling, mission, and spiritual intimacy occurred *amid* the hardships of later life. Moses faced myriad disappointments: the people's disloyalty in worshipping the Golden Calf, endless kvetching by the Israelites. He struggled to sustain his people, and fought off enemies. He confronted the deaths of Nadab and Abihu, his young nephews, and eventually of Miriam and Aaron, his siblings and closest companions.

A midrash suggests that Moses and Aaron were so preoccupied with grief for Miriam, God had to goad them into responding to the people's thirst.[12] When it came time for Aaron to die, Moses was to become a "last twig," the last remnant of his family of origin. God instructs Moses to inform his brother of his impending death. Moses cannot bring himself to tell him directly, so he invites Aaron to study the book of Genesis together. Moses says:

> "During the night I meditated on a matter in Scripture that I found distressing, and so I rose early and came to you." "What was the matter?" Aaron asked. "I do not remember, but I know it was in the book of Genesis. Bring it and we'll read it." They took the book of Genesis, read each and every section in it, and said about each one of them, "The Holy One wrought well, created well." But when they came to the creation of Adam, Moses asked, "What is one to say of Adam, who brought death to the world, so that I, who prevailed over the ministering angels, and you, who held back death—are not even you and I to have a like end? After all, how many more years have we to live?" "Not many," Aaron answered. Moses continued talking, until finally he mentioned to him the precise day when death was to come. At that moment, Aaron's bones felt the imminence of his own demise. So he asked, "Is it because of me that you found the matter in Scripture so distressing?" Moses answered, "Yes."
>
> YALKUT SHIMONI, CHUKKAT 764

Moses went on to bury Aaron and to confront the community's grief for this towering leader and peacemaker. Aaron and Miriam's absence must have cast a pall over the rest of Moses's days.[13] All who are blessed to grow old must, like Moses, learn to endure the absences. We must cope with the loss of beloveds, of witnesses to our childhoods, of supports and companions without whom life seems less beautiful.

Facing (and Resisting) Death

When God told him that he would not live to cross the Jordan, Moses was crestfallen. The midrash expands on the terse biblical narrative, asking how Moses received the news that he would die before entering the Promised Land. It traces his complex and tortured reaction in a narrative that touches every stage of response to dying outlined by Elisabeth Kübler-Ross: denial, anger, bargaining, depression, and acceptance.[14] Moses's incredulity and indignation that his life must end gave way to negotiation for a final favor:

Moses said, "Master of the universe, give me permission, and I will become a bird and fly in the air by the power of the Name, or make me into a fish, and I will make my two arms like two fins, and my hair like scales, and I shall jump into the Jordan, and at least see the land." The Holy One said, "If I do this for you, I am violating My oath." Moses said, "Master of the universe, lay me upon the clouds ... that I might just see the land from above the Jordan." God said, "This, too, would constitute a violation of My oath." Moses said, "Master of the universe, cut me limb by limb and cast me across the Jordan, then bring me back to life that I might see the land." God said, "This, too, is a violation of My oath." Moses said, "Show me the land in the blink of an eye." God said, "To this request I shall accede, for it is written, 'You may view the land from a distance, but you shall not enter it'" [Deuteronomy 32:52]. So the Holy One showed him the land four hundred miles by four hundred miles ... and gave his eyes the power to see it all, lowlands and heights, hidden and visible, far and near, and said, "This is the land I gave to Abraham."[15]

MIDRASH PETIRAT MOSHE

Letting Go

The midrash describes Moses's other attempts to evade his destiny as the angels warn that death approaches. When God suggests that Moses must die to make room for the next generation, Moses offers to hand leadership to Joshua. Joshua takes up the mantle as Moses stands by.

> The people who had gathered as usual before Moses' tent to hear from him the word of God, failed to find him there, and hearing that he had gone to Joshua, went there also, where they found Moses standing and Joshua seated. "What are you thinking of," they called out to Joshua, "that you are seated, while your teacher Moses stands before you in a bowed attitude and with folded hands?"[16]
>
> *MIDRASH PETIRAT MOSHE*

The people cannot accept Moses in this reduced role, and they blame Joshua. This arrangement also proves intolerable for Moses.

> Joshua now began his discourse with Moses sitting at his right, and with Aaron's sons, Eleazar and Ithamar, at his left. But hardly had Joshua begun his lecture with the words, "Praised is God who has delighted in the pious and their teachings," when the treasures of wisdom vanished from Moses and passed over into Joshua's possession, so that Moses was not even able to follow Joshua's discourse. When Joshua had finished his lecture, Israel asked Moses to review with them what Joshua had taught, but he said, "I know not how to reply to your request!" He began to expound Joshua's lecture to them, but he had not understood it.... He [Moses] now said to God, "Lord of the world! Until now I wished for life, but now I put my soul in Your hands."[17]
>
> *MIDRASH PETIRAT MOSHE*

Here Moses becomes recognizably old. He cannot be who he has been, now that he has lost his cognitive acuity. My mother-in-law, who held fast while suffering horrifically in the Shoah, has refused to give up on life in old age. She has borne the loss of her husband, sisters, and dear friends, as well as chronic physical pain. When we ask about her advance directive, she says, "As long as I am *zhitomnye* [Polish for 'clearheaded'], I want to live. If I don't know who I am or who you are, then let me go." For Moses, as for my mother-in-law, the loss of cognitive capacity is the one thing he cannot accept. Upon asking God to take him, Moses meets a gentle death, a kiss from God.

Moses as a Model

Moses represents vital and complex aging, though he does not endure protracted frailty and dependency. He is vital *and* hurting; he is broken *and* whole.[18] Moses provides a rich model for later life. His is not the "just do it" model that envisions vigor and adventure without loss, failings, and dying. Nor is Moses's example what Dr. Bill Thomas calls "declinism," the assumption that aging can only be an inexorable downward spiral.[19]

Moses offers us the possibility of becoming *more* in later life. He shows us that the blessing and the wisdom of later life come not despite the hardships, but precisely because of them. As a friend says of caring for her aging parents, "The blessing is the challenge; the challenge is the blessing."[20]

The Lesson for Us

Moses is the receiver of the commandments, or *mitzvot*, even their embodiment. By his example he teaches the *mitzvah* of leading Israel, the *mitzvah* of studying Torah, the *mitzvah* of mourning the dead, the *mitzvah* of loving God. These *mitzvot* call to Jewish elders in our time as well.

Moses's journey, as depicted in the text and midrashic expansions, prompts us to cultivate qualities for the callings, missions, and losses of later life. Moses's process should also inspire congregations to empower people for a new calling and mission in later life. Are we only relating to older members as recipients of care or service, or are we also helping them to discern and use their talents? In addition to needs assessment for elders, we should conduct *gifts* assessments.[21]

Our communities and our elders will be enriched as we tap their wisdom, passion, and experience.

Moses's model may help us to avoid the catastrophization of the age wave, or "apocalyptic demography."[22] The midrashic Moses can teach us that a surging number of elders is not a problem to be solved but a boon. Elders can help to heal and transform our world.[23]

7

Narrative and Loss

Eitan Fishbane, PhD, is assistant professor of Jewish thought at The Jewish Theological Seminary in New York. He is the author of *As Light Before Dawn: The Inner World of a Medieval Kabbalist* and the coeditor of *Jewish Mysticism and the Spiritual Life: Classical Texts, Contemporary Reflections* (Jewish Lights). The following essay is drawn from Fishbane's *Shadows in Winter: A Memoir*.

Words in the Dark
A Personal Journey

Eitan Fishbane, PhD

Words in the dark: like blazing lanterns in the night-forest.

And then silence: trying to speak in the place of the speechless.

"What happened to her is tragic." *Tragic.* The words of the neurosurgeon still ring clearly in my ear, and the haze of those hours comes back to me again—my own private lamentation.

> *Lonely sits the city*
> *once great with people!...*
> *Bitterly she weeps in the night,*
> *Her cheek wet with tears.*
> LAMENTATIONS 1:1–2

People are still roundabout me, but I am alone.

Alone.

At that point we didn't expect anything different; not after two days of feeling the shadows creep in, of hearing one doctor after another deliver the message that there was little hope to hold on to.

"Right now all we can do is pray for a miracle," said one of the physicians who had been with us since the nightmare began on Tuesday morning. He said it with great compassion. But all I could hear was the unreal knock of the angel of death.

177

Lying on that hospital bed in the ICU, the respirator inhaling and exhaling for her, was my Leah—the center and anchor of my life. Sweet love, she lay there so helpless and so gentle, and there was nothing I could do to stop the train wreck of our life together, happening right before my eyes.

Hands laid at her sides, placed there by the nurses. I almost think she is sitting at that angle deliberately, her arms set out in perfectly calm composure. Until of course the blanket shifts and her hand slips uncontrolled. But they are still her hands. Warm. Soft. Holding her hand I can almost feel the familiar squeeze of her palm, the closing of her fingers in mine. I am still waiting for her to open her eyes of a sudden, to whisper hoarsely to me: "Eitee ... bring me some cold water ... Eitee, my throat is so dry ..." And the other half of me expects to hear the sound of her healthy voice, familiar as my own blood, as close as the inside of my own head.

So many memories. A thousand moments that circle now through the wheels of my mind like gleaming leaves in late autumn—floating through the air in waves, and the new chill that bears them whispers of the coming winter. Suddenly I feel hollowed out inside, emptied by her absence. She can't put her hand on my heart, or hold me tightly to her chest. She can't bring me back from the edges of my worry and my fear to tell me that we will be all right after all. She was slipping from me, and with her, the whole of my life was slipping too.

So here it is: I am stunned by how quickly the ordinary fabric of life can be upended.

Time passes against my will; memories take on a life of their own. Once we *just were*: living didn't require any reconstruction or evocation, it was the pure pulse of presentness. Now it is different: now we are fragments of a story that yearns for reunion. A reunion in the telling.

We build our lives knowing that things will end, that they may end suddenly and harshly. (Isn't that what purchasing insurance represents?) But who really *believes* that it will happen to us? Careers, homes, marriages—we enter into their shelter, never quite accepting how fragile they really are. Like the bridges that are constructed over rivers, or the towers that stand above cities: not until the moment of their sudden collapse is it ever imaginable. And then, in the flash of an instant, it's all gone: the security we relied on, the world we knew. To feel the impact of the sudden—it is to witness the disappearance of all that was taken for granted in our lives.

And there is Aderet. A daughter, only four years old.

Will her memories fade entirely? Will they dissolve into the unstoppable passage of time?

I don't know if anyone really remembers life in that distant recess of early childhood, or if what we recall is mostly the composite of narratives we are told and the pictures that remain. What will she remember of her mother and the devotion with which Leah surrounded her for four magical years? Will all the details be held only in the transmission she receives from me? Will her mind's eye become dominated by the *emotion* of memory, instead of by the particularities of remembrance? The idea that the immediacy of her memory will fade strikes me like a dagger in the heart: for how can such an immensity of love ever be forgotten? How can the heart not preserve the sanctity of those formations, those powers of deep embrace? I want to scream out against the injustice dealt to a daughter for whom this was supposed to be only the beginning.

The nights fall in with their heavy force, and I am awakened by the voice of my little girl:

"Abba, I'm having a bad dream."

Three times, just this night. I lie next to her and stroke her head—she holds her picture of Imma tightly to her chest.

"I'm feeling Imma's *keppie* and I'm smelling Imma's hair-smell. Abba—I miss my Imma."

"I know, sweetheart—I do too."

"But, Abba, Imma's alive in my heart and in my room, right? 'Cause that's where Imma would sit on my bed."

I don't know what to say. *Not really.* So I lie next to my baby girl until I gradually hear her breathing turn to sleep. It's only then—lying in her room so still—that I can see the shadows return to me.

I am now the bearer of her bad dreams.

Moments of togetherness; moments of transcendence.

I can feel it with all of my senses—as though I am absorbed back into the realm of dreams—the sleepless midnights, the paths open and alive to us. The 2:00 a.m. feedings: Aderet cradled in my arm and resting on the soft green pillow from the living-room couch; she drinks in the milk I have prepared for her, long deep inhalations—her tiny cheeks moving to the rhythm of her sucking, her wide-open eyes gazing up at me with all the wonder of pure reception and pure giving. The night outside is run through with a dark freeze—it reaches round this inside space, it curls its cold breath along the walls and walkways. But the silence of that time feels luminous to me—the hush-hush embrace and the whisper of new life setting the room to its perfect warmth. The feeding done, I kiss my little child on her face—I lie her down in the bassinet beside our bed, and I crawl in next to Leah. Through her sleep my wife takes hold of my hand and pulls it close. There, in the quiet, the world regains full balance; all my fears are now forgotten.

The house is strangely quiet. Aderet fell asleep on the couch, and it is 4:30 p.m.—the blanket of Shabbat is slowly approaching. And my chest and stomach feel weighed down—it is an ache that is not like an acute pain, just a lingering deep heaviness that is at once light from sheer emptiness. My breathing is rapid—like the trembling just before the body collapses in weeping. Suddenly I am conscious of being so utterly alone in the world; as though a vital part of my body has been removed—no, ripped away—whatever anesthetic had been given is now wearing off, and my amputated soul, my bleeding insides, are viscously present in awareness.

You died on the edge of spring, lilacs unbloomed, the snow still on the ground. So many things unfinished. Still so much love.

The truth is, my mind keeps returning to the image of her six feet beneath the earth's surface. Standing over Leah's open grave on that Friday noon—the dismal rain of the early morning having been replaced by a clear and bright sun, the false promise of spring whose overtures would be taken back only days later with the last whip and snap of winter snow. Measure by measure, her space in the ground was filled in as the hole in my heart was torn wider. And then, as now, I could suddenly understand why people have been so determined to believe in the reality of a soul, in some form of immortality—any transcendence of these terrifying shadows of death. For what is the essence of a person, and what endures in this lifetime of fleeting moments and images? What lasts beyond this physical lifetime?

I am.

She was.

You always walked together, and now she is gone.

So reads the card of a friend—memories of our years in Boston.

What was bound has come undone; what was whole is now torn: the shattered mirror of lost reflections.

Still your body lies concealed in that graveyard, and though I know what I must teach our daughter, I myself don't know where to go to find you. Against every rational thought in my head, I am filled with sadness at how horribly alone you must be now, at the bottom of all that earth.

I think of how my ninety-two-year-old grandmother cried out after my grandfather died, and we couldn't understand her. Not then.

"But he'll be so cold and lonely there all by himself," she wailed through a pain that I only now understand. "My sweetheart, my sweetheart—I can't leave him there all alone."

Were you cold the other night when it was raining? Does that simple pine box protect you, or are you just surrounded by so much darkness? Is that you under the earth? Or am I right in what I tell Aderet, desperate for the words to console her? Does your spirit live on?

I want to halt time in its tracks. I want to demand that the earthwheel cease its unending spin.

My all.

My breath.

My space and my time and every inch of me—to know if it is day or night, the moments seen and those hidden from all others; coming apart, coming undone. Past and future collapsing into memory. *My secret midnight moments, holding your soft black dress—there, in the*

*quiet, your scent and self returns to me for a while, a time that evapo-
rates and then disappears.*

Tonight I sit in the plush reading chair that we picked out together for
the living room. Beige. Soft. Aderet is asleep, and the house is once
again a chasm of quiet—sometimes a welcome and pensive silence,
other times the bottomless abyss of disorientation and fear. Do I still
linger in the haze of disbelief? Have I crossed the invisible threshold to
become aware of this massive hole in my chest—a heartache that
makes me feel like my insides are sinking while the shell of my body
floats in a dream-fog on the surface of things?

I hold my favorite mug, filled with hot peppermint tea, laced with
honey.

Steam rising like the vapor of life.

I am aware of the warmth, and of the sensation of swallowing.

It fills me, and I exhale.

Faith

At a deep level, I cannot really separate her identity from mine. And so
her absence leaves me feeling incomplete in the most basic of ways—
the rest of me has been removed and buried, I try to understand what
it is that I am without her. For more than ten years we defined ourselves in relation to one another—there was no real separation
between us; the presence of the one was the presence of the other.
Consciousness and feeling, regret and hope—all of these and more
were filtered through the intimacy of relationship, through the oneness
of our merged selfhood. So what does it mean to untangle that thread-
weave of binding and inseparability? Can it ever be unbound, untan-
gled? Who am I without her?

And where is she? Where is she now?

Four-year-old Aderet intuits this with a depth that frequently
leaves me stunned.

"Imma is everywhere, Abba. In my room, in the air— But, Abba,
can you reach up to the sky and pull Imma down from heaven for me?"

Part of me wants to try.

But all I can do is pull my little girl in closer as I carry her up the hill for the evening prayers. We stand there with the other mourners, all of them from another generation. Even amidst community our experience is solitary. Whose wife dies at thirty-two? Who loses a mother at age four? We stand within a vast abyss—our screams go unanswered.

> *May God's great name be blessed for ever and ever ...*
> *May great peace and life from heaven be drawn down onto us*
>   *and onto all of Israel, and let us say: Amen.*
> *He who makes peace in the heavens, He will bring peace*
>   *upon us ...*

These are the words of the *Kaddish*: the prayer we Jews recite aloud in the daily presence of our community. The words are said as announcement, as reminder; they call our fellow Jews into the momentary awareness of our ongoing condition. But do the words themselves really mean anything to me? Is this the God of *my* faith, or is it merely a relic of an older, outmoded theology—one that we hold onto with the desperate clutch of childhood simplicity?

"Abba, you know what? I think Imma and God are playing checkers together! And when God is gonna make it rain, Imma can say: No, God. I don't want it to rain on my Aderet and my Eitee! And you know what? God listens to her, and it doesn't rain!"

Blessing. Peace. Life. The refrain of my outward grief, my communal grief—words spoken for generations and generations. But these words ring hollow. What peace? And where am I to find blessing and life in all of this? The liturgy refers to God as the Compassionate One, but I see no compassion and no mercy. I want to rewrite the language of the prayers: *He who curses. He who makes war. He who doles out death with a merciless hand.* This is the refrain of my inward grief, my private world. And yet the problem of injustice was never my theological problem. I could never believe in that kind of God anyway: not in the God of Justice who controls and destines everything; the God who is portrayed as the Great King and grand puppeteer of the universe.

For me, God was always more of an animating life-force in the world; the breath that lies at the center of things; the pulse and lifeblood of the Great All of Being. And so there was never the presumption that some Hand was guiding the destinies of life. I think of that image even more so now when I recall Leah's final passage from the physical realm. The departure of breath: the withdrawal of life's vital center and spiritual essence.

But my daughter's speech encapsulates our most basic religious dilemma, the reason so many feel they have lost their faith in the wake of tragedy and injustice:

"Abba, I'm mad at God. I'm mad at Him for making Imma die. I'm gonna hit God, and I'm gonna make him throw up! Are you mad at God, too, Abba?"

I see that this struggle is instinctual; it's burned into the psyche even at a young age. But I think it's different for me. To place that kind of blame on God is to operate within a particular structure of belief—one that is not my own. But the God of my religious life is not the "Our Father, Our King" of the classical liturgy. I do not believe in a God who is represented as the ultimate arbiter of cosmic justice.

I have always felt much closer to a neomystical theological path: to the idea that God's mysterious presence is to be found in all the ordinary shadows of worldly life; that the river of divinity courses through the body of the world like the circulation of blood in the human being.... In the cycles of our being we reflect the tragedy and the brokenness that is a part of God; but we also reflect the sublime beauty and the redemption that is God's presence as well.

Descent into Hell

We thought it was just a bad run of pregnancy sickness—never imagining that we were entering the final days of your life. Now, in retrospect, I know the tumor was putting increasing pressure on her brain—making her weaker, torturing her with violent headaches and horrible hours of illness. I find myself (against my better judgment) allowing my mind to go down the dangerous road of *what if* and *if only.* The headaches she suffered for nearly ten years—what if we had done more CT scans more recently? Would we have found her invader in time? How is it possible that the best neurologists in Boston, the headache specialists who took no insurance—how could they not have found her killer before he surfaced? Was he not really there inside of her yet? Is this all just a bizarre series of coincidences?

Back in time.

If only.

What happened to her is tragic....

All of a sudden I am in the middle of complete unreality—Leah lying on the floor of the hospital room, a code team of doctors working on her—Dr. A., the high-risk obstetrics doc, kneeling over her—*finding your pulse, finding your breath.*

"Leah—wake up. Leah, can you hear me?"

He taps her gently on the cheek.

"Give me thiamine—I need *thiamine!*"

Another doctor comes in—now there are six of them, and me, cramped into the little bathroom where she passed out in my arms.

"Is she breathing?" the other one asks.

"This is the husband," one of the nurses says, gesturing in my direction.

They have an oxygen mask over her face, which she keeps trying to pull off.

Through delirium, she says:

I don't want ... to be ... pregnant ...

I don't ... want ...

If nobody else knows, I know: she very much wanted to have another child, she yearned for a second baby. But the suffering was so great, the pain was wrenching open her soul.

And then:

Where ... am I...? What's ... happening?

"Come with me, sir—we're going to lift your wife onto a stretcher."

"Is she stabilized?" says another.

"I want her put in the room across from the nurses' station," Dr. A. directs.

"She needs close monitoring. Get an EKG, and put her on a pulse-ox monitor right away. And page cardiology and neurology."

"She's gonna be OK," he says to me with kindness. "We'll figure out what's wrong with her."...

And more tests would come.

~

They took Leah to a new room where she could be closely watched. She was still very disoriented and out of it. About twenty minutes before the fainting she had started expressing that confusion.

Where am I? I don't know where ... I am ...

Was that the dehydration talking?

Can't you get a neurologist to see her any faster?!

She still knew her name, still recognized me—but her mind was going quickly at that point.

We just didn't know it yet....

I stood by the door to the room, watching—my heart in my throat.

"Sir, why don't you come with me to a quiet waiting area. We'll come and get you with any new information." I could see their considerable discomfort in having me stand there.

"I'll stay here," I said. I had to watch—these people were trying to save her, but she was a patient to them. A medical case. *No—someone who loved her had to be there.*

I still thought that I could protect her.

"I'm thinking we're looking at a cerebral edema," one doctor said to another, coming out of the room.

I interrupt. Cerebral edema?

"Yes. That's a swelling of the brain. We just don't know what's causing it yet."

What did they think it could be?

"My hunch is that she's experiencing an extreme fluctuation in her blood-sugar levels. Or it could be an unusual reaction to the medications she is taking. We're just going to have to wait and see."

I didn't know it then, but those moments before the seizure would be the last time I would speak to Leah (at least when she was conscious)—and it was the last she would speak to me. From that instant she would never regain consciousness. Remembering it now, I wonder what her last thought was before slipping under: Was her mind thinking clearly enough at that point to harbor any organized consciousness, or was it just the moving slides of fleeting perception? Did she intuit that these would be her last moments of awareness and seeing? Was she thinking of Aderet? Was she thinking of me?

A strange daze had begun to settle over me as I watched the doctors and nurses coming and going. At short intervals my cell phone would ring, and I would deliver updates on Leah's condition to members of the family.

"Mr. Fishbane, I have some important forms for you to sign over at the nurses' station."

"What are these?" I ask, barely able to hear any response. My movements are slow.

"Hospital waivers. We need to do a CT scan to see if there's any swelling that might be causing your wife's symptoms. This waiver is necessary since Leah is pregnant...."

I look over to Leah's OB doctor, a petite woman who would show me great humanity in the hours that were to follow.

"Is there any reason I should be concerned about signing this?" I ask her.

Funny. I was still thinking about the pregnancy. Still thinking about my Leah as an expecting mom.

"It's absolutely necessary," she reassures me. "Our first priority is to find out what's going on with Leah and to get her better. Afterwards we can reassess the pregnancy."

Afterwards.

I nod and sign the papers....

"You can wait here for us," one of the doctors says.

"I can't come inside?" Of course I already know the answer.

"No—I'm sorry. We won't be long, though."

So I wait. Quiet, empty halls. The faint sounds of them working behind the closed doors. Even at that moment I feel reality unfolding outside of myself. As in a dream.

Is this happening?
At what point is Leah going to wake up and relieve me of this terror?
She had had scans like this before.
Years before, when the headaches began.
But there was never anything alarming in the scans: just the unlucky fate of chronic headaches. *Just.*

"Feel my forehead," she would say to me. "Do I have a fever?"

"Honey, I just felt it a little while ago—you don't feel warm."

Then she makes that playful sad face—our little game of love. So I sigh and put my palm on her head.

Other times, she says:

"Eitee, do you think I'm sick—you know, really sick?"

But how could we have ever imagined?

Waiting here, I think of your softness, I think of your touch. Sitting in the dark of the movie theater—the lights dimming, the music beginning. *Holding your hand then I always felt like a kid again.* Happy. Content.

I remember nights when my parents would babysit at our little house on Shenandoah Street in L.A., and we would head over to Beverly Drive—to Mulberry's, for the best white pizza in town, or to Urth Café across the street, where the atmosphere was a perfect romance—little tables tucked into corners, low candles lit on each one—and an exotic array of teas and pastries. We would stand there for long moments smelling each canister—inhaling the perfume of dried leaves. I can still recall the scent of blackberry—or was it peach?—jasmine, Ceylon, and mint. And of course there was the banana cream pie. Two spoons—and again the rising steam of tea.

Those moments stand like sanctuary now, a quiet set aside deep within. All the secrets we shared on those early nights of Pacific wind—the cool that washed over us together as we obsessed about what seemed important at the time. What frustrated us, what we hoped for—planning for a future that seemed like a broad expanse of adventures and possibilities. Only our togetherness was taken for granted, expectations for Aderet, and wonder about children yet unborn. Of what will come.

Of what will come.

The doors to the CT scan room open, the team of doctors emerges. It is Dr. A. who speaks to me first.

"Mr. Fishbane." The haze of my waking dreams drifts out and passes over me again.

"The scan shows a large mass in your wife's brain. From the CT we can't tell whether it is a tumor or a bleed, and we'll need to do an MRI to determine that."

Again I am outside of myself, observing the scene in which I am but a character. The odd sensation of unreality. *Did he actually just say that? Did I imagine the whole thing?...*

"It doesn't look good," Dr. A. replies in a soft voice. "All we can do right now is pray." He places his hand on my shoulder in a gesture of healing. My chest and abdomen rise and fall with the heaviness of breath.

I feel the blood receding from my face—fear rising slowly in me from an unknown interior space.

I can't believe this is ... happening ... I can't ... believe ...

I can see how they are all looking at me then—the critical-care specialist, the high-risk obstetrics people, the radiologist. Suddenly I am that person—the recipient of the news the physician dreads delivering, the one standing in the inner circle of tragedy.

The wheel of life as it is known spins, and I am (in an instant) lost and adrift. From the morning to the afternoon—not even a day—from presence to absence, from knowing to unknowing—I reel on the sharp edge of Being.

Crying never came easily for me—the feelings there hidden out of sight, in the silence of my insides. *And that always frustrated you— wanting to know I could weep, that I would weep for you, if it ever came to that.*

It has come to that.

"If I ever go, you better cry for me," she said to me in her playful way. *Can you see me crying for you now?*

There, outside the MRI room, the tears rose in my throat, they pummeled my lungs. My chest and shoulders convulsed, my face was quivering and wet. I couldn't even remember when last I cried. Not like this.

In your time of dying.

The time when memories of the life we had made together burned in my chest, weighed on my breathing.

Dr. R. found me there—your obstetrician with the sweet face—and she did what none of the others could do. She held my left hand in hers, and she cried with me.

"You shouldn't be alone," she kept saying to me.

"You shouldn't be alone."

And we talked through the tears.

"I just keep thinking about my little girl," I breathed, barely sounding the words through my choked throat. "I try to imagine her growing up without her mom, and my heart breaks all over again."

"She has *you*," Dr. R. says—her voice also shaking with tears. "She has you."

I smile for a short moment—I am comforted by the presence of this kind person, a person I barely know.

The team of doctors comes out again, this time to confirm that it is indeed a tumor in her brain. They speak gently. They tell me they have asked the Jewish chaplain to come sit with me.

I feel numbed by the haze that has descended onto me.

"I'm not giving up on her yet," says Dr. H., the critical-care specialist who, less than two days later, would be the one to confirm and pronounce brain death.

Suffering

I can barely recall a time when you did not suffer from headaches—it became part of your daily life and our shared frustration, even when you had learned to disguise your pain to others, to go about your life as if nothing was really wrong.

But I always knew. The way her posture would shift ever so slightly, the way her eyes would dart to the side or up to the ceiling. While we were sitting with others over dinner, she would lean over to me and whisper her request for some Advil or Aleve; and I would find a subtle way of handing these to her under the table—our secret language of pain and coping. And when the façade was finally withdrawn, I would retrieve the blue ice packs from the freezer; I would massage the top of her neck. Our closer friends came to know this as an unyielding part of Leah's life....

And so we sought out the headache specialists: first in Chicago, with the doc who never made eye contact, and then in Boston with the memorable Dr. S.—the Dutch neurologist who always wore a bow tie and greeted us with a distinctly European gentility and formality. In the waiting room there was a table with cookies and coffee, Dr. S.'s wife sitting as the receptionist who would welcome us when we entered, who would process our payment when we were finished. Dr. S. would often spend forty-five minutes with us in his office—looking up at Leah and me kindly over his desk (I vividly remember the model brain that sat on the front of that desk, but mostly I remember his compassion and the authentic *presentness* of his care), writing down detailed notes in a condensed yet elegant handwriting. Going to that place together became a kind of pilgrimage—each time hopeful for some breakthrough in healing, and yet always protecting ourselves with the caution made of so many fruitless attempts....

I think now of the vulnerability of the patient as she places her faith in the discernment of doctors. At what point must we simply trust in their judgment, hope that their skill will bring healing? Can we ever really be certain that they have the right answers, that they have not missed the most important clues? Looking back on it now, I am suspicious of all the "experts" we consulted, and I am sharply aware of the degree to which medicine is an art and not a science. I recall the stories told to me of gravely ill patients who received radically contradictory advice from different medical luminaries. What are we supposed to do with that? How much of this search for healing is utterly relative, and how much of it is objective?

My mind returns again to Joan Didion's reflections. Despite what you may think, despite the ambiguity the medical professionals assert, there is a clear line between life and death. Until then she is here—really just asleep, peacefully unconscious. Until then I am able to hold her warm hands in mine, to watch her torso rise and descend with the influx of air from the respirator. Surely there must be something there. Some glimmer of life, some trace of Leah hidden beneath these shadows of coma? I remember thinking: she will still come out of it, she will still wake up. Is there a difference at that moment between believing and hoping?

Where Are You? What Endures?

Now, at the close of Passover: not even five weeks out. The heartache washes over me, and I am in its inescapable grip. My breathing becomes both heavy and shallow, my chest filled with the sorrow of sinking. When it fills me I am pulled into a forest of darkness—the black hole of dissolving futures tumbling in my insides. I try again to breathe. In through my nose, long exhalation through pursed lips. But it is not the same as stress. It is a more unconquerable ache. Heart-ache. Soul-ache. A hollow ache at the very center of my body. My stomach feels it too, and my throat and my legs. How is it that some-one can burrow down so deep inside of you as to dwell in your very bones, to inhabit the pathways of your circulation? A presence so thor-ough that its withdrawal feels like a dying in my own self, a death inside of me?

Your wife died, but you did not die—so I read in one of the books on my night table.

You did not die.

But am I living?

We lit a memorial candle for Leah this Passover holiday—she took her place on the dining room table, next to Nana—my father's mother (*who would have imagined that you and Nana would die in the same Hebrew year—she in December, you in March?*), aglow next to the remembrances of other lives. Incandescence of memory, slow-burning marker of a soul-spark.

And what endures? A presence?

My mother said she had the strangest sense of your presence watching over her as she played with Aderet on her bedroom floor.

The traces of what was written by her hand in the house? What of her body that lies concealed by earth? Does that which was Leah return to an undifferentiated continuum of Being? Is it truly *dust to dust*—elements recalled to their most basic roots in the world's fabric? I think of what Aderet asks about the time before she was born, before she was even conceived and carried in Imma's tummy.

Was I in the stars then, Abba? she asks.

To imagine a state of nonexistence, a time when there was no *me*, is instinctively difficult, even impossible. And to imagine the space of death is just the same—to have crossed the boundaries of what we know as real, an inability to accept that what we know as *living* ever morphs into something else. *Not living? Dead?* What is that? I can't fathom it—how could I ever expect a four-year-old child to grasp it? I read the calming advice of Thich Nhat Hanh, paraphrasing the wisdom of the Buddha: in this world we are but manifestations, disclosures of the always enduring continuum of Life. To die is to withdraw from manifestation; it is not to cease to be.

In the stars.

Is that too the ethereal house of your presence? The same stars we would count on Saturday nights at the close of Shabbat—the three of us standing in the backyard of our home in Los Angeles, lights of another world peering down at us in our earth-time. And I think of how those lights are but the remnants of a place in the galaxy now long gone, burned up in the expanse of time it has taken to reach our perception down here. So do they live? Or are they but the traces of what once was?

To Aderet I read Tomie dePaola's classic story *Nana Upstairs & Nana Downstairs*—his gentle narration of death, of love and loss in a child's world. I remember the magic of this story from my own childhood: a shooting star as the kiss of memory, the flash of transcendent presence. She kisses you good-night from that luminous place, from the great Beyond in the brilliant vault of heaven. She is there—radiant and in motion in the night sky.

Read it again, Abba, she says. *Read the dying part again.*

~~~~~

Thinking to myself, I wonder if I can pinpoint the moment when Leah's spirit began to depart, when the person who lived this life was no longer, and all that remained was the physical shell. Can I even try to do this? Do I even believe in any of it? It's just so difficult to talk about her, think about her, in any way that is removed from that physical presence. How can I separate her spirit or soul from the voice that spoke to me (in a way that could reach me like no other voice could), from the touch of her skin, from the scent of her hair and face, from the movements of her legs and arms and back as she went about ordinary living?

It is the great irony of our resistance to mortality—our pushing back against the finality and haunting emptiness of death. We cling to this notion of an enduring soul, of a spirit that lives on, though dislodged from its physical chamber.

But I want to scream out against it.

It's your living body that I want! Gone to your eternal rest in the heavenly Garden of Eden?

The hell with that, I want you here!

But Aderet and I do still talk to Leah each night as our final bedtime ritual—a deep testimony, I suppose, to a stubborn belief that some measure of a life transcends death. I encourage Aderet to tell her mom about the day she has had—what little things we did that would have made Imma smile, that would make her proud.

Tonight she tells me that Imma can't really hear what we are saying (her own awareness of death's elusiveness), and to my surprise I find myself insisting that she can. *She can hear us. We really are speaking to her. Even in death she is somehow alive, reachable.* I realize that despite my disbelief, there is something powerfully true in that. Something immediate and real: a truth that I want to affirm. As we talk out loud to Leah (Aderet playfully insisting that Imma guess what fun things she did today), I feel an unmistakable lightness filling my heart and throat—as though my suspension of disbelief takes me into the embrace of an alternate universe, a place where time has been suspended in the days before tragedy struck. Aderet smiles and talks with love to her mom. Things are good again, safe again—if only for a short while.

In the morning she has something urgent to tell me:

"Abba, I ripped a napkin in the kitchen. Do you know why? Because that makes me feel sad about Imma."

Is this her way of reenacting what she saw me do during the first week of mourning? The rip in my shirt just over the left side of my chest? The cutting of cloth that symbolized the tearing of my heart? I think of the moment of Leah's death in the hospital, when, as is the custom, we each ripped a piece of our clothing. The rending of garments as the wordless testimony of our bearing witness: witnesses to the passage from life to death; witnesses to the horrible mystery of life's threshold; testifiers to the agony of the heart's breaking, to the tearing open of a hole that can never really be repaired....

"Do you understand what happens at the cemetery?" I ask. "Do you know where Imma is?"

"Yes," she says—"she's under the ground!"

I don't remember really explaining this to her; if I did, I certainly didn't expect her to understand it.

I see from her face that she is very eager to go, to have something concrete and visual to associate with "Imma's bed." I think of the tender way Leah's sister Stephanie recalled to me our act of shoveling soil into Leah's open grave. We were tucking her in. Pulling the covers up nice and tight.

Fishbane family, good-night.

Imma, good-night.

Am I projecting a fear of graves onto her? We talk about visiting the earth where Leah is buried, we talk about bringing flowers for Imma and a special note for Imma too. "I want to do that," Aderet says. "I want to put flowers on Imma's bed." In what world of unimaginable suffering is this the destiny of a little child?

We are up again much of the night—Aderet calls to me every ten minutes from her bedroom. She is plagued by bad dreams—the on-and-off crying lasts from 3:00 to 5:00 a.m. At a certain point I feel like I am losing my mind—a tumult of sleeplessness and frustration—in and out of bed without rest. Here is the life of a single father. My partner is gone. And my child's grief surfaces in these dreadful mid-night moments—together we are adrift at sea with unkind winds.

She wakes wailing and crying. It takes me a while to realize what she is saying, but gradually it becomes clear. She is crying out for her Imma:

"I want you ... I want you ..."

I come into her bedroom. She is so tired that she has already fallen back asleep, but when I go to fix her covers she wakes for a moment.

"Did you see Imma in your dream?" I ask her.

She nods. Her thumb in her mouth; her voice soft and sad.

"What happened in your dream?"

"Imma was falling off a cliff! She was falling and falling to her death!"

My God.

On the couch downstairs she clutches a white blanket to her chest; she pulls it up close to her face.

Imma used to lie with this blankie, she says. *It still smells like Imma, so I like to hold it and I like to smell it.*

She slides herself off the couch—thumb in her mouth, blanket held tight. Then from the shelf she retrieves the special purple box we have designated as "Imma's box"—inside she keeps all the little items that somehow connect her to her now absent mother.

"You see this mirror, Abba? If you look in it, you can see Imma!"

Oh, that's terrific! I say. Just like the mirror that the Beast gives to Belle when she leaves the castle! So she can always find her way back to him.

"Yeah, that's right! And in this one, I can see my Imma!"

What's she doing in the mirror, what do you see in there?

"Well, I see her cooking dinner! She's making pizza and other things. Oooh! And here's an Imma bear! If you cuddle with this bear, you'll feel Imma softing your back. And here's a magic bracelet! If you wear this bracelet, you'll feel Imma stroking your *keppie*."

What are these, I ask, holding two small drawings between my fingers.

"Abba, those are pictures that Imma made of me, and if you hold these pictures to your ears, you'll hear Imma saying *I love you, Aderet*."

———

At long last I find the courage to watch the videotapes that we had recorded, knowing I would come before the realness of her voice, the apparition of her living movements. And as I enter into the wondrous nostalgia of Aderet's second birthday party (how amazing to now recall Aderet's voice and speech from that stage of development; I had forgotten how much change there has been in just two years; how she speaks now like an articulate little girl!), I am overcome with the degree of Leah's familiar sound, expressions, gestures. I can feel the welling up of a deep sadness that had hidden itself for a short while, and I know the sting of bittersweetness in the most immediate of ways.

There she is: the knower of my soul, the healer of my pain—my tenderness, my calm, my ache. And there she is not: captured in the merging illusions of dream, remembrance, and the trick of digital lights and images.

This is the housing of memory: the chambers of long cultivation, the concealment beneath the soil of a gardener's winter, the season of its reemergence and the flowering of new life. I am filled with an overpowering desire to have her back; for my life to be restored to the way it was.

———

The *Shema* before death: eyes closed like the *Shema* we recite in bed each night with Aderet. These are the last words on our lips before the unconsciousness of sleep descends; and they are the last words on our lips before consciousness disappears forever, before the last inhalation and exhalation of breath.

I return to the hospital well before dawn on Thursday. After a few hours of rest at home, I am on my way back—through the empty silence of blackened streets. Passing again into the ICU, I find Leah's parents, Barbara and Jack, still there—sleepless from having stayed by Leah's side through the night. I ask them if they managed any sleep. They didn't go home at all to rest?

"We'll take what we can get," Jack says in a voice that reveals a parent's broken heart.

Later they would tell me, "We did not want her to be alone; we couldn't bear to leave her there alone...."

In the excruciating torment of a mother and father's collapsing world, they cry out to their child.

So many experiences of devastation: each one erupting in the same hour, and yet each so unknown to the other. All we can do is embrace. Are there words?

"Sweetheart, you know how sometimes people can get so sick that even the doctors can't make them better anymore?"

"Like Nana and Bapa [my mother's father]—and they died."

"Yes, love. Usually people are very old when they get that sick. But sometimes, and it doesn't happen a lot, people who are young like Imma can get so, so sick that they just can't get better anymore."

"And then they die? But what kind of sick is Imma?"

"Imma has a special kind of sickness, sweetheart."

(Much later, I overhear another child innocently ask Aderet where her mommy is now. And without hesitation, she responds: *In heaven. My Imma had a special kind of sick.* I am amazed at how these words leave their mark on the mind and imagination of a little child).

I tell her that the doctors think Imma will not get better from her sickness; they think she is going to die.

"She's going to die?" she repeats—"Oh, Imma ... Imma!"

We hold each other. *My baby ...*

"Abba, does that mean that Imma will have a new bed in heaven? Will Nana and Bapa be her mommy and daddy in heaven? I think God will be her blankie in heaven!"

And within a few moments she begins to compose drawings—notes for me to deliver to Imma on her deathbed: one the image of her traced hand, to be placed as soothing comfort on Imma's heart. The other picture contains a long, winding line, drawn with a purple marker. When I ask her to tell me what she has made, she says:

This is Imma's bed in the hospital, and this is her path to heaven. This is her bed in heaven.

Her drawing and her narration reflect something more profound than I could ever find the strength to say. Imma endures beyond this bodily life; she undertakes the journey across the threshold of time and space, from the world of the living to the world of the dead....

That's beautiful, I tell her. Imma will love it.

And with new tears beginning their descent, I hug her tightly—I stroke her back and hair with the palm of my hand.

Months later, looking out the car window at the blue bright presence above her, she says, "Abba, I think that white in the sky is God's face. No, actually, I think it's Imma's bed up there. It's Imma's bed in heaven. I'm sad and I love her. Abba, I wish Imma was still in the hospital so she could come home."

Endings

As the doctor conducts the final test, I am holding Leah's hand in mine—I am envisioning an array of scenes from our life together; imagining that this here is our last walk together, our last journey of holding hands. I am weeping from a place so deep that my whole body is overtaken. It is as though a core section of my own soul is being pulled out from my own *neshamah*, my own spirit-breath.

And then, as the respirator is disconnected, I place my head on her chest and listen to her heart beat until I can't hear it anymore. Is that the last pulse of life? Is it in her brain or in her heart? If this feeling in my chest is any indication, it is surely something of both. The brain may give consciousness and control of the body's function, but the heart feels like it lives on its own, the throbbing energy of life and the yearning for its return.

Her body grows cold—her lips become white, then darkened with the color of death. In accord with an ancient Jewish custom, we lift her onto blankets set out on the floor. We bend down one at a time, giving her one final kiss good-bye. *Good-bye, love....* We cover her with the white sheet, a veiling of death.

My father and I wait in the sacred silence of that hospital room—fulfilling the religious obligation not to leave the dead unattended. Such a powerfully strange feeling to sit there with her—with her body as presence and her spirit as absence, the fragments of her departed soul strewn in the air that I breathe. Am I here with her, or is she already gone? And if she is *gone*, to where does that departure lead?...

If I can believe that something called *Leah* survives this (if I can believe that for even the most infinitesimal of moments), then I wonder if she has gone to a realm without words, a place without speech. Or has she perhaps not really departed at all? Does her spirit remain in our company, in the heart of her daughter, in the endurance of memories? Does she remain in me, whispering in words without sound, telling me what I must do in my moments of greatest helplessness, guiding me with her soothing presence?

Perhaps that is the greatest gift of community and friends as we try to find our way through the unknowing ineffability of grief: in their standing before us, in their eliciting of our stories, they teach us to speak again—to rediscover the need for words as we emerge from the place of no words. From the silence of death's presence—the absence that is the most complete presence I have ever known—I pass into the muteness of life's unmaking, I travel through the mindscapes of articulation's withdrawal, through the disappearance of understanding and rational thought. I need to re-learn my ability to speak as much as I must learn the ways of a single parent.

The way forward: what does it hold for us?

Is there any redemption, or are we now the ones exiled from love?

Lost together in the dark plains of terrifying expanse, wandering together in the shallow waters of unsurpassable horizons, in the caves of endlessly echoing sound.

All at once I understand the words of the psalmist:

> *I lift up my eyes to the mountains—*
> *From where will my help come?*
>
> PSALM 121:1

But unlike the psalmist I see no answer to the question, no divine resolution in the desperation of quiet loneliness.

In this valley of winding paths, we still search for a trail out of the darkness.

It's hard to believe that more than six months have passed. Some days the whole thing still feels unreal, other times the steady weight of awareness settles in and it occurs to me that this is what life has dealt me. This is the inescapable reality of our days.

On Rosh Hashanah I stand and chant the liturgy that speaks so bluntly about mortality—of our living and our dying. Who will live and who will die this year?

Who will be inscribed in the Book of Life?

The human being is dust, and it is to dust that she will return.

As I recite these words my inner eye flashes to the visage of Leah's grave, of me seated on the grass beside that place on the afternoon before Rosh Hashanah.

Dust to dust.

I try to speak to her in this place, but I can feel her returning to the earth.

Six months.

All at once I am aware that this time has proven to be a process of evolution for me, the slow rebirth of my self from the embers of a violent fire. At this moment I am aware of my first steps along a path of a new kind of walking. I think of those magical days when Aderet was taking her first steps in our California living room—toddling a few paces and then falling down again. That's me.

The griever needs someone to *hold* his pain: to take in some measure of it, to listen, to embrace.

If I can identify one thing that has helped me survive these last months, it is that, in holding us up when we are at our weakest, true friendship and community step into the breach to hold our pain. It is a holding that is not a transfer of suffering, but a *being present* that is embodied in the one who comes to hold the mourner's hand in silence. Sometimes there are no words worthy of being said—then it is just the company of another person, there to hold us in our darkest place....

And as I remember my passage through the Jewish rituals of mourning, surrounded as I was by the warmth and love of a caring community, I realize that these structures of time come to us from the tradition as a buffer against the tidal waves of crushing solitude. From within those walls of grief's terrain, I hear the ancient words recited to me again and again:

> *HaMakom yenachem etkhem be-tokh she'ar avelei Tzion ve-yerushalayim.*
> *"May God comfort you among all the other mourners of Zion and Jerusalem."*

Comfort within the fellowship of those who have experienced this pain themselves. For who else could really understand us? Who could fathom our pain and our despair?

But the name used for God in this traditional formula is what sets me to thinking. *HaMakom*—simply, "the Place"—one of those recurrent names for God used in classical Rabbinic literature. God as Place. Indeed, the Place of all places—the cosmic space in which this world is inscribed and enfolded. And despite this global image, I think the real power of *Makom* is far more local. It is the *Makom* of community; the *Makom* of the shul where we meet our friends and call up the power to pray; the *Makom* of this house where Leah's traces are so present. For as I can believe that God is to be found in everyday reality—not secluded above in the transcendent heavens—I find that Presence, that divine indwelling, in the ordinary and extraordinary acts of kindness that have been given to me these last months.

A teacher of mine who visited the house during shivah said: "I would say *HaMakom yenachem*, but I really think *HaZeman yenachem*—that Time will bring comfort." He too offered that play on words as a fragment of hope.

God as Place. God as Time.

The healing power of time's passage is itself a divine manifestation—we put the pieces of a broken life back together as best we can, and each moment is layered on top of the others, each day building to the slow crossing of unforeseen thresholds. But as I think of these months gone by, and of our attempt to cut a path in the thorny brush of a dark wilderness, I am drawn again to this image of Place—to God as the energy that underlies the place of community....

In the symbolic language of Jewish mysticism, the *Shekhinah* (the feminine divine presence, the tenth emanative stream within the One God) is often represented by the term *Kenesset Yisrael*, "The Assembly of Israel." In its kabbalistic context, *Kenesset Yisrael* refers to a heavenly dimension of God, the earthly terminology but a symbolic marker in an otherworldly meaning. But today I want to read it much more literally. That dimension of God that is most associated with an Indwelling in the human world; that part of divinity that is most revealed to human consciousness—it is manifest and present in the living breath of community. The community that takes care of its weakest in their times of need and desperation; the community that works divine miracles in bringing fragments of light to those who are submerged in the darkest of spaces.

That is Creation, revelation, and redemption bound up in One—all of those divine forces show themselves in the working of community to lift up the fallen, to bring comfort to those whose spirits have been ground into the dust. That, I believe, is the true meaning of *HaMakom yenachem*—in and through the places where we are, where we suffer, and where we begin to rise. For it is in that getting up—the elevation that can only come through the loving hands of friendship—it is there that the ultimate reconstruction of *divine* space (*Makom*) can begin. Indeed, it is the repair and the rebuilding of God's own broken self— the divine face shattered like the first vessels of Creation, fragments that reflect the pain and the broken heart of this world. But the pieces are melded back together, even if they can never be the Whole that they once were. For it is also a world of love—a place where simple acts of kindness and generosity have the power to bring redemption: to redeem the person bound in the chains of despair, to heal the fractured state of this earth.

Linda Raphael, PhD, is director of medical narrative and humanities at George Washington University. She is the author of *Narrative Skepticism: Moral Agency and Representations of Consciousness in Fiction* and coeditor, with Marc Lee Raphael, of *When Night Fell: An Anthology of Holocaust Short Stories*.

Reflections on the Dark

Linda Raphael, PhD

In the last few decades there has been a proliferation of autobiographical writing in the genres of loss and grief memoirs and personal illness narratives. The confessional mode of self-presentation, from television talk shows to academic conference talks, set in motion a trend in self-reporting; at the same time, the term "bearing witness" that became indispensable for the history of the Holocaust added legitimacy to recounting stories of trauma.

Eitan Fishbane's moving essay is a lamentation on loss set in a narrative time six months after the death of his wife, Leah, as well as it is an account of the dramatic story of Leah's unexpected hospitalization and death during her second pregnancy. While reflecting on one's loss and continuing grief has potential value for writers and readers, the inclusion of Fishbane's essay in this volume owes to the author's engagement with ontological, theological, and existential questions. The questions can sometimes be answered by his scholarly and personal understanding of Judaism and by his personal faith, and at other times his doubts resist the dictates of his learning and belief.

The essay opens with a further challenge, one indirectly aimed at the difficulty of finding language to describe the fact of Leah's death and to express the enormity of the writer's grief:

Words in the dark ... trying to speak in the place of the speechless....

Tragic. The words of the neurosurgeon still ring clearly in my ear.

The intensity of the bereaved husband cannot find words, yet he writes. He remembers the word "tragic"—a term once associated with the genre of tragedy in which terrible events result from a character's flaws. The word's power to convey the contemporary meaning, "deeply sad," has been somewhat mitigated by casual and frequent use (similar to the use of "horrendous," "awesome," "absolutely," and so on). However, even were it to retain its power, the difference between saying or writing that something is "tragic" and experiencing the emotions during and following the tragic event cannot be completely bridged. At one point, Fishbane asks, "But do words themselves really mean anything to me?" The difficulty of language informs both the limitations and the significance of writing about personal experiences of grief or illness: the effective writer works to find words that will create symbols and images that convey meaning when a statement, such as the one Fishbane remembers the neurosurgeon uttering, "What happened to her is tragic," inevitably makes the particular general and collapses the past, present, future into a word.

From the first line, Fishbane structures the essay in such a way as to engage the reader in the agony that follows the loss of a loved partner. As in Tolstoy's *The Death of Ivan Ilych*, the death is reported at the onset, and so one reads to find out how the event occurred and what the reactions to it have been and are rather than to find out if Leah survived. The narrative of Leah's history of severe headaches and the failure of physicians' exams, of tests conducted with the latest technology, and then terrifying days in the hospital tell the medical events that ended in the neurosurgeon's pronouncement, quoted in the first lines. But this is not a story about failures in the world of medicine— such a story would likely take the reader on a trip from the beginning to the end of the illness, revealing the fate of the patient late in the story. While the details inform the reader of the horror of what the author experienced and now remembers, the accounts of his relationship with his four-year-old daughter, Aderet, and each of their relationships with Leah open for the reader scenes of beauty that end abruptly and, so the writer and reader may feel, unjustly. The narrative moves fluidly among many time periods in no particular chronological order, in a style to which readers have become accustomed, at least since Virginia Woolf wrote *Mrs. Dalloway*. The modernist stream-of-consciousness in fact offers the reader a realistic image of the way the human mind works—no one is at all times in the present moment.

Fishbane's inclusion of scenes from his and Leah's early days of marriage, including precise locations that some readers may be able to identify (e.g., Urth Café in West Los Angeles) help readers to relate to the Fishbanes even as they may unconsciously be creating a distance between themselves and the events of the story. At the same time, the specific details of medical events in the hospital play an important role in the reader's ability to imagine what Fishbane experienced, from following the gurney transporting Leah to the MRI room to the obstetrician who stays with Fishbane, holds his hand, and cries with him.

Some of the metaphors and similes have complex meanings: "the blanket of Shabbat is slowly approaching" (after Leah's death) sounds comforting, but at the same time, the writer's "chest and stomach feel weighed down ... a lingering deep heaviness that is at once light from sheer emptiness"; or "I am outside myself, observing the scene in which I am the center figure."

Memoirs of the loss and grief are sometimes celebrations of the lost person, as is Calvin Trillin's *About Alice*. Others are attempts to resolve a particular problem by giving it narrative form and thus a sort of logic. Joan Didion's *The Year of Magical Thinking* works very much in this way, as Didion expresses remorse that takes the form of "If only I had done...." Didion continues to imagine that she could have prevented her husband's sudden death, repeating the same thoughts obsessively, even after seeming to have resolved them, until finally it seems she has expiated her (undeserved) guilt and remorse through writing. Fishbane's essay is different; he explores questions about the materiality of life and death: Where has Leah gone? How can Eitan imagine her being "six feet beneath the earth's surface"? What does it mean that he believes that she is a part of him, in some way that is more profound than just in his mind? Why do such things happen? How can a person who experiences something that seems so unfair and so devastating, not just to himself, but to his four-year-old daughter, not only find solace but continue to believe in his God? These are the questions that Fishbane has the courage to raise and to share with others in a profoundly sad story of loss.

8

The Dilemmas of Psychotherapy; the Healing Response of Midrash

Philip Cushman, PhD, is core faculty in the doctor of psychology program at Antioch University, Seattle, Washington. He is the author of the book *Constructing the Self, Constructing America: A Cultural History of Psychotherapy* and many articles on the history, politics, and philosophy of psychology and psychotherapy.

The Danger of Cure, the Value of Healing
Toward a Midrashic Way of Being

Philip Cushman, PhD

We live today in a psychological world. The therapeutic worldview is a complex, highly creative, idiosyncratically Western, and surprisingly ahistorical discipline regarding its own theories and practices. Psychotherapists have a tendency to forget that their theories and practices are cultural artifacts; instead they act as if those theories exist outside of history and are thus unaffected by the larger forces that frame our understandings about ways of being human. As a result, therapists become unable to notice the ways their practices fit with the political arrangements and practices that contribute to emotional suffering.

Because of the hegemony of what writers such as Philip Rieff and Jackson Lears have called the therapeutic ethos,[1] any successful healing practice in contemporary American society must be able to think psychologically and conceive of human being in ways similar to the self that psychology has "described" and treated. The Jewish healing movement, a relatively new force in the American Jewish community, cannot escape that imperative. In order to be considered legitimate in our early-twenty-first-century world, the Jewish healing movement must be able to speak the language of psychology. And yet, some interpretations of Jewish tradition, applied to the current moment, call on the helping professions to avoid reproducing psychotherapy's more problematic elements.

Many social commentators, such as Robert Bellah, Anthony Giddens, and Charles Taylor, have argued that self-contained individualism has been the increasingly dominant ideology of the last four hundred years. These critics suggest that the valorization of individualism contributes to the isolation and mistrust characteristic of our time and makes for the society-wide self-centeredness Christopher Lasch identified in 1979.[2] When people suffer from loneliness and self-blame they seek out psychotherapy. But, ironically, the treatment they receive is often based on theories that are informed by notions such as the naturalness of separation-individuation processes and the unquestioned correctness of an instrumental approach to relationships. Therefore the therapy they receive may reproduce the way of being that initially contributed to their suffering.

The Jewish healing movement has a unique opportunity to give comfort and guidance to those suffering and in need without falling prey to the growing trend in mainstream psychotherapy that treats human suffering in highly mechanized and scientized ways. But how can the Jewish healing movement find a way of avoiding the problematic aspects that inhere in therapeutic practices, especially given the emotional and economic pressures of everyday therapeutic work? This is a genuinely difficult intellectual and moral task. In order to successfully undertake it, I believe the Jewish healing movement must draw from a resource that resides at the heart of Jewish life. It has provided our communities with inspiration, intellectual guidance, interpretive skills, and moral integrity for over two thousand years. This resource is midrash, a form of Jewish biblical commentary and interpretation that has a uniquely democratic and dialectical tone.

To embody midrashic process is to be able to hold both sides of the hermeneutic paradox: to question rigorously, creatively, and thoughtfully within a historical tradition of moral understandings deeply held. It is to refuse to accept texts or authority without interrogating and exploring their inconsistencies and contradictions. The process includes awareness that critical activity and imaginative artistry are achieved only by virtue of a set of moral commitments and beliefs framed by the historical tradition a person lives within and continually modifies. Midrashic study is training in critical thought, moral discourse, and political resistance; from it we learn that no text, interpretation, person, theory, or practice should be exempt from being evaluated according to the tradition's standards of social justice, compassion, and personal respect.

Many claims from clinicians of past eras, such as those made about the coercive methods of the mad doctors of the early-modern-era asylums; S. Weir Mitchell's Victorian "rest cure" for neurasthenic women; American mesmerism's hypnotic cures that promised to create a "wider, truer self" for the emerging nineteenth-century urban middle class; and American ego psychology's mid-twentieth-century tendency to conflate conformity with "normality," have in retrospect been evaluated by critical historians as harmful to patients, justified by theories considered fanciful at best, and (despite claims to scientific objectivity) implicated in the political status quo.[3] Psychotherapy's inability to historically situate its own practices has led to a paradoxical situation: its practitioners have a decided tendency to develop innovative and colorful practices that claim remarkable successes with claims that are not tested critically.

The Dilemma

In this chapter I hope to add to the discussion of how the Jewish healing movement is situated in this historical moment and to support one of its central philosophical commitments: to inspire, enhance, comfort, and heal even when cure is not possible.[4] This commitment places the Jewish healing movement in the difficult position of joining with aspects of the therapeutic ethos and yet also opposing others. One hopes the Jewish healing movement could develop healing practices that are psychologically sophisticated and yet avoid some problematic aspects of contemporary psychotherapy. For instance, mainstream psychotherapy's implicit reliance on self-contained individualism has contributed to the alienation and lack of human connection that is characteristic of our time. Peter Gilford and I have maintained that a technicist understanding of healing practices, in concert with the insurance industry and managed care arrangements of treatment, has continued to grow in power and influence, affecting how therapists conceive of and implement their work.[5] An instrumentalist vision of human beings is infecting psychotherapy theory just as it has academic psychology and our larger society. And some, such as Susan Bordo, have persuasively argued that the Cartesian dualism of mind and body has contributed to difficulties and conflicts, including, for instance, eating disorders such as anorexia.[6]

Fortunately, the Jewish healing movement's commitment to certain Jewish values could be utilized in order to avoid the dilemma. One of the most significant expressions of that commitment is found in the literature of midrash, biblical commentary in the form of storytelling and intricate interpretive processes, based on creative readings of the biblical text. The more the Jewish healing movement can draw from and apply the values derived from the midrashic process, the better it will be able to avoid the problems that inhere in reductive psychotherapy theories that focus on solutions, techniques, and procedures established by manualized procedures at the expense of human contact. My suggestion as to the importance of midrash and how it achieves its goals is consistent with the work of several contemporary scholars who have been working in what is called the "interpretive turn" in the humanities and social sciences. The work of these scholars, among them Daniel Boyarin, Michael Fishbane, and Peter Ochs, emphasizes interpersonal engagement, critical interpretive processes, and playfulness. These scholars suggest that midrash can be an anti-authoritarian practice and a hedge against fundamentalism (the literal and authoritarian readings of the biblical material). My interpretation of these issues is one of several contemporary interpretations, and I acknowledge that not all Judaic scholars would agree with my assessment.

The Movement

The Jewish healing movement is an interdisciplinary movement dedicated to bringing Jewish practices to patients who suffer from illness, chronic pain, significant life challenges, loss, or the approach of death and to the family, friends, and caretakers who are involved with them. The movement was founded in response to unmet needs in the community for services that would combine traditional Jewish literature and liturgy, nontraditional Jewish healing and spiritual traditions, Western medical science, psychotherapy and counseling practices, and spiritual wisdom and medical knowledge from other cultures. Practitioners are usually rabbis, Jewish communal workers, social workers, and counselors.

Among the potential problems that emerge as the Jewish healing movement evolves is the aforementioned infrequently examined connection between psychotherapy and the political status quo that has plagued therapy practices since its emergence in modern Europe. Critical interpretive traditions within Judaism, like midrash, might help the Jewish healing movement avoid the problems that come with the early-twenty-first-century therapeutic ethos while embracing (and improving upon) the good in it. One way of avoiding the pitfalls of popularity is to historically situate your own practices and the social practices from which you hope to draw, and then evaluate the understanding of the good that they embody and the personal and political consequences that flow from them, according to your own moral commitments and the standards of your culture.

Jews in America

"Hello America, goodbye God" was a familiar Jewish saying in the late nineteenth and early twentieth centuries. Today, unfortunately, we might well wish our difficulties were as few and straightforward as that, because American Jews face a range of profound and interrelated psychological and political challenges.[7] One such challenge is the continuing effect of the traumas and culture shock that were the products of European anti-Semitism, the ongoing flight from Europe, the Holocaust, and subsequently the everyday attempts to survive, fit into, and finally thrive in a society that at times is conformist, highly competitive, politically conservative, and sometimes militaristic. A second challenge is the identity struggles that seem common to all ethnic groups in the United States, caused in part by the undermining of cultural traditions that was the result of industrial capitalism and the shift from feudal patterns to modernity. Among these identity struggles are the oscillations between ethnic group self-hatred and inflated self-regard, intergenerational conflict, language difficulties, and a sporadic, often conflicted search within one's tradition for meaning and relevance. A third challenge is the emptiness and destructiveness characteristic of mainstream American consumer culture that takes its toll on all groups, causing various experiences of brokenness and alienation in a social world that sometimes appears materialistic, hypercompetitive, and anti-intellectual. This concern was voiced by Christopher Lasch, among others, when he suggested that post–World War II American culture routinely produces narcissism as a predominant way of being.[8]

All ethnic groups in America struggle with how they are positioned within the social hierarchy, with what they will be required to jettison both socially and personally in order to move up the social ladder, and with whether they will be willing to do so in order to escape the fate of being "nonwhite."[9] At the same time, all ethnic groups also get glimpses of the destructive elements of American mass culture. Much political and personal suffering has been caused by the American prescription of giving up ethnicity and tradition in order to survive in the American mainstream.

Of course, antimodern movements that emphasize tradition and compliance do not automatically supply a solution to the complex dilemmas above. These movements promise to reconnect followers with the cultural traditions and social structures of their people and a group identity meant to counter twenty-first-century alienation. However, ultimately, there are no quick solutions to these problems and no airtight guarantees. The dream of an unproblematic return to the world of the past is often shattered by the limitations and coercions that inhere in an attempted escape into fundamentalism.

Psychology and Its Problems

Many psychological problems have emerged out of the absences of communal and cultural guidance and the destructive pressures of a minimally regulated capitalist marketplace. In order to address these problems over the last three centuries there have appeared many new psychotherapeutic technologies, each complete with a scientific theory, scientific experts, and often a pop-psych explanation for the interested layperson. Usually these new therapeutic innovations turn out to be much more problematic than their practitioners' scientific claims make them out to be. In retrospect, most highly regarded psychotherapeutic "breakthroughs" turn out not only to reflect, but also rather insistently to reproduce the political status quo, albeit in unintentional and remarkably subtle ways. Practices as dissimilar as the previously mentioned nineteenth-century rest cure for female neurasthenia, mesmerism's *fin de siècle* promise of abundance, mid-twentieth-century ego psychology's affinity for social conformity, psychoanalysis's late-twentieth-century allegiance to the true self, or psychology's current romance with cognitivism and "evidence-based treatment" and how they conveniently enable managed care, all contain a similar flaw: they are unable to historically situate and politically interpret their own practices.

Psychotherapy, of course, does not hold a monopoly on addressing human suffering; in fact, it is a relatively new addition to the disciplines of care. Religion has not yet surrendered its place as protector of the soul; it won't do so without a fight, and rightly so. The behavioral and emotional responses to the problems that inhere in modern life in the United States are often interpreted as scientifically derived psychological symptoms, but that is not the only interpretation possible.

However, religion is also not immune to the philosophical and political trends of the day. Over the last 150 years in the United States, religions have sometimes suffered from various degrees of mediocrity and irrelevance. In order to boost their appeal, religions have sometimes taken on the protective coloration of, or even merged with, secular ideologies and their practices. In the 1890s, for instance, mainstream Protestantism, in order to increase its diminishing appeal, adopted the worldview of an increasingly high-powered capitalism by incorporating the spirit and language of advertising and salesmanship.

The current social world is one that has delivered a profound challenge to mainstream religions. The Jewish healing movement is an attempt to address needs in the community to which previous Jewish institutions and practices were not adequately responding. One way of attempting to fit with new social trends and meet those needs was to apply a more nonmainstream psychological way of treatment for patients and their caretakers.

This has become a legitimate and often extremely helpful response to the many ways community members suffer. But with the immersion into a more psychological world of practice come different challenges and new potential problems.

For instance, assurances that the practitioner uses various therapeutic techniques located in a metaphorical "spiritual toolbox" indicate the influence of the technicist, instrumental worldview of today that might well be a source of the client's distress. This is a common phrase in psychotherapy jargon in the era of managed care. And while every professional has particular strategies and interventions that fit with certain problems or situations, we would do well to remind ourselves that the patient is not a machine that needs a "tune-up."

It would help our patients and our community if we make it a conscious practice to notice when our therapeutic explanations fit too well with current mechanistic or consumerist metaphors. When we use idiomatic expressions indiscriminately or unquestioningly or, worse yet, proudly, we run the risk of contributing to the larger sociopolitical arrangements of our current world and thus reproducing current psychological ills. It is the repetition of social practices that makes our ways of being so difficult to question. A critical perspective then becomes difficult to locate.

Some healing centers encourage patients to "take responsibility" for their personal health and wellness, an oft-used phrase in recent American health-care language. This is well-intended. But the concept of personal responsibility can be misused to commodify health care, turn the patient into a consumer, and industrialize patient care by suggesting an assembly-line approach to treatment and an advertising/marketing approach to medication.

Above all, the emphasis on a noncontextual understanding of suffering and a focus on the value of individual action shift the focus away from institutional causes of suffering and the ways those political arrangements impede good treatment. Preoccupation with the intrapsychic tends to obscure the effects of the material causes of suffering and blames the victim; when cause is misidentified, therapeutic solutions are by definition compromised. Also, the emphasis on individual action serves as a justification for industry-wide practices in managed care that insist on short-term treatment plans and a reliance on psychotropic medication, which in turn force therapists into a psychologically reductive way of thinking and intervening.

Further, individual and intrapsychic approaches have broader sociopolitical ramifications. "In medical culture," Crawford wrote, "health has become the secular salvation of a society ... for which this one and only life becomes everything. Health is conceived as the condition of possibility for the good life or even the good life itself."[10] The moral and philosophical consequences are obvious. The political ramifications are even more disturbing:

> Individual responsibility for health has become a model of and a model for the neoliberal restructuring of American society.... Middle-class optimism and identities are invested in the ideal of personal control.... Health *is* the language of a class that, even as it disintegrates, continues to believe in its self-making salvation. Health practice lends itself to a logic of survival: individuals must do what they can to protect themselves from harm.[11]

Crawford demonstrated how the current concept of health, in its professional and pop-cultural manifestations, has both reflected and initiated important political arrangements of the last quarter of the twentieth century. Hyperindividualism and personal responsibility carried to their extreme have justified the undermining of public health initiatives and furthered the deregulation and privatization of medical care. They have reinforced the neoconservative vision of a dangerous, unsafe world in which governmental limitations on the private and corporate sectors (such as environmental regulation) are understood to be inefficient, immoral, even un-American—only individual, personal solutions can be trusted.

The Jewish healing movement is a promising response to the difficult issues facing American Jews. The movement attempts to integrate Jewish traditional observance with new forms of spiritual practice, psychotherapy, pastoral counseling, and sociology. It faces the limits of human influence in the universe, reflected especially in its faith in the ability of the sufferer to face difficult truths that may well have no immediate or certain solution, such as personal loss, chronic illness and pain, or even death. At its best, the Jewish healing movement embraces the values of respect, compassion, and courage and has the potential to resist the seductiveness of both religious fundamentalism and contemporary therapeutic ideology.

It is possible to resist these trends, as, for instance, relational psycho-analysis has demonstrated. Relational psychoanalysis has combined aspects of interpersonal, object relation, self-psychology, feminist, critical, postmodern, and hermeneutic traditions into a practice that often resists the mechanistic, instrumental trends so influential in psychotherapy.[12] The intellectual integrity and vitality of the relationalists provide an inspiration and a philosophical model for other contemporary movements.

Midrash

I have written about the similarities between some basic characteristics of midrash and relational psychoanalysis. I came to realize that some ways of studying midrash were congruent with opposing authoritarian group processes and fundamentalist ways of thinking. I want now to expand this exploration by relating ideas about midrash to the concept of healing and to certain contemporary political topics in a concluding section. Please keep in mind that I am not an expert on midrash or Judaic studies; I am a psychologist with a research interest in the cultural history of psychotherapy, especially American psychotherapy.

From the philosophical, hermeneutic perspective I favor, midrash is important because it engages us in a continuing group experience of interpretive study that helps develop a way of being. This way of being is profoundly shaped by ideological content and narrative form, but of equal importance is that its content is *embodied* in the practice of group interpretation. That is part of the genius of midrashic process: its study requires an emotional, intellectual, and critical engagement that necessitates the living out of some of its central moral understandings.[13] In other words, studying midrash requires the enactment of its values, and the enactment of its values over time has been meant to necessitate the embodiment of its values. It was this interpretive dynamic that created in late antiquity a particular way of being—an embodied moral understanding of the good—that has helped fashion Jewish life in powerful ways for the last two thousand years.[14]

American Jews have become increasingly estranged from that way of being for many reasons, including, I think, because most of us have not experienced an ongoing involvement in the kind of group study that has characterized traditional ways of learning midrashic/Talmudic literature.

The practice that was one of the central social institutions of Jewish communal life has become for all too many of us a thing of the past.

The way of being that gets developed by participating in the interpretive midrashic process—including a dyadic relation called *chavruta*—can be an important part of living a fuller Jewish life in the early twenty-first century in the United States. How we develop that way of being in our current American lifestyle is an open question, and I do not presume to know its answer. But I do think that without some ways of living out the values and commitments embodied in the study of midrash, our emotional and psychological lives are likely to become increasingly impoverished, our ability to resist the worst aspects of American consumer and political culture increasingly compromised. Without an ongoing group practice like interpretive midrash, our capacity to interpret our Jewish heritage and creatively apply it to the most important aspects of our daily lives will become misplaced almost to the point of being entirely lost.

Fortunately, aspects of a midrashic way of being or at least aspects of its central ideas and values have shown up and will continue to show up in various social practices from time to time in American society. One such site, as noted earlier, is the practice of some types of contemporary psychotherapy, notably the synthesis today referred to as relational psychoanalysis. In our contemporary world, some of the values and commitments that in past historical eras were routinely expressed as religious show up today in disguised ways in the putatively secular practices of the human sciences.

But of course, just as there are some psychotherapy values that oppose the current cultural framework and its political arrangements, there are some that support them. Often psychotherapists are handicapped in their attempts to find their way through these dilemmas in part because their professional and financial legitimacy has traditionally been tied to a modern-era scientific warrant that cannot allow philosophical discussion about these issues. They are not trained to think philosophically about therapy and often are actively discouraged from doing so. And, sadly, there are therapists who actively support the status quo and those who are simply uninterested in this dilemma. As a result, some therapists find ways of working through these issues, but many do not.

Surely, what has happened within American Jewish communities reflects much of what has gone on in our Western culture at large. We are a social world, after all, that values productivity and procedural efficiency on one hand, and gravitates to more romantic, transformational practices that stress individualistic mystical experiences on the other. To their credit, many psychoanalysts have resisted these pressures. Relationalists such as Irwin Hoffman, who has written about the dangers of scientism; Donnel Stern, who writes about the mystery of human change; Roger Frie, who discusses psychological agency and choice within the frame of the postmodernism and hermeneutics; and the anti-Cartesianism of intersubjectivists Robert Stolorow, George Atwood, and Donna Orange have contributed to a more philosophically sound approach to these issues.[15] The Jewish healing movement, necessarily, has to face the seductions from both the mechanistic and the transformational poles. Fortunately, Jewish healing movement practitioners have an advantage that might not be available to more conventional or secular therapists: they have Jewish tradition, and especially the values that inhere in midrashic practice, to guide them in this difficult task.

Five Midrashic Qualities

Five aspects of midrashic practice seem to be particularly germane for the challenges facing American Jews (and thus the Jewish healing movement) today. They are the values of interpretation, intertextuality, interpersonal engagement, the absence/presence dynamic, and the prohibition against idolatry.

Interpretation

Interpretive practice is at the heart of midrashic study. What the Rabbis called biblical commentary is really the interpretation of the Bible that took place over many centuries. They told stories to illustrate, explain, rewrite, justify, critique, and teach about the Bible. And then they told stories about their stories. In this essay I draw in particular from two important views of midrashic practice.[16]

Perception is a profoundly complex, social, problematic process that is in large part contingent upon the interpretation of what is perceived. It is one's cultural framework that makes interpretation possible; without it, human perception would be chaotic and meaningless. Interpretation is crucial not only in the process of how humans make sense of the world, but also in how we make sense of ourselves—we are "self-interpreting animals," in Charles Taylor's famous phrase.[17]

Philosophical hermeneutics sounds like serious business. But, surprisingly, one of the distinguishing qualities of midrashic literature and study is playfulness. The Rabbis not only interpreted the Bible, they did so consciously and sometimes boldly and humorously. They believed that every word, every letter in the Hebrew Bible, sometimes even every mark, was from God, that God implanted meaning in every written symbol. It was thus their job to interpret every word, letter, and mark in order to understand what God was communicating. But by doing so they developed an appreciation for imaginative interpretations and the concept of multiple truths in a single text. Therefore, they often included fictive, varying, even competing interpretations in the compilations of midrash that they produced over the centuries.

Their playfulness seems particularly courageous to me. While on one hand they seemed to have a belief that they were "discovering" God's word, on the other hand they were aware that their ideas and stories were dependent on their interpretative imaginative abilities. For instance, there is a story that illustrates the paradox at the heart of midrash: The Rabbis once got into an argument about what in Jewish literature was the exact, direct word of God, and what was human interpretation. They argued and discussed this for days or perhaps weeks on end. Finally, one opinion carried the day: neither the Hebrew Bible, nor the Five Books of Moses, nor the Ten Commandments, nor the first commandment, nor even the first word of the first commandment, but the first letter of the first word of the first commandment is the only instance of God's direct, unmediated voice. That letter, the *aleph*, was declared the only sound of God's voice that humans had ever heard. All the rest, in Gershom Scholem's understanding of this narrative, was interpretation.[18] Imagine the implications of this line of reasoning! Everything, except for one letter, is of human origin, and therefore imperfect and contestable. The Rabbis decided that that one moment of sound contained all that God wanted to communicate to humans; it contained for all time God's immense truth. For that reason, the Rabbis have referred to that first *aleph* as "the Immense *Aleph*."

But there is more: the letter *aleph*, the first letter in the Hebrew alphabet, is a silent letter. It has no sound. The Immense *Aleph* contained all sound, but it made no sound. It contained all truth, directly spoken from God to Moses, in one immense silence. There is a great deal that the world offers, an immensity, we might say, but it makes no sound until humans interpret it. The potentiality of all understanding is out there, waiting to be heard and comprehended, but first it must be interpreted by a human voice, imperfect but hopeful, limited and prejudiced, but full of ideas, grand plans, and high ideals. Even God's voice, the Rabbis understood, was unhearable, until generations of sometimes poor and anonymous Jewish scholars put pen to paper and imaginatively interpreted God's silences through their own cultural understandings. The Immense *Aleph* is without end, pregnant with what is possible, but it can only be communicated through human interpretation. Only then can God's voice be heard. Midrashic process could help Jewish healing movement practitioners remember that there are no unproblematic diagnoses, apolitical therapeutic techniques, or natural outcomes of therapeutic interventions. Whatever the outcome of a therapeutic intervention, it must necessarily be the product of a series of interpretations, and interpretations are necessarily social products. There are no perfect, foolproof techniques that produce natural, asocial results.

Diagnostic categories, therapy theories, the interventions they prescribe, and the tools used to evaluate them are always in danger of becoming elements of a self-sealing doctrine. As such, they tend to reflect and reproduce the moral understandings and political arrangements of their social world. Hermeneuticists and critical psychologists argue that there are no asocial, universal diagnostic categories, therapy theories, intervention practices, or evaluative methods; they are best thought of as historical artifacts.[19] This doesn't mean they are necessarily bad—they are just, to paraphrase Michel Foucault, "dangerous," meaning they are political. Foucault's point is that categories, theories, practices, and methods are human inventions that should be historically situated and politically interpreted. Therapy, in other words, is not a positivist, scientific procedure; it is a kind of moral discourse.

Intertextuality

Intertextuality is the relation between the many Jewish texts that appear in midrash: how texts refer to, inform, echo, mirror, oppose, reinforce, and modify—in general, engage with—one another. Intertextuality implies that texts are what we have to turn to when interpreting texts.[20]

In the social world the midrashic Rabbis inhabited, direct experiences of God, such as the witnessing of miracles, direct interventions, or communications from God, were not usually thought to happen. Because the Rabbis knew God only through the interpretations they compiled about God, there was no way to turn to some putatively unproblematic and unmediated experience of God or a text that specifically and concretely defined God. Humans, they seemed to think, learn about the world through imperfect, historically contingent, human-made sources. In fact, in one of the few instances when the Rabbis claimed God tried to intervene in midrashic deliberations, the Talmud relates a story in which the Rabbis brushed off God's miracle making and refused God's advice. They did so by using a phrase that became an idiomatic expression in Jewish interpretive tradition: "It is not in heaven." This phrase indicates that midrash is properly decided through textual interrogation and human debate, not by recourse to the claim that God has spoken and announced the one truth. God is pictured in heaven laughing with pleasure in response and saying, "My children have defeated Me" (Babylonian Talmud, *Bava Metzia* 49b). Midrash consists of the human processes of interpretation conducted with human skills and human concerns—God was to have no direct role in the textual determinations the Rabbis decided upon.

In order to create and understand their sometimes remarkably complicated arguments, the Rabbis had to know and understand well the literary and historical contexts of the biblical sources from which they drew. Even though they often treated proof texts as if they existed apart from time, they couldn't have used them in the ways they did in their arguments and expect their readers to follow their arguments unless the literary and broad historical context of the texts were well understood.

An important aspect of intertextuality is the interdependence of biblical and midrashic texts. Although the written Torah is preeminent, no one text was deemed to hold all the truth, as each contributed to the meanings of the others; each was part of an overarching fabric that opened new possibilities and especially brought to light each individual text and the creative interpretations of the Rabbis. Without each one of them, the whole could not have emerged as it did.

Midrashic process could help Jewish healing movement practitioners remember that the psychotherapy theories they sometimes utilize are not composed of unquestionable truths. They are human inventions that reflect a particular historical time period; in order to adequately appreciate them, practitioners have to be able to situate them and develop interpretations about the functions they play within that sociopolitical world. We can interpret them by comparing and contrasting them and evaluating them according to our best understandings of the good.

Interpersonal Engagement

Parallel to intertextuality is interpersonality. By that I mean a recognition of the importance of depending on one's fellow humans, turning to them to learn about and affect the world. As in intertextuality, understanding one person through another sheds light on both. The Rabbis mined the spaces between letters, words, and concepts, explored the gaps and puzzles in their texts, and turned to other texts and their study partners to explain those gaps.

The insistence on communal activity mirrors the main mode of literary study, and both activities reflect and enact one of the strongest of Jewish values: the commitment to honor the cultural-historical space between persons, to recognize the existence and importance of the other, as other, and to encourage a meaningful engagement with the other. It is the "space between" that is the terrain in which meaning is made. In tandem with the content of its ideas, it is the interpretive process of engaged, critical, compassionate, respectful, communal involvement that renders texts understandable and heals souls, psyches, and communities. Midrashic process could help Jewish healing movement practitioners understand the dangers of hyperindividualism and be wary of theories or practices that define humans as isolated monads who live best when they are separate, distant, and disengaged from others. Midrashic process takes place within a working group; it is the antithesis of hyperindividualism or at least can be used to counter hyperindividualistic trends.

The Absence/Presence Dialectic

In the social world of the early midrashic Rabbis, unlike that which was described by the biblical texts they studied and interpreted, God, with rare exceptions, was understood as neither intervening directly in the affairs of humans nor communicating directly and personally with them. The contrast must have been difficult for the Rabbis to come to terms with. The Temple in Jerusalem was destroyed, the nation defeated, much of the population exiled, and the God who promised to protect them did nothing to intervene. Over time, however, the ability of the Rabbis to face the fact of God's absences, while somehow remaining in relation with God, helped them shape a new understanding of presence. The tension between the two poles of absence and presence appeared to open up a space dominated neither by hopeless despair over God's absence nor a defensive inflation or exaggeration of God's presence.

In that dialectical space emerged the literary practices of midrash. The Rabbis maintained a type of presence in the face of absence in two ways. First, they drew forth new stories and meanings from a text that, to the untutored eye, contained little of what was subsequently developed by the Rabbis. And second, through communal study and ongoing artistic creativity, the Rabbis created a new way of being with one another and with God in a social world that, to the untutored eye, contained little or no precedent for what was subsequently developed. By relying on one text to aid in the interpretation of another and by relying on a group of study partners to support, encourage, challenge, and care for one another, the Rabbis created a way of enlivening and relating to a God who, to the untutored eye, might have seemed removed, disinterested, and perhaps even uncaring. They created a way of being that brought presence into what had appeared to be an absent space. Midrashic process could help Jewish healing movement practitioners appreciate the dialectical nature of God's absence and presence. Communal and interpersonal relating defeat the barrenness of absence, an absence in clinical work often disguised by the claims of a disengaged objectivity. The courage and wisdom that come out of a commitment to honesty and humility defeat narcissistic self-inflation and the wish for a transformation, a "special," unique, immanent experience of God or the universe. It is in a limited, paradoxical, and often painful dialectical space that meeting happens and a healing can occur—even when curing does not.

The Prohibition against Idolatry

It is ironic that in our secularized world, the fight against idolatry is usually thought of as either an antiquated issue long since dispensed with or one too obvious to be important in modern Western society. However, two important figures in philosophical and critical social thought, Karl Marx and Erich Fromm, have made important contributions to understanding the reason for the prohibition against idolatry and explained its contemporary relevance.[21] Marx's concepts of alienation and commodity fetishism have been used by contemporary Marxists and postmodernists to explain (1) the seductive power of commodities over consumers in advanced industrial economies, commodities that inspire reverence, devotion, wish, desire; and (2) the perplexing way that the proletariat did not make a revolution but instead, as the twentieth century rolled on, often supported politicians and policies that opposed their class interests.

Fromm argued that idolatry is the process by which certain qualities become disowned or disavowed by an individual or society and are then projected onto something else—either a particular person (e.g., a charismatic leader or celebrity), a type of person (e.g., a person of color), or an object (e.g., a commodity such as a car). The disavowed quality is then worshipped from afar (as in placing a movie star "on a pedestal") or feared and attacked (as in believing that African American males are naturally hostile, Jews dishonest, women irrational, Latinos lazy). Both worship and attack take on the quality of a submission to idolatrous processes, an inability to question the dynamic or resist its power. Fromm used the concept of idolatry to explain such noxious late-modern-era social phenomena as consumerism, racism, and blind patriotism.

Fromm's point is that the dynamic of either worshipful or hateful idolatry is a deadening process. It freezes human creativity because it stops critical thought and meaningful engagement with oneself and with the other. The most prominent aspect of idolatry, according to Fromm, is the alienation of the individual from his or her creative human qualities. Submission to the idol is complete and uncompromising. It is a kind of slavery, a dangerous way of "escaping" from freedom.

Midrashic process could help Jewish healing movement practitioners fight against the tendency to treat behavioral theories and their techniques as unquestioned, universal truths. It teaches that humans are not static, deadened, one-dimensional "things" that can be diagnosed and studied in a disengaged, procedural fashion, understood in a formulaic manner, or cured by using predictable, mechanistic instructions. A respectful, thoroughly engaged appreciation for the other, as other, a commitment to situate theories and practices historically, a willingness to recognize what one does not—and cannot—know, while acknowledging and honoring the mystery that is human life, seem like ways of avoiding idolatrous processes.

Midrashic Lessons

In Fromm's terms, then, midrashic process can be understood as a fight against idolatry. Midrash can inspire us to develop a way of life that features intellectual honesty, flexibility, and an openness to difference always informed, necessarily, by the historical traditions that value and enable these qualities. It is a definition of the good in Jewish life. Interpretive midrashic process requires the capacity to think critically and to discuss the good. It is predicated on both the freedom to question and the freedom to be part of a larger tradition; the capacity to be open to new ideas and different practices and the capacity to have a place to stand, to know what one stands for, and who one stands with; the freedom to know but to know incompletely and uncertainly. These qualities are the products of a life less influenced by idolatry. When texts, religious belief systems, leaders, therapists, or healers lose sight of the simultaneous power and fragility of human interpretation, they lose touch with an essential aspect of humanity. When a text becomes an idol, God becomes a thing (visible, named, and known), and human creativity and relatedness become deadened. The less people believe in their ability to be engaged and effective in the world, the more they look toward and begin to depend on a magical figure (or a miraculous

cure) to save them. Subservience follows idolatry and leads to apocalyptic visions and inflated fantasies. In our desperation, God is thought
to be an intimate and immanent presence who stands ready to intervene whenever needed, to provide a sign, a spouse, a remission for
cancer, or an irrefutable justification for war.

An idolatrous dynamic and its products run counter to the understandings midrashic traditions developed. "To really understand the concept of the coming of the Messiah," a wise old rabbi once told me, "you
must realize that he will never come." An important Jewish understanding is that, contrary to the Christian Bible (see John 1) the word is not
made flesh. The word remains the word, and the word, as always,
remains contingent, imperfect, incomplete. "Midrash refuses," Judaic
scholar David Stern contends, "to make the identification between God
and Torah literal."[22] Words are surrounded by gaps, puzzles, inconsistencies, self-contradictions. Readers, rabbis, counselors, and patients fall
into those textual gaps, engage with their interlocutors there, wrestle
with God there. We live in those gaps; we are our best selves there.

Midrashic Lessons and Jewish Healing

During vulnerable moments in a person's life, especially a young person's life, the wish to be cured can be overwhelmingly powerful. Under
the right conditions, to be delivered from the pain and confusion of life
in a bewildering and hurtful world can drive the best of us to extreme
forms of self-deception. In those moments it appears the only remedy,
short of death, is to be delivered from human misery, to be lifted out of
the dilemmas and uncertainties of human consciousness, to be saved
from an unsolvable problem, to be removed from human imperfection
through contact with God or with the one truth.

When the magic seems to happen and the true believers think they
have stumbled upon the one great truth, the relief is enormous.[23] It
floods them with the sensation of being saved not only from their
momentary problems and despair, but from all problems and all
despair for all time. In effect, they believe they have been saved from
being human.

But in order to be vulnerable to that experience, you must live in a
social world framed with the understanding that God might, just might,

speak directly to you at any given moment—or that there is one perfect messenger speaking the one perfect truth, whatever form it might take, and it could visit you, or you could stumble upon it, today, or tomorrow, or sometime soon. In other words, you must live in a social world in which the miraculous is thought to be possible at any time—a world in which presence is an unchallenged, immanent possibility.

One strength of the midrashic Rabbis is that they had to learn how to live in a world without God's direct presence. They had to face God's absence in their world, and as a result they developed ways of living together that created a way of being reconciled to God's absence, or perhaps a new way of understanding God's presence—not a direct, personal, active presence in the world, but a presence somehow located in the space between one student of midrash and another, when they studied and worshipped and celebrated together.

That understanding of God's presence, or rather an understanding of the *dialectic* of presence and absence, is an aspect of a midrashic way of being that is important for us to dwell in today. It is a capacity to tolerate uncertainty and death, the impermanence and incompleteness of human understanding, the ongoing vulnerability of a human life, the arbitrary nature of illness and suffering.

The presence/absence dialectic in midrash can help us attenuate the yearnings for the one truth, for the wish to follow the one perfect leader or discover the perfect healing intervention, for the fervent belief that God or God's messenger is right around the corner, just about to visit us with a divine, perfect message or perfect cure. The desperate yearning to be visited by God's truth causes humans to believe that there is only one right way to be, one truth in the text, one correct interpretation of the Bible or the Constitution, only one correct political party, psychotherapeutic technique, or healing practice.

This interpretation suggests that the wish to be removed, or saved, from the fate of being human is one of the reasons why people come to believe that there is a personal and interventionist God who will speak to humans directly and intercede in human life directly if only they believe faithfully or enact the correct rituals or say the correct words or give enough money to the one perfect sect. Believing all that makes life so much simpler and easier. It assures us that God wants us to make a lot of money, achieve fame, or attain peace of mind or enlightenment if we just relinquish all control to this higher power. It made President Bush believe that the decisions that faced him as president were easy decisions that didn't require a great deal of study or deliberation or agonizing. All he needed was to hear God's voice telling him to invade Iraq, no matter what the moral or financial cost. It makes all things simple. It makes life itself simple.

But the primary sense I have gotten from my study is that learning midrash in community should move us to be wary of those who claim they have the one truth, the direct line to God's ear, or the foolproof request form that unleashes God's healing miracles. Midrash demonstrates, as I see it, that narrative truth moves in a circle, not a straight line; that there are many truths in a text; that when our brothers and sisters have different opinions it doesn't necessarily make them or us wrong. There may well be moments of loving, of meaning, of understanding, but they will come in the space between us, as we help one another through the difficult times and enjoy the good times, as we commit to life as it is and try to make it slightly better for one another, given the losses and limitations that are a necessary part of daily life. We will, reluctantly, develop the capacity to face the presence/absence dialectic within ourselves, with one another, and with God. And somehow if we are lucky, we will learn to take ourselves more lightly than before, learn to play a bit, laugh a bit at our fantasies, and cherish the time we have together, because it is all we have; and enjoy one another and life itself precisely because of its limitations.

That way of thinking, it seems to me, is what the Jewish healing movement means by healing, and why it is not called the Jewish curing movement. And that is why I have come to appreciate it, even though I first approached it with a chip on my shoulder. I suppose I am still a bit wary, and always will be, but I think their workers are headed in a good direction, especially if they maintain a historical perspective on the therapeutic ethos, continually examine the implications and consequences of the therapeutic techniques they use, and by so doing, guard against the cultural traps that lie in wait.

At their best, the practices of the Jewish healing movement embody a kind of midrashic way of being. Founders of the movement realized, as Rachel Cowan explained in 1991, that they were motivated in part by a feminist understanding "that even though illness might not be curable, there were many ways to relieve the suffering.... We knew that relationships and community were the key to healing."[24] Jewish healing movement practitioners don't claim to call on God to magically erase pain or cancer, or save us from arthritis or especially death. They sit with us, listen and sing and laugh and tell stories with us, introduce us to others and to community experiences, and hope for something important and helpful and, yes, for healing to happen. Healing is, after all, all that we can hope for in an unredeemed world not unlike the world of the midrashic Rabbis. But it is enough, because we have one another.

Rabbi Lewis M. Barth, PhD, is professor emeritus of midrash and related literature at Hebrew Union College–Jewish Institute of Religion, Los Angeles, where he
was formerly the dean of campus. He has authored studies of midrash and is a
research candidate at the Institute of Contemporary Psychoanalysis in Los
Angeles.

Midrashic Thinking
An Appreciation and a Caution

Rabbi Lewis M. Barth, PhD

Philip Cushman continues to challenge us in his chapter "The Danger
of Cure, the Value of Healing." In an appeal to the Jewish healing
movement, whose statements of purpose he cites with great appreciation, Cushman urges reflection from the perspective of "critical history" so that the movement does not find itself falling into the traps
that have ensnared psychology and especially psychoanalysis. He
argues this in the hope that "the Jewish healing movement could
develop healing practices that are psychologically sophisticated and
yet avoid some problematic aspects of contemporary psychotherapy."
These include "implicit reliance on self-contained individualism ..., a
technicist understanding of healing practices ..., an instrumentalist
vision of human beings ..., the Cartesian dualism of mind and body,"
in addition to the most negative features of capitalism, racism, and
pop culture that impact so many aspects of American life. The antidote to falling into this nonreflective and overly mechanistic and
materialistic trap is found in the processes of midrash, a fascinating
aspect of Rabbinic culture that "emphasizes interpersonal engagement, critical interpretive processes, and playfulness." He notes that
this understanding "suggest[s] that midrash can be an anti-authoritarian practice and a hedge against fundamentalism (the literal and
authoritarian readings of the biblical material)." The processes of
midrash, as well as the community or group context in which

midrash is studied, represent the best values from within Jewish experience to withstand the worst of modern culture, economics, and politics and the best chance for the Jewish healing movement to remain committed to its core values.

Cushman's very rich description of the problematics of psychoanalysis, historically and in the present, and the benefits of midrashic processes, is meant to challenge our thinking, and he succeeds in that goal. In responding to his challenge, it is not my goal to reject his arguments, but to raise questions about Cushman's descriptions of psychoanalysis and midrash, to see in what way the solutions he offers need correction, refinement, and expansion as we enter the second decade of the twenty-first century.

My sense is that the negative view Cushman has of the field of psychoanalysis is shaped primarily by his focus on classical psychoanalytic tradition and the overemphasis on science represented by "cognitive behavioral therapy." The excesses of the past, and the neat fit of cognitive behavioral therapy with the fiscal motivations of insurance companies, certainly demand our concern.[1] However, the positive qualities Cushman sees in midrashic processes—"interpersonal engagement, critical interpretive processes, and playfulness," as well as strongly anti-authoritarian attitudes—have informed much of the writings of contemporary psychoanalysis for more than a quarter of a century. Diverse schools of contemporary psychoanalysis (e.g., relational, interpersonal, intersubjective, self-psychology, among others) have shifted the ground of psychoanalytic focus from the classical authoritarian model going back to Freud to a two-person "dyadic" model that focuses on the relationship between the therapist and the patient.

These schools, each in its own way, parallel Cushman's strong relational orientation. Specifically, Cushman notes with appreciation the writings of the relationalist Stephen Mitchell. We might add to Mitchell the writings of Stolorow, Atwood, and Orange, all of whom have argued for the rejection of the Cartesian worldview and emphasized the importance of various streams of modern philosophy for helping shape psychoanalytic theory. Lachmann, Ringstrom, and others have written extensively on the role of humor and playfulness in the clinical setting.[2] Findings and clinical practices that draw from infant research and contemporary attachment theory emphasize the importance of mutuality and connection in human development and functioning.[3] What characterizes these and other psychoanalytic theorists and ideas is a deep and critical awareness of the problematic history of psychoanalysis and psychoanalytic theory and its overemphasis on the individual and the intrapsychic (i.e., that which takes place within the patient's psyche). In addition, one has to be impressed by the generally lively level of debate within contemporary psychoanalytic journals, reflective of serious intellectual efforts to sharpen distinctions between psychoanalytic schools as well as to find the common ground that distinguishes the contemporary from the classical. Consequently, Cushman's appropriate concern about the limiting and corruptive impact of contemporary culture has to be balanced against highly creative theoretical changes in contemporary psychoanalysis as well as new understandings of the human brain, the development of which relies on the essentially relational nature of human experience.[4]

Many of the positive dimensions found in midrashic processes that Cushman emphasizes are *already* represented in their own way in contemporary psychoanalytic thinking. And that makes for a very interesting fit between these two aspects of human endeavor, one ancient and deeply embedded in the activity of meaning making through transforming Scripture to speak to Jews in postbiblical historical settings, and one modern, seeking to provide healing for the pains and illnesses of mind in the modern (and postmodern) world.

In relation to midrash, Cushman's argument can be expanded as well to touch on the modern world, not just through the communitarian and hermeneutic process of midrashic study, but also by looking at the *content* of midrash specifically in the areas of social and institutional critique that inform so much of Cushman's writings.

The following section of this essay contains a brief presentation and assessment of a midrashic text that deals with issues as disturbing in contemporary American and Jewish life as they were in antiquity. My purpose is to demonstrate that midrashic processes are designed to communicate messages that can be as meaningful for sick societies as communal midrashic study might be for individuals and small groups. Process and meaning (content) are inextricable. I introduce this midrashic passage to demonstrate that midrash—openly hermeneutic though it may be in theory—often has very specific didactic purposes.

As will become clear, this passage is neither collaborative, nor open-ended nor anti-authoritarian.

The midrashic text to be discussed is taken from a Rabbinic homily found in chapter fifteen of *Pesikta D'Rav Kahana.*[5] This midrash is based on Isaiah 1:21–27, a traditional *haftarah* (prophetic) reading for the Sabbath before Tisha B'Av, the ninth day of the month of Av, memorializing the destruction of the First and Second Temples in Jerusalem. The biblical text speaks for itself: the prophet Isaiah (active c. 740–700 BCE) describes the transformation of Jerusalem from a once-faithful city to a place of murder, corruption of standards, corruption of the ruling class, and corruption of judges and the judicial system. The passage concludes with a description of a vengeful God who will cleanse the city of its perverse ways and reestablish its leadership as of old—so that Jerusalem will once again "be called City of Righteousness, Faithful City."

> *Alas, she has become a harlot,*
> *The faithful city*
> *That was filled with justice,*
> *Where righteousness dwelt—*
> *But now murderers.*
> *Your silver has turned to dross;*
> *Your wine is cut with water.*
> *Your rulers are rogues*
> *And cronies of thieves,*
> *Every one avid for presents*
> *And greedy for gifts;*
> *They do not judge the case of the orphan,*
> *And the widow's cause never reaches them.*
>
> *Assuredly, this is the declaration*
> *Of the Sovereign, the* LORD *of Hosts,*
> *The Mighty One of Israel:*
> *"Ah, I will get satisfaction from My foes;*
> *I will wreak vengeance on My enemies!*
> *I will turn My hand against you,*
> *And smelt out your dross as with lye*

And remove all your slag:
I will restore your magistrates as of old,
And your counselors as of yore.
After that you shall be called
City of Righteousness, Faithful City."
Zion shall be saved in the judgment;
Her repentant ones, in the retribution.[6]

ISAIAH 1:21–27

However, this biblical text, as do so many others, cries out for explanation and concretization. How can we engage in a process of reading and discussion that helps us understand more deeply the prophet's words and their midrashic amplification *and* experience them in a way that shapes our own conscious and unconscious being in the world? What kind of examples could make this text come alive? How are the examples related to the words of Isaiah? Finally, in what ways will this text help us expand Cushman's description of midrash?

Of the many comments in the midrashic elaboration of Isaiah's words found in *Pesikta D'Rav Kahana* 15, three in particular provide examples of problems the Rabbis encountered in their own society: the problems of just weights and measures, the possibility of receiving justice under the law, and the judiciary itself. Put another way, the Rabbis present vivid stories demonstrating the perversion of standards and legal institutions, the corruption of judges, and the exploitation of the powerless.

Thy silver is become dross, thy wine mixed with water [Isaiah 1:22]. At one time coins made of silver were current. As tricksters grew numerous, however, coins made of copper but silvered over were put into use, so that when a man went to a silversmith [for currency], he was apt to hear him mutter to his apprentice, "Copper it [over] for him." So, too, when a man would go to buy a pint of wine at a wine dealer's, he was apt to hear him mutter to his clerk, "Water it [down] for him." Hence it is written *Thy silver is become dross* just as *thy wine is mixed with water.*

This midrash, a commentary on Isaiah 1:22, probably has its historical background in the rampant inflation and debasement of coinage of the late Roman Empire during the late third and fourth centuries.[7] It singles out practices that undermine trust in weights and measures. In antiquity as today, government was responsible for setting and regulating the marketplace and those who work in it. The *agronomos*, the market inspector, was the responsible officer in villages and towns; his authority in various historical periods had life-and-death implications for violators. If he were taking bribes, trust in the system could not be sustained. Our midrashic example does not play on specific words, but on the juxtaposition of the two parts of Isaiah's rebuke: "Hence it is written *Thy silver is become dross* just as *thy wine is mixed with water.*" The rhetorical tool is amplification of examples: coinage is debased, just as measures are corrupted—adding up to a picture of a society undermined from one end to the other by the very people on whom we rely. Sound familiar?

Thy princes are rebels, and companions of thieves [Isaiah 1:23]....
Thy princes are rebels against the law: every one of them loved stolen goods. *And companions of thieves:* every one of them associated with thieves. Rabbi Berechiah told the story of a woman whose kettle was stolen. When she went to a judge to report the matter, she found her kettle sitting on the judge's stove. Another story is told of a man whose cloak was stolen. When he went to report the matter to a judge, he found his cloak spread out on the judge's couch. Rabbi Levi told the story of a woman who presented a silver lamp to a judge. Thereupon her opponent in the suit went and presented him with a foal made of gold. The next day the woman found that the judgment which had been issued in her favor was reversed. She said: "My lord, should not the previous judgment in my favor shine before you like a silver lamp?" He replied: "What's to be done? The foal has overturned the lamp." Of such it is written *Every one loveth bribes* [Isaiah 1:23]—every one of them has larceny in his heart. *And followeth after payments* [ibid.]—you scratch my back and I'll scratch yours [literally "you pay me and I'll pay you"].

In providing *stories* to exemplify Isaiah 1:23, the midrash responds to two unstated questions: Who are "thy princes," and what is the connection with the next phrase in the verse, "Every one loveth bribes"? Rabbi Berechiah's tale specifies that the princes, companions of thieves, are judges who themselves are receivers of stolen property; Rabbi Levi reconfirms this and also uses the attempt of the woman to bribe the judge as the connection between the two parts of the verse. "*Every one,*" including the woman, her opponent, and the judge loves bribes. Corruption is universal.

> They judge not the fatherless, neither doth the cause of the widow come unto them [Isaiah 1:23].... Rabbi Yochanan said: In times past when a man would go up to Jerusalem to plead a lawsuit, the judge would say, "Split a couple of logs for me," "Fill a couple of casks of water for me," [and so on]. While the man was doing such chores, his money ran out, and he would have to leave Jerusalem with a broken spirit. When a widow happened to meet him on the way and asked him, "How did your lawsuit come out?" he would reply, "My money ran out, and I got nowhere at all." The widow would then say [implied: to herself], "If this person, who is a man, got nowhere at all with his case, all the more certain will I, who am a widow, get nowhere with mine." Thus the words They judged not the fatherless, nor doth the cause of the widow come unto them were fulfilled literally [ibid.].

In commenting on this final passage on Isaiah 1:23 I want to focus on how the midrash concretizes the concluding biblical phrase. Referring to the judges, "*nor doth the cause of the widow come unto them,*" an entire narrative is created to explain the reasoning of the widow who, out of utter despair, does not proceed with her case. She understands that her neighbor, a man who went to a judge in Jerusalem, was returning home despondent because a venal judge exploited him for the judge's own benefit. The result was simply that the neighbor had no resources left to pursue his case. Hearing that, the widow knows that she will get nowhere with hers. That is the lot of the powerless in society—they cannot afford justice and have no hope to achieve it. They give up before even starting.

From the perspective of literary midrashic analysis, it is interesting that the woman is portrayed as using a Rabbinic hermeneutic rule, *kal vakhomer*, an inference from a minor or less weighty matter to a major or more weighty situation—or the opposite, as in this case—to rationalize her decision not to go to a judge in Jerusalem. The presumed power of men is greater than the powerlessness of women; the "broken spirit" of the neighbor, a man, is significantly telling for the widow's lack of possibilities. Noting the use of the hermeneutic rule is a technical observation on modes of argumentation in midrash and Talmud and how such rules of interpretation were used in Rabbinic narrative, even to represent a kind of stream of consciousness. But our recognition of the style of the widow's internal monologue should not blind us to the utter, totally realistic despair that has embraced her. And this is the point at which we see that the midrashic process—discussion, analysis, attention to Rabbinic playfulness, and all the other qualities we ascribe to midrashic literature and its study (study whether by an individual alone or in groups)—is instrumental for the primary purpose of conveying or deriving specific meanings.

The Jewish healing movement has nothing to fear from the worst examples in the history of the psychoanalytic movement if it focuses on the best of psychoanalysis—those contemporary approaches that emphasize genuine relationship, a nonauthoritarian therapeutic environment, a sensitive understanding of the pain that goes with being human, and a constant shared commitment to achieving a healthier way of being in the world.

The prophet's message and our midrash portray God alone as having the power to change society and to restore judges, counselors, and magistrates as they were in the idealized past. But note: this midrashic theology provides no room for *tikkun olam* in the modern sense—that we are partners with God in the ongoing perfection of the world. Perhaps for the creators of *Pesikta D'Rav Kahana* 15, the reason God alone can make the world better is because they, following Isaiah, thought that human society could not right itself.[8] We recognize, of course, that Jewish life and values did not stop developing with these texts or with the world of the Rabbis. In spite of this somewhat authoritarian midrashic passage, and in spite of the belief it contains that *tikkun olam* resides only with God, in our time, we feel that we have the obligation to heal this world, as partners with God. We have the responsibility, as well, to work with individuals to heal themselves while helping us grow. In such beliefs and the actions that flow from them, we need not feel that we are either alone or powerless. This is where Cushman's emphasis on collaborative attitudes—whether toward *tikkun olam* or processes of collaboration in understanding classical Jewish literature—come into play. Relationship and partnership can be developed, whether in the understanding of midrash or of psychoanalysis. We—within the religious community—need connections to the healing professions just as the healing professions have a shared need to study and understand the prophetic, midrashic, and oh-so-ancient and yet contemporary critique. In that sense, Philip Cushman is correct.

9

The Narrative Turn in
Jewish Bioethics

Rabbi Leonard A. Sharzer, MD, was formerly clinical professor in the Department of Plastic Surgery at the Albert Einstein College of Medicine of Yeshiva University in New York. He received rabbinic ordination from The Jewish Theological Seminary, where he now serves as senior fellow in bioethics of the Louis Finkelstein Institute for Religious and Social Studies.

Aggadah and Midrash
A New Direction for Bioethics?

Rabbi Leonard A. Sharzer, MD

When I was a young medical student working in obstetrics in the mid-1960s, it was the standard of care for a woman undergoing a second cesarean section to have a tubal ligation at the time of the C-section. The reason for this was that the risk of uterine rupture in a subsequent pregnancy was thought to be unacceptably high. I did not know at the time, nor do I know as I write this today, whether this assessment was the result of scientific studies, received wisdom from earlier generations of obstetricians, or a paternalistic desire on the part of (mostly) male obstetricians to protect their female patients. Although the patient was at liberty to refuse for religious or other reasons, the recommendation was made strongly and the overwhelming majority of patients consented.

The hospital at which I worked had house officers (residents in training) who were mostly women, all Filipino, and all Roman Catholic. These house officers would assist with the C-section, but when the time came to perform the tubal ligation (or occasionally oophorectomy) they would leave the operating room. The sterilization procedure would be carried out by the attending obstetrician with my assistance. Once it was complete, the house officer would return to the operating room to assist with the conclusion of the operation.

As I look back at those experiences, I realize there were several narratives playing out. There was the narrative of the physician, advising,

245

guiding, and caring for his patient according to the best scientific information and medical wisdom of the day. There was the narrative of the patient, experiencing childbirth and undergoing a surgical procedure that would permanently end her fertility. There was the narrative of the resident, living in a foreign country, reconciling her medical milieu with her religious background. And finally, though I would not have said it in those terms at the time, there was the effect of the convergence of all of these on my personal narrative as a Jew and a physician in training.

I did not know then, nor would have it occurred to me ask, what the Jewish position was on elective sterilization to protect against the risk of a future pregnancy. It may have been that for me and all the Jewish medical doctors I knew, our religious and professional medical lives existed in separate realms. We were physicians in the clinic and Jews in the synagogue. Or it may have been that we exemplified what Rabbi Immanuel Jakobovits wrote in his groundbreaking *Jewish Medical Ethics* in 1959, that Jewish law was almost entirely consistent with good medical practice, and that "Jewish law clashes with medical opinion very rarely indeed."[1]

Rabbi Jakobovits is widely considered to be the father of modern Jewish bioethics, and the enterprise, as he envisioned and formulated it, became halakhic discipline. "Jewish law," he wrote, "does not know of any division between *jus* (legal law) and *fas* (moral law) in its principles or administration."[2] As the field of bioethics has developed over the half century since Jakobovits published his magnum opus, and especially in recent decades, in both the secular and Jewish worlds there has been a recognition of the important role of stories, of narrative, in bioethical decision making. In most Jewish bioethics discussions, narrative has been used primarily to provide supporting arguments for halakhic decisions. Some thinkers, however, have suggested that the Jewish narrative tradition, or *aggadah,* has a place as important as, and perhaps more important than, traditional halakhic analysis in guiding us in vexing bioethics issues. It is my goal in this essay to support the argument regarding Judaism's narrative tradition in the field of bioethics and expand it to include Judaism's exegetical or midrashic tradition as it applies to both narrative and legal texts.

Physicians' Codes of Conduct

Codes of ethical conduct for physicians have for centuries been governed by physicians' oaths. One of the oldest and certainly one of the best known is the oath of Hippocrates. According to Steven Miles,

> [The oath's] age is debated; 400 BCE is a reasonable estimate of when it was written.... There is no evidence that Hippocrates wrote it, knew of it, or approved of it.... We do not know how long or how widely it was used.... [It] is neither a scripture nor a legal code. It appears to be designed for the swearing in of a person at the beginning of a medical apprenticeship.... Ludwig Edelstein asserts that ancient Greek physicians commonly performed euthanasia, abortion, and surgery [procedures oath takers swore to avoid] and that the Oath reflected the views of a sect of philosophers rather than the medical ethics of the day.... The Oath was neither widely used, nor influential, until the last 500 years or so.[3]

Many of the provisions of the Hippocratic oath[4] are found in the oath of Asaph ben Berakhyahu and Yochanan ben Zabda, dating from the fifth or sixth century CE.[5] The oath of Amatus Lusitanus, a sixteenth-century Jewish Portuguese physician, is remarkably similar to both previous oaths in its tone and particulars, and places the Jewish physician squarely in the tradition of rationalist medicine:

> I have never in my medical practice departed from what has been handed down in good faith to us and posterity.... In short, I have done nothing which might be considered unbecoming an honorable and distinguished physician, having always held Hippocrates and Galen before me as examples worthy of imitation and not having scorned the precepts of many other excellent practitioners of our art.[6]

Although Galen, the Greek physician of the second century CE, wrote disparagingly of both Christians and Jews because of their acceptance of "revealed" truth not subject to empirical observation,[7] references to Galen in Rabbinic literature tend to approve of his rationalist approach to medicine even while disagreeing with him regarding the truth of revelation.

Miles suggests that we should read the oath as a text, a "coherent whole, a kind of case presentation," a text to be interpreted, rather than simply a list of aphorisms. In this way the details of what the oath says about surgery or abortion become less important than the way it holds together as a text. The structure of the oath, he says, is similar to ancient Greek medical records and to the Deuteronomic code in that both suggest specific consequences for specific behavior:

> The physician comes from this heroic family.
> A physician acts this way and not that way.
> If the physician acts this way, this is what can be hoped for.

> Israelites come from a heroic family.
> They [ought to] act this way and not that way.
> If they act as they ought to, this is how they will be rewarded,
>   and otherwise this will befall them.

These two texts appear very different on first encounter—a Greek oath for apprentice physicians and the final testament of the greatest of Jewish teachers. Although the details enumerated in each may have limited application to the modern-day physician or Jew, when read in this manner, they may be understood as transmitting values, Jewish and medical, that have remained remarkably constant through the millennia.

The Dual Patrimony of the Jewish Physician

Jewish physicians, then, have a dual patrimony. How they ought to balance the two is not always clear and has certainly not been constant. Since Jakobovits first published his book, the field of secular bioethics has undergone a sea change, and his statement that there was rarely any conflict between Jewish law and medical opinion is no longer obvious. One of the most salient elements of this change has been a move away from the paternalism of earlier eras, in the doctor-patient relationship, toward a paradigm that values patient autonomy as a fundamental right. It is precisely with regard to this principle of autonomy where secular and Jewish medical ethics have come into the most direct and profound conflict.

For Jakobovits, a physician's religious obligation may outweigh his duty as a physician:

> In advising his patient, particularly in sexual matters, he may have to decide whether or not he is morally justified in recommending a procedure which, while physically beneficial, conflicts with the dictates of his faith.[8]

Maimonides had a different take on the obligations of the physician and the autonomy of his patient:

> The physician, because he is a physician, must give information on the conduct of a beneficial regimen, be it unlawful or permissible, and the sick have the opportunity to act or not to act. If the physician refrains from prescribing all that is of benefit, whether it be prohibited or permissible, he deceives, and does not deliver his true counsel. It is manifest that the Law commands whatever is of benefit and prohibits whatever is harmful in the next world, while the physician gives information about what benefits the body and warns against whatever harms it in this world. The difference between the edicts of the Law and the counsels of Medicine is that the Law commands compliance with what benefits in the next world and compels it, and forbids that which harms in the next world and punishes for it, while Medicine recommends what is beneficial and warns against what is harmful, and does not compel this or punish for that, but leaves the matter to the sick in the form of consultation; *it is they who have the choice* [emphasis added].[9]

As the field of Jewish medical ethics has developed over the half century since the publication of Jakobovits's work, certain ideas have become fundamental principles. As is often the case, however, once such principles become solidly entrenched, the reasoning behind them may be forgotten. One such idea is the notion that when it comes to medical decision making, our autonomy is limited because God owns our bodies and we are merely leaseholders or stewards of God's property. This idea is accepted among several strains of Jewish thought. Rabbi Elliot Dorff, one of Conservative Judaism's most eloquent spokespersons in the field of bioethics, says explicitly in his book *Matters of Life and Death*:

> For Judaism, God owns everything, including our bodies. God lends our bodies to us for the duration of our lives.... Consequently, neither men nor women have the right to govern their bodies as they will; ... God can and does assert the right to restrict how we use our bodies according to the rules articulated in Jewish Law.[10]

But where does this idea come from? Dorff cites a number of biblical verses that allude to God as the possessor of heaven and earth, that is, everything: "Now, if you hearken to my voice, and guard my covenant, you will be my treasure among all the peoples because the entire land is mine" (Exodus 19:5); "So to *Adonai* your God are the heavens and heavens' heavens, the earth and all that is in it" (Deuteronomy 10:14); "The earth and its fullness are to *Adonai*, the world and its inhabitants" (Psalm 24:1).

Rabbi J. David Bleich, an Orthodox authority on bioethics issues, makes the same claim:

> Man does not possess absolute title to his life or to his body; title to human life is vested in the Creator, and man is but the steward of the life which he has been privileged to receive. Man is charged with preserving, dignifying, and hallowing that life. He is obliged to seek food and sustenance in order to safeguard the life he has been granted; when falling victim to illness or disease he is obliged to seek a cure in order to sustain life.[11]

In a commentary on *Parashat Behar*, Rabbi Michael Chernick, professor of Jewish jurisprudence and social justice at Hebrew Union College–Jewish Institute of Religion, writes as follows:

The concept that we belong to God, that we are God's servants, also has far-reaching implications. It means that our rights over others [are] limited. In fact, our right to treat ourselves poorly, whether physically, spiritually, or emotionally, is limited so as not to deny our true Owner the very best service we can give.[12]

To be sure, this idea is neither new nor specifically Jewish. One can find similar ideas in Locke, Kant, and indeed going all the way back to Plato.[13]

Most of the early Jewish references to the idea of humans as God's property come in the context of discussions about suicide, not necessarily related to health-care decision making. In fact, one is hard-pressed to find this idea explicit in Jakobovits's treatise, which is subtitled "A Comparative and Historical Study of the Jewish Religious Attitude to Medicine and Its Practice." I would pose two questions: First, how and when did the idea of God's ownership of our bodies in the context of health-care decision making become so integral a part of the Jewish imagination? And second, is this a meaningful and useful metaphor at the beginning of the twenty-first century?

The late Rabbi Eliezer Yehudah Waldenberg, writing on the prohibition of hastening the death of a *goseis* (one whose death is imminent) and mercy killing (*Tzitz Eliezer*, part 5, *Ramat Rahel*, chapter 29), begins by quoting Rabbi Yechiel Michel Epstein, author of the nineteenth-century code *Arukh HaShulchan*:

> It is forbidden to do anything to [a *goseis*] that will hasten his death ... and despite the fact that we see that he is suffering greatly during the dying process, and he would be better off dead, it is still forbidden to do anything to hasten his death, for the world and all that is in it are God's and that is his will.
>
> ARUKH HASHULCHAN 339:1

Waldenberg explicates the above by asserting that the soul of a person (*nefesh adam*) is not his own property but the property of the Holy Blessed One. He goes on to cite three rulings from Maimonides' *Mishneh Torah* to support this idea: (1) a person may not injure either himself or his fellow and may not even strike his fellow (*Hilchot Chovel* uMazik 5:1); (2) a court may not accept payment (ransom) from a convicted murderer in lieu of a death sentence, even with the agreement of the next of kin of the victim (*Hilchot Rotzeach* 1:4); and (3) a court may not accept a confession in a corporal or capital case (*Hilchot Sanhedrin* 18:6). Though Maimonides never gives a reason for any of these laws, Waldenberg states that the reason is the same for all, namely that no person owns his own soul, but it belongs to God. It should be immediately apparent that none of these instances has anything to do with the kind of end-of-life decisions that individuals or their surrogates regularly face.

Moreover, Waldenberg seems to be addressing concerns about active euthanasia and assisted suicide by, and on the recommendation of, physicians. These are clearly issues that pose ethical dilemmas, but they are not the only or even the most common questions faced by individuals or their surrogates in end-of-life discussions, where typical questions involve the discontinuation of therapies deemed futile, removal of mechanical devices that seem only to prolong the dying process, such as respirators and artificial hydration and nutrition, and even whether to attempt resuscitation after cardiorespiratory arrest.

Even the prohibition against injuring another person would be attributed to the idea of a person's soul being God's property (*Shulchan Arukh, Choshen Mishpat, Hilchot Nizkei Guf*, paragraph 4 and subsequent).

So the idea of God's ownership of our bodies seems to have been derived from the principle of God's ownership of our souls, which developed from capital criminal cases and a prohibition against self-injury and has been used to explain a general prohibition against any act or omission that would have the effect of hastening the death of a terminally ill patient. Ultimately, this became a fundamental principle used to support the limitation of individual autonomy in health-care decision making.

In an era in which secular bioethics has stressed autonomy as a fundamental right of individuals and obligation of health-care deliverers, how useful is the metaphor of God's ownership, and is there an alternative? For those for whom the metaphor of being God's property resonates with their sense of themselves, it may indeed be helpful. But for many people in our day, their sense of personal autonomy, of the "sovereign self," renders the idea of God's ownership of our souls or bodies unhelpful at best and irrelevant at worst.

When Jakobovits wrote *Jewish Medical Ethics*, he was responding, in part, to changes in Western society in the mid-twentieth century in the way medical care was viewed and the way it was practiced. It was a time of major advances in medical science that posed challenges to conventional medical ethical thinking. Within most physicians' codes of conduct, perhaps the most widely known tenet is "Do no harm," which is often referred to in secular bioethics writing as the principle of nonmaleficence. Along with technological advances in medicine and the development of life-prolonging treatments, it has become less clear what treatments are helpful and which are harmful, and in whose opinion. Perhaps the greatest impetus to the development of the field of bioethics and the notion of individual autonomy has been concern regarding unwanted interventions on the part of the medical profession.[14] Questions were being raised not only as to whether "enough" was being done, but whether "too much" was being done, whether recommended treatments were even for the benefit of the individual patient, for someone else's benefit, or purely for the advancement of medical science.[15] As technology has improved over the decades, these questions have become even more prevalent and more pressing.

Physicians and Rabbis Are Storytellers

Miles has pointed out that "physicians are storytellers" using methods such as grand rounds, in which historical background, symptoms, and clinical findings are reported to create a narrative that will lead to a diagnosis—in essence, an exegesis of the medical history.[16]

Just as physicians are storytellers, so are rabbis. The aggadic tradition is long and venerable. However, when told in the context of halakhic discourse, or ethical discourse couched in halakhic terms, stories are cited to exemplify or support halakhic positions. I believe that for many of the questions raised by modern medical situations, *aggadah* may be more helpful at arriving at decisions that are within the Jewish tradition than halakhic reasoning. It is in the nature of stories that they are open to multiple interpretations and invite the active participation of the listener, be she physician, patient, or family member. In the introduction to *Stories Matter*, Charon and Montello note that narrative "locates the work of bioethicists within a universal search for authentic human communion through language and an effort to create meaning in our lives."[17]

Stories transmit values rather than prescribe specific courses of action and are thus well suited to dilemmas where context is of utmost importance. I would argue, in fact, that stories are the primary way we transmit values to children and an important way we communicate them to our fellow human beings. I would suggest further that halakhic analysis, because it relies on precedent and casuistic reasoning, often uses ancient or medieval paradigms to deal with modern situations where the analogy is often tangential and forced.

It is a universally accepted principle in Jewish bioethics that it is not permissible to hasten a death, but it is permissible to remove an impediment to the dying process. Nearly every discussion that enunciates this principle cites two stories from the Talmud, the story of the execution of Rabbi Chanina ben Teradyon by the Romans and the story of the death of Rabbi Yehudah HaNasi. Although most citations note that *halakhah* (normative standards of behavior) cannot be derived from *aggadah* (narrative), the stories are often said to support and, one might argue, validate the principle that although it is not permissible to hasten death (actively), it is permissible to remove an impediment to death.

The Tale of Rabbi Yehudah HaNasi's Maid

The story of the death of Rabbi Yehudah HaNasi, the redactor of the Mishnah, related in the Babylonian Talmud, Tractate *Ketubot*, is one of the most well-known stories in Rabbinic literature and is often cited in discussions of end-of-life decision making, notably by the editor of this volume, Rabbi William Cutter.[18] I would like to examine this story in some detail and ask whether the principle cited above is the only interpretation or even a reasonable interpretation of the story, or whether it is an instance of *halakhah* as stated in the various codes retrojected back onto a Talmudic narrative. The story as usually presented is as follows:[19]

> On the day when Rabbi [Yehudah HaNasi] died, the Rabbis decreed a public fast and offered prayers for heavenly mercy.

They, furthermore, announced that whoever said that Rabbi was dead would be stabbed with a sword.

Rabbi's handmaid ascended the roof and prayed, "The immortals desire Rabbi [to join them] and the mortals desire Rabbi [to remain with them]; may it be the will [of God] that the mortals may overpower the immortals." When, however, she saw how often he resorted to the privy, painfully taking off his tefillin and putting them on again, she prayed: "May it be the will [of the Almighty] that the immortals may overpower the mortals." As the Rabbis incessantly continued their prayers for [heavenly] mercy, she took up a jar and threw it down from the roof to the ground. [For a moment] they ceased praying, and the soul of Rabbi departed to its eternal rest.

{"Go," said the Rabbis to Bar Kappara, "and investigate." He went, and finding that [Rabbi] was dead, he tore his cloak and turned the tear backwards. [On returning to the Rabbis] he began, "The angels and the mortals have taken hold of the holy ark. The angels overpowered the mortals and the holy ark has been captured." "Has he gone to his eternal rest?" they asked him. "You said it," he replied, "I did not say it."}

BABYLONIAN TALMUD, *KETUBOT* 104A

The protagonist of the story is Rabbi's handmaid. She is known from elsewhere in the Talmud to be a wise woman and one who is familiar with Rabbi. But looking only within the boundaries of this story, what do we know of her? Her vantage point is the roof, an elevated position, compared to both Rabbi and the disciples. It is in effect a godlike vantage point. In fact the Hebrew translated here as "immortals" is *elyonim*, literally "the elevated ones," the ones in the high place, to whom according to the narrator she is closest. Furthermore, her words are all in Hebrew in contrast to the narrator's Aramaic, a reflection of her greater authority. She observes a conflict between two groups, each desirous of Rabbi joining them, each concerned with their own wishes, not what is in the best interests of Rabbi or what his wishes would have been.

At the beginning of the narrative, the maid prays that the prayers of the disciples prevail. However, from her vantage point, where she has access to the big picture, she becomes aware of not only the disciples and the immortals but of Rabbi himself. Remarkably, we never actually hear his voice in this narrative, only the assessment of a woman who knows him well, who sees the situation not from the standpoint of her own needs and desires, but those of Rabbi. And what does she see? He is afflicted with an illness manifested by painful diarrhea, presumably some type of dysentery. He goes to the privy frequently, and each time he must remove his tefillin. The translation above suggests that the act of removing and replacing the tefillin is physically painful, but the Aramaic reads *v'halatz tefillin umanah lehu v'kamitzta'er*, literally, "he would remove his tefillin and put them on again and thereby he would suffer." Rabbi, it may be supposed, was a man who lived his life in intimate relationship with God, manifested and exemplified by the tefillin that he would wear during all his waking hours.[20] It is certainly plausible to understand this passage as saying that by having to spend so much of his time without his tefillin was a spiritual existence so diminished that it caused him great suffering. However, only the maid, who knew him well, recognized this. Once she recognized this suffering, her prayer changed. She now prayed that the prayers of the immortals prevail over the prayers of the disciples. For her this is still a contest between two groups, each looking after its own needs and desires. Notice, she doesn't add her own prayer to those of the immortals, nor does anything she says suggest that she can or should play a role in the outcome.

She throws a jar from the roof to the ground and the disciples interrupt their prayers, presumably because they are startled by the noise of the jar breaking. The presumption in the story is that she threw the jar down with just that end in mind, and the conclusion of those telling the story is that the maid, the heroine of the story, acted appropriately in removing an impediment to the death of Rabbi, namely the prayers of the disciples. But nowhere are we told her motivation or intention. It may be that having finally become aware of the suffering of Rabbi, both physical and spiritual, she became angry at her impotence to alleviate his suffering and in her frustration threw the jar off the roof. It is the first and only time in this brief narrative that anyone acts exclusively out of concern for Rabbi. I would suggest further that it is no mere coincidence that the protagonist is a woman or that the object broken is a jar, a clearly feminine allusion. After all, it could have been a brick, a stick, or a post she threw off the roof. But no, it is a jar, a womb, a symbol of nurturing, caring, and selflessness that is broken. She sees his suffering, feels helpless to alleviate it, and responds to that helplessness with an aggressive act.

The traditional interpretation, of course, is that the noise startled the disciples, who momentarily ceased their prayers, permitting Rabbi to die. Alternatively it may have been a signal to God, something like the sound of a shofar, and this is God's way of answering her prayer. God permits the immortals' prayers to prevail, perhaps by silencing the prayers of the disciples, or perhaps even more directly by causing Rabbi to die. Perhaps the noise of the shattering jar startles and shocks Rabbi so severely that it provokes his death.

The disciples, meanwhile, seem not to have learned or changed from the beginning of the story to the end. The story begins with them praying for heavenly mercy but does not make clear for whom or how that mercy would manifest itself. Is it mercy for Rabbi, and does that entail prolonging his life or ending his suffering? The former interpretation is that of the maid but is not explicit in the narrative. Or is it mercy for themselves, that they not lose their teacher? Furthermore, there is this strange statement that anyone who stated that Rabbi had already died would be killed with a sword. Is this magical thinking, that mere statement of a fact will render it true? Or is it that they live in a fantasy world where as long as they can believe that something is true, they can act on that belief and be comforted by the act? Whatever their motivation, it seems clear that it has nothing whatever to do with "the infinite value of human life." Furthermore, in light of my suggestion about the feminine symbolism of the jar, I believe it is no coincidence that the disciples' warning is that the one who claims that Rabbi has died will be run through by a sword.

In the coda to the story, Rabbi Kappara, the one who discovers the death, acts appropriately in rending his garment, but does so in a way that his appearance will not reveal to his cohort what has happened. He speaks symbolically of the holy ark (the repository of Torah and the source of its dissemination, i.e., Rabbi) being fought over by angels (*er'elim*) and the righteous on earth (*metzukim*), different terms than those used by the maid, and perhaps a bit self-serving. In any event, the disciples learn the truth of Rabbi's death, and as far as we know, no one is stabbed.

Halakhah and Aggadah

The law concerning a *goseis* as stated in the *Shulchan Arukh* reads:

> A *goseis* is (to be considered) like a living person in all respects. One does not bind his jaw, anoint him, purge him, stop up his orifices, remove his pillow, nor place him on the sand, floor, or ground. One does not place a plate on his belly, nor a bit of salt. The announcement [of death] is not made, nor flute players or mourners hired. And one does not close his eyes until he has died. Anyone who closes another's eyes at the moment the *nefesh* is leaving has shed blood. One does not tear one's clothing, remove one's shoes, give a eulogy or bring a casket into the house where the dying person is located until the person has died. And one does not recite *tzidduk ha-din* until the *nefesh* has gone out.
>
> SHULCHAN ARUKH, YOREH DEAH 339:1

And Isserles' gloss on the above affirms the principle that one may remove the impediment to death, even though one may not hasten death actively. Is this a principle or value found in the story of Rabbi's maid? If so, is it the only plausible one? And if not, do the narrative and the *nomos* have any relationship at all? And finally, how can either of them provide any guidance in dealing with end-of-life dilemmas? Cutter, in his discussion of this story, notes that "the prayers [of the disciples] can be defined, in the later halakhic language, as an impediment (a *mone'a*) to the dying process."[21] That is, the idea that the prayers are an impediment to the dying process is one that becomes normative only in support of halakhic dictates.

Since the law cited above deals specifically with a *goseis*, an initial question to ask is, is Rabbi a *goseis* in this story? A *goseis* is a person who is actively dying.[22] It is clear that a *goseis* is more corpselike than living being–like. Rabbi, on the other hand, is in and out of the privy, is putting tefillin on and taking them off. Nothing about the way he is described remotely suggests that he is a *goseis*. The only part of the story that might imply this is the disciples' warning that no one state that he is dead, similar to the prohibition in the *Shulchan Arukh* that one does not announce the death of a *goseis* before he has died.

Any similarity of the so-called impediments—feathers of certain birds, a nearby woodchopper, salt on the tongue—to the prayers of the disciples is doubtful. Their only similarity, it would seem, is their lack of efficacy. More importantly, whether the impediments suggested have any relevance whatever to any of the modalities or interventions we are faced with in modern times—respirators, pacemakers, feeding tubes, dialysis, ventricular assist devices—is even more doubtful. The relationship between the provisions in the codes and modern end-of-life questions is a matter for another, more detailed discussion. Suffice it to say, the analogy between the values embodied in the story and the principle stated in the codes is tenuous at best.

What then can we take to be the values of this story? First, be realistic! Do not look at the world as you would wish it to be, but as it is. Second, step back and look at the big picture! Look at the person about whom you may have to make a decision, empathize, and take all you know about the person and the world into account. Act! If you are the one who knows what the person would want, do not hesitate to act on that knowledge. There is considerable debate among bioethicists regarding the appropriateness of the "best interests" standard (*letovato*) as compared to the "substituted judgment" standard (*bim'komo*). If we understand the action of the maid as intended to cause/allow Rabbi to die and his suffering to end, it could be a manifestation of either of these standards or even a combination of both of them.

Aggadah, story, narrative, has from the very beginning of Jewish tradition served to articulate matters that defy statement in rigorous philosophical form. Fiction teaches truths accessible in no other way; it has long helped Jews, adopting Heschel's words, to take up the lessons learned from experience and "tell [them] to our minds."[23]

I agree with Peter Knobel, who has argued that "most contemporary Jews are not halakhic in their approach to Judaism."[24] Few could argue with this proposition. And yet, while I consider myself to be a halakhic Jew, I often find that in the realm of bioethics specifically, *halakhah* is often at odds with my life experience, in general, and my experience as a physician, in particular. In his response to Knobel,

Newman notes that "just as most liberal American Jews have rejected the divine authority behind Halacha, they have similarly rejected the same authority behind the aggadah."[25] He makes a straw-man argument against *aggadah*, presupposing that divine authorship, which could at most apply to biblical or Toraitic narrative in any event, is the source of its authority and value. I would suggest instead that the value and authority of these stories is not that they are of divine origin but that they are Jewish. They contain and transmit Jewish values, and many of the nonhalakhic or "posthalakhic" Jews to whom Knobel and Newman refer want to be guided by Jewish ideas and values in these very difficult decisions.

Moreover, Cutter points out, citing Bruner, that "there are two irreducible modes of cognitive functioning.... One seeks explications that are context-free and universal, the other seeks explications that are context-sensitive and particular."[26] Bioethical dilemmas in the clinical setting are always context-sensitive and particular, as are issues of public policy.

In addition to making the case for the value of narrative in Jewish bioethics, however, it is necessary to address the role of *halakhah*, which has been for generations of Jews the gold standard for ethical decisions. In areas of modern end-of-life decision making, *halakhah* has several drawbacks. There is the danger of taking directives too literally. For example, the *Shulchan Arukh* states explicitly that a *goseis*, a dying person, should not be moved, yet can we really argue that a dying person should not be moved to prevent the development of pressure sores, or to be cleaned, or to relieve positional discomfort?

More importantly, however, many of the situations envisioned in medieval writing are too dissimilar to what we encounter in modern medicine to be of analogic value. The paradigm of the *goseis* has been cited by most *poskim*, halakhic decisors, as the basis of decisions regarding treatment at the end of life. Some state that discontinuation of a ventilator in a terminally ill patient is tantamount to murder. Others base their permission to discontinue use of a ventilator on the notion that it is conceptually the removal of an impediment to the dying process à la Isserles.[27] But is the paradigm of the *goseis* even appropriate?

The classical understanding of the term is that a *goseis* will die within three days of attaining that status. In the modern era, with the medical interventions currently in use, a time-based understanding of *gesisah* is anachronistic. Rather, I believe the term should be applied to those actively dying.[28] This phase of the dying process is characterized by specific patterns of breathing, changes in level of consciousness, secretions, skin-color changes, bowel- and bladder-function changes, and more. It generally lasts a matter of hours to a day or two, and health-care workers who regularly care for dying patients recognize when patients enter this final phase. This seems to me to be what the Rabbis were referring to by the term *goseis*. Many, perhaps most, people who die in modern times never go through the period of being a *goseis*.

My personal narrative includes the experience and extraordinary privilege of being part of a family vigil when my maternal grandmother and both my parents died at home. They died after long illnesses, having made the decision not to medicalize the end of their lives by having it occur in the context of an ICU. Those experiences, in addition to those of the dying patients I cared for as a young physician, made it clear to me that active dying is a distinct and recognizable phase of the dying process. The literature referred to above describes, defines, and clarifies active dying in order to guide caregivers, but in terms of recognition, even for laypeople, it is like Justice Potter Stewart's comment about pornography—you know it when you see it.[29] In my view, ventilator-dependent patients enter this phase only *after* discontinuation of the use of the ventilator, and the halakhic paradigm of the *goseis* is of no help in deciding whether or not to discontinue use of the ventilator.

Some might suggest that I am unfairly citing poorly done casuistry. That may be so. Nevertheless, it seems to me that narrative, *aggadah*, may be useful because it transmits values rather than rules and is open to multiple interpretations. *Aggadah* can offer guidance that may be helpful for many of today's Jews who do not feel bound by *halakhah* and who may distrust authority figures in general, but who still want to be guided by and act within a broadly Jewish framework.

Those who, like Newman, prefer a halakhic approach argue that "stories are rich and ambiguous and subject to multiple readings," and that even if a given interpretation could be agreed upon, it would not identify a specific course of action to be pursued.[30] The same criticism can of course be leveled against the halakhic approach. How else may we explain diametrically opposing attitudes toward the diagnosis of brain death, or removal of ventilatory support in dependent patients, or the withholding or withdrawing of artificial hydration and nutrition, to cite but a few examples.

In the end it may be the very ambiguity of the story that is its most valuable characteristic, that and the fact that stories by their very nature are, like the problems we face in the bioethical realm, context-sensitive. As Abraham Joshua Heschel wrote in his remarkable essay "The Patient as Person": "Physical vigor alone does not constitute total health. Nor is longevity the only purpose of living. Quality of living is as important as quantity of living."[31]

Autonomy Revisited

Finally, for those of us for whom the metaphor of God's ownership does not work, I would suggest substituting the metaphor of a gift. We find this notion in our prayer book: our morning prayers begin with the statement *Elohai neshamah shenatata bi tehorah hi*, "God, the soul You have given me is pure." We find it in the Psalms: *Ha-shamayim shamayim l'Adonai v'ha'aretz natan livnei adam*, "The heavens are for *Adonai*, but the earth God gave to human beings" (Psalm 115:16). We would still feel obligated to care for our physical selves, not because they are the property of another, but because they are the gift of a beloved. The difference is that as a gift, a gift intended to be of finite duration, they belong to us, and we bear the responsibility of making decisions regarding how to treat this precious gift. Charon and Montello make the point in their introduction to *Stories Matter* that "a narrative approach focuses on the patients themselves: these are the moral agents who enact choices."[32] Maimonides recognized that his job as a physician was not to control his patients' decisions but to give them the information necessary to make decisions for themselves, right or wrong. That is as close to a contemporary understanding of autonomy as I can imagine.

Jonathan Cohen, PhD, is associate professor in Talmud and halakhic literature at Hebrew Union College–Jewish Institute of Religion in Cincinnati and director of Hebrew Union College–University of Cincinnati Center for the Study of Ethics and Contemporary Moral Problems.

Jewish Bioethics
Between Interpretation and Criticism

Jonathan Cohen, PhD

Jewish Bioethics, *Halakhah,* and *Aggadah*: Setting the Stage

Jewish bioethics is at something of a crossroads. It is now a recognizable academic and applied discipline that attracts the interest and involvement of members of all Jewish streams and denominations. Yet, the relationship between Judaism and ethics remains subject to debate. For centuries, if not millennia, the dominant voice of normative Judaism has been *halakhah* (Jewish law). These days, Jewish bioethicists seek to speak using "Jewish voices," to use established terms and categories, and to anchor their contributions in Rabbinic tradition. At the same time, many reject the normative claims entailed in *halakhah*, and seek nuanced yet less authoritative, nonbinding forms of Jewish discourse. Increasingly, Jewish bioethicists resort to Jewish narrative in general, and *aggadah* in particular, to engage with medical issues. In the spirit of dialogue with Rabbi Leonard Sharzer, I argue that this use of *aggadah* can be as problematic and controversial as the reference to *halakhah*.

The argument is inspired by the writings of Geoffrey Hartman, a noted scholar and critic of reading. Hartman suggests that both oral discourse and reading can be comforting and difficult, healing and wounding, and that our engagement with text is therefore suspenseful and ambivalent. The impact of the reader's engagement with words is largely dependent on one's approach; it is a function of the willingness or capacity to experience the challenges that words represent. The focus then shifts to interpretation and to the suggestion of an analogy between legal interpretation and clinical decision making and health-care policy discussion. The conclusion to this chapter highlights the relevance of preceding observations to the engagement in Jewish bioethics. The purpose of this contribution is not to reinforce one par-ticular tendency or to present a definitive position in this debate, but to emphasize the potential contribution of literary criticism and certain aspects of legal theory to the ongoing conversation.[1]

On Reading, Healing, and Wounding

In "Words and Wounds," a prominent chapter of his important book *Saving the Text*, Geoffrey Hartman addresses our ears' vulnerability to words that we cannot block or filter and the function of language in healing the wounds that words themselves create. Describing the kinds of wounds words can inflict, Hartman explains that "the word-wound may be *real* in the sense of *being ... actually experienced* or fan-tasied."[2] Further, the implications of the word-wound should not be underestimated; it may alter the hearer's self-understanding and engagement with the world. In some cases, oppression serves to release the potential genius.[3]

Not only is the violent impact of the word-wound potentially life-altering, Hartman explains that it transcends the pure auditory func-tion. Reading is an activity filled with suspense because we constantly recall the pain inflicted upon us by words and anticipate being wounded again in the process of reading. As Hartman explains, while reading we simultaneously seek and try to avoid the injurious word that may present itself to us, knowing that we are destined to fail.[4] Indeed, reading can be perceived as healing and comforting; at the same time, it is both suspenseful and dangerous.

The complexity, tension, perhaps even danger, in our encounter with words figure prominently in the lectures of Yish'ayahu Leibowitz. In one lecture on life guided by the commandments, he describes the required mindset for approaching the words of Torah.

Concerns with the ethical value and implications of Torah are pursuits that characterize the atheist, he argues. Ethics cannot constitute the criteria or evaluative tools of the believer who recognizes the presence of his Creator at all times. In his analysis, all ethical systems require action on the basis of one of two assessments: either the call of inner duty and conscience or the observation of truth in one's reality. Leibowitz identifies Immanuel Kant as the leading advocate of the former, and Socrates as a principal proponent of the latter. However, Leibowitz reminds us, the Torah requires that we follow neither our hearts—that is, our sense of duty or conscience—nor our eyes—our assessment of reality. Rather, as the text we repeat daily elucidates, the exclusion of the eyes and the heart occurs because "I am the Lord your God" (Numbers 15:39–41). In other words, true submission to the Word of God requires its elevation beyond ethical (and for that matter all other) considerations and values. Leibowitz's description is interesting because it would shut out both the inner voice of conscience (the "heart"), and the audible challenge coming from without (the "eyes"). The safety that Leibowitz's focused, directed approach to God's words aims to achieve would certainly lend itself to internalization or identification with the claims made upon the believer in the sacred, revealed text.[5] Yet, this intimate, religious reading also exacts a cost: the conscious exclusion of those sounds and voices that we are accustomed to hearing; sounds that we seek, that we have been conditioned to seek, and that sometimes wound us. To Leibowitz, acceptance of the yoke of Torah requires safety. There is safety, in other words, in yielding.

Hartman associates a similar notion of safety and intimacy with Christian hermeneutics. Commenting on chapter 13 in the fourth part of *Anna Karenina*, he focuses on the exchange between Kitty and Levin. There, understanding is achieved *in spite* of the awkwardness of language, the fear entailed in wielding it and exposing yourself, and the consequent difficulty in expressing your thoughts. Hartman comments on the understanding achieved between Kitty and Levin, a connection that transcends words and argument. In this example, the extraordinary communication between Levin and Kitty renders unnecessary the "enormous expenditure" entailed in argument and represents an overcoming of the fear associated with exposure of yourself through words. Hartman proposes that for Tolstoy "religious as well as ... erotic intimacy ... bases capable understanding on a *pre-understanding* associated with benevolence."[6] However, if understanding requires a connection before words are ever uttered, he points out, "the result is that words become mere tokens. The lovers exchange glances as well as words, and the context points to something beyond speech. Here [in Levin and Kitty's meeting] as the language exchange is restituted, words are paradoxically left behind."[7]

There are differences between Tolstoy's sense of communicative intimacy and the prescription for religious commitment outlined by Leibowitz, and there are also noteworthy resemblances. In contrast to Tolstoy, Leibowitz identifies the Word as the exclusive and indispensable means to realize the Jewish (religious) experience. Yet, both Tolstoy and Leibowitz offer responses to the difficulty involved in achieving understanding, and both present preconditions for intimate communication to succeed. Further, both reflect a need to minimize the potential wound that may be generated in our encounter with the word, and both construct a sense of safety that becomes associated with and reinforces this encounter.

Reading, Safe Reading, and Regulation: Between Criticism and Interpretation

If for Leibowitz the revealed Word and our approach to it are key, Hartman highlights the need for emotional connection that transcends verbal exchange. As he explains, whether or not they agree, Levin and Kitty understand each other. Levin's yearning for happiness and contentment with others, realized in this set of exchanges with Kitty, is coupled with his disclosure that he misses music. Hartman points out that Levin's need for community and understanding as well as his interest in music are not merely coincidental. He explains, "The recurrence of music as theme or metaphor ... reminds us that interpretation is not an argument that resolves arguments or dissolves words. It brings understanding without agreement, or charts the very space between understanding and agreement."[8]

The implications of the differing approaches to the word are far-reaching, and it is hardly possible to do them justice in these few pages. Yet, Hartman does us great service when he refers to a historical distinction between the interpreter and the critic. He writes:

> The Interpreter was often defined as someone who translated strange or unknown tongues into edifying idiom, or who could bring contradictory words and aspects of a text into harmony. The Critic was often defined as one who distinguished the authentic text from the inauthentic, or authentic from inauthentic in a text. What has happened is that those who call themselves interpreters now claim an edifying or reconciling function even when the language of the text is well known; while the critics adopt a methodically suspicious or doubtful attitude toward the value of every text, secular or sacred.[9]

Herein lies a great challenge for Jewish bioethics: writers and practitioners must exhibit greater self-reflection and transparency regarding their own engagements with Jewish text. Leibowitz's reading of the Word would likely be closer to Hartman's interpretation. Yet Leibowitz himself would expect the normative ethicist to subject the sacred text to the test of "higher values," to those injurious voices, and to the critic's skepticism. He would expect it and reject it.

Robert Cover and Michel Foucault: On Violence, the Law, and Bioethics

To some, the concern with bioethicists' readings of the Jewish tradition's textual resources may seem "academic" or detached from the contribution of practitioners to the exercise and regulation of medicine and to patients' experiences. In partial response, setting aside arguments regarding the implications of reading, let us ground Jewish bioethics firmly within the field of normative ethics. In other words, let it be clear that as Leibowitz's reading of Torah informs his approach to God and humankind, normative ethics is also "prescriptive rather than descriptive and seeks to grapple with live moral issues and to come to normative conclusions about them."[10] To the extent that Jewish bioethics addresses decision making in clinical settings and policy debates regarding care and research, it too constitutes a normative discipline.

The implication is that the wound or potential wound entailed in the engagement with Jewish bioethics transcends the encounter with the Word. Indeed, following Robert Cover's observation that "legal interpretation takes place in a field of pain and death,"[11] we may argue that the practice of medicine may be similarly characterized and, by extension, the work of the bioethicist as well. In the context of this short essay, it is both impossible and unnecessary to fully articulate the strengths and weaknesses of the analogy between the legal interpreter and Jewish bioethicist. Yet there is value in describing certain aspects of it and highlighting its potential value.

Two main objections may be raised to an analogy between the legal interpreter and the health-care professional or advocate. First, it may be argued that the jurist, and especially the judge engaged in sentencing—the focus of Cover's essay—deals in sanctioned repression, in the assignment of guilt and its consequences. In contrast, the care provider seeks to improve the patient's condition or quality of life regardless of personal attributes or past actions. Or, it may be said that the judge's utterance directs the punitive powers of the state against an individual, while the health-care team and those who support it try to release the victim from the oppressive, punitive grip of illness. After all, medical professionals commit themselves to beneficence and the avoidance of maleficence.[12] Although we cannot do justice to this objection here, it is nevertheless important to briefly address it. To begin, we may note that mental health care and the violence or societal repression it has entailed has been attracting considerable attention over the past two generations.[13] Foucault also expresses concerns with regard to centralizing and decentralizing tendencies in the development of modern, institutional medicine and the transformation of the doctor-patient relationship.[14] In a passage that describes medical decentralization and the function of the local physician in early modern France, he writes of the increasingly quasi-judicial function of the doctor. The medical profession, he argues, would acquire more pronounced distributive and policy-making capabilities, and these necessarily entail moral judgment.[15]

While the roles of physicians and other health-care professionals have evolved (especially in the United States), centralizing and decentralizing tendencies continue to exercise their powers over medicine and its administration and regulation. To date, the distributive aspects of medicine retain a political, sometimes quasi-judicial quality.[16] It can hardly be denied that medicine is shaped by socioeconomic, political, and otherwise ideological environments and that its exercise is not a neutral, objective activity. Where the allocation of lifesaving resources to a patient necessitates the privation of another, the association of doctor with magistrate becomes more credible. Needless to elaborate, a number of medical practices and procedures, ranging from selective reduction in multifetal pregnancies to the administering of certain kinds of palliation toward the end of life, entail judgment, prioritization, and a balancing of benefit and harm on the part of physicians and other care providers. Each instance of this kind of balancing of wellness and suffering occurs in a medical or medicalized context that generates meaning and entails quasi-judicial characteristics, as well as decisions that are potentially life altering, life enhancing, and life diminishing.

A second objection that may be raised to this analogy regards the discrepancy between the legal interpreter's power over the life of the accused and the autonomy that characterizes the patient. The accused standing before the judge faces the overwhelming force of the state and is no longer in control of his destiny. On the other hand, the patient meeting the doctor presumably can reject medical advice, refuse treatment, and sometimes insist on the continuation of therapy against medical advice. While the judge may be seen as directly causing the pain of the accused, the physician's contribution to medical decision making is more difficult to define. Cover's study focuses on judicial interpretation and its seamless association with a range of mechanisms that threaten or inflict institutional, state-sponsored violence, the kind of force that judges rarely witness or experience and that may be ignored in the activity of legal interpretation. Physicians typically cannot wield such force and are often exposed (at least to some degree) to the consequences of their administration of treatment. The stark contrast in the levels of autonomy enjoyed by the convict and patient suggests that the relationships of judge–accused and physician–patient are incomparable. Yet, Cover himself indicates that a concentration on the judge engaged in sentencing, or judge–accused relationship, would be too narrow. He writes:

> Legal interpretation may be the act of judges or citizens, legisla-
> tors or president, draft resisters or right-to-life protesters. Each
> kind of interpreter speaks from a distinct institutional location.
> Each has a differing perspective on factual and moral implica-
> tions of any given understanding of the constitution ... consider-
> ations of word, deed, and role will always be present in some
> degree. The relationships among these three considerations are
> created by the practical, violent context of the practice of legal
> interpretation.[17]

In other words, the engagement of various stakeholders in the debate over legal interpretation generates an "ecology" or framework of social cooperation and dependence that lends coherence to acts of legal interpretation. At the same time, it is anchored in the practical, violent implications of these interpretive acts. The same may be said of the contributions of physicians, other medical professionals, administrators, patients, and advocates to the system of health care. Our engagement with and participation in it lend health-care practices coherence or meaning; at the same time, their context is the pervasive reality of the struggle with suffering and death and the violence and potential violence entailed in the experience lived in clinical settings. The judge's interpretive act may be readily identifiable as a cause of the now-powerless convict's punishment. However, Cover teaches, even where causation cannot be established, participation in legal interpretation only makes sense in the context of what the law does. Similarly, even assuming autonomy and an implied lack of formal authority to impose particular procedures upon the patient, participation in health care and its "interpretation," including that of chaplains, advocates, and ethicists, is anchored in the continuum of suffering and healing, in what health care does.

Halakhah, Aggadah, and Jewish Bioethics: Reading and Communicating Our Tradition

If Jewish bioethicists were to demonstrate greater reflection and sensitivity in their encounter with the oral-written tradition, they would perhaps also highlight our participation in the complex of suffering and healing that characterizes the practice of medicine. Yet, a direction increasingly explored among scholars and practitioners risks under-emphasizing the impact of Jewish tradition's presence in the clinic. The danger is of Jewish bioethicists' excessive leaning toward a discursive exchange that grows ever more remote from its organic and violent context and that regulates our engagement with tradition to render it safer, less painful. The resort to a corpus of Rabbinic narrative, *aggadah*, as a platform for participation in this complex of suffering and healing (widely construed) is symptomatic of this approach. A number of scholars, and surely my partner in this book's dialogue, appropriately identify aggadic materials as intricate and open to a variety of interpretations, and—most important—to a communication that favors values or sensibilities over particular rules of conduct. Also, the exploitation of *aggadah* in Jewish bioethics reflects two observations that are both astute and valuable. On the one hand, nowadays most North American Jews reject *halakhah*'s own claims of authority as well as halakhic reasoning and rules as a firm basis for medical decisions. On the other, as we already noted, during the last two generations, health-care professionals have increasingly emphasized patient autonomy and relinquished the prerogative to act in the patient's best interest. Thus, while Jewish patients seek new ways to integrate their religious identities with medical experiences, the task of Jewish health-care professionals, clergy, and bioethicists is to promote such integration and encourage the Jewish growth it may entail. With this aim in mind, Jewish exploration is deemed more productive than an evaluation of potential treatments or any pronouncement of permissibility or prohibition.

While the use of aggadic material bears great promise, it must also attract a note of caution. To begin, it is worthwhile to recall that narrative can change readers' lives and alter their behaviors. Stories can "make us do things," rather than merely influence our worldviews or inform general principles and values that guide our action. It almost goes without saying that the impact of stories on behavior is highly dependent on readers' engagements and situations.[18] Narrative can also be constructed or presented in specific ways to engage particular readers, or to promote the reader's friendship with the implied author. American literary critic Wayne Booth writes:

Our fullest friendships are with those who seem wholly engaged in the same kind of significant activity that they expect of us.... Most of the great stories show characters of a moral quality roughly equal to that of the implied reader ... the plots are built out of the characters' efforts to face moral choices. In tracing those efforts, we readers stretch our own capacities for thinking about how lives should be lived, as we join those more elevated judges, the implied authors. We cannot quite consider ourselves *their* equals: they are more skillful than we at providing such exercise in moral discernment. But they imply that we might become their equals in discernment if we only practiced long enough.[19]

Further, the construction of such relationships with or in readers in large measure is a product of the able author-storyteller's set of strategic choices. The story is built, constructed, refined.[20]

The same characteristics may also describe Rabbinic narratives. An *aggadah* may have a powerful impact, to the point of altering the listener's conduct or behavior, depending on her engagement and situation. The student's reaction to the story of the death of Rabbi Yehudah HaNasi in class discussion may differ from that of the hospital-bound daughter of a sedated patient who is nourished and hydrated by machines and who requires assistance in breathing. Indeed, the influence of the storyteller's tale in a clinical setting may be greater than the teaching of any halakhic rule. The selection of the story and its delivery are never free of context and often reflect pragmatic, tactical choices, rather than preferences that are grounded in one's perception of the contemporary status of *halakhah* and *aggadah*.

Perhaps more important, *aggadah* may serve its presenter in creating a "literary friendship" with the listener in ways that could not be achieved in the context of a pronouncement of halakhic rules. The type of encounter engineered through the use of Rabbinic narrative would plausibly generate a safe space or sense of common purpose between the storyteller and listener, perhaps almost a "pre-understanding." The Rabbinic story could be their meeting ground and medium toward a measure of intimacy and sharing. As in every encounter, here too this imagined hospital conference-room meeting would be choreographed. In clinical settings, this approach would be more likely to give rise to a reading that is closer to Hartman's interpretation and more distant from criticism. The question we would have to ask is not "What corpus of Jewish text is employed in this setting (*halakhah* or *aggadah*)?" but rather "How do we read the text?" *Aggadah* may well be the material preferred, but it might be employed as halakhic material would be in the hands of an able rabbi in conversations with Orthodox or ultra-Orthodox patients and relatives. The narrative could well be communicated in ways that suggest prescription and be stripped of its richness and openness. This would plausibly occur in settings of constraint, violence, and pain, as well as a profound thirst for healing and comfort. In short, *aggadah* would no longer be *aggadah* as our Sages understood it, and something of it would be lost.

In other words, we must consider how we describe our connection with the Jewish tradition and our communication of its messages as bioethicists, especially but not exclusively in clinical contexts. There is likely no simple answer to this question. Yet, the temptation to achieve communion and understanding on matters relating to health care using a Jewish voice, as strong and seductive as it is, must not lead toward a shortcut. Jewish bioethics is an evolving, growing field that now requires a conversation about the import of the words of our tradition to health care and to debates about it. Recent explorations of *halakhah*, *aggadah*, and their contemporary functions constitute a solid foundation for such a conversation.

10

What Takes Place and What Can Be Changed

Rabbi Julie Pelc Adler is the director of Jewish student life at Santa Monica College Hillel and serves as the director of the Berit Mila Program of Reform Judaism. She is coeditor of the anthology *Joining the Sisterhood: Young Jewish Women Write Their Lives.*

A Midrash on the *Mi Sheberakh*
A Prayer for Persisting

Rabbi Julie Pelc Adler

During rabbinical school, I spent more time in doctors' offices than in classrooms. Whereas initially my illness was "acute," and the traditional *Mi Sheberakh* and other prayers for a *refuah shleimah* were appropriate, the years of recovery and the resulting permanent disability no longer qualified for such a hope or wish.

At a prescribed moment during Jewish formal prayer, throughout the world, the Torah is unrolled and the reader pauses so that prayers for healing might be offered. The *Mi Sheberakh* is offered by individuals and communities: hearts and sanctuaries overflowing with requests for healing of body and healing of spirit. Sometimes people carry long lists of names inside their hearts, and sometimes on lists in their pockets, looking forward to this prayer when their aching list of names becomes public.

Although the prayer itself differs from one community to the next, the need for this ritual remains constant. There is never a dearth of ill people, nor of people wishing to pray for their healing. The text of the traditional *Mi Sheberakh* requests "complete healing, healing of the soul and healing of the body, along with all the ill among the people of Israel—soon, speedily, without delay." There are variations on this prayer, but that is the template.

I think of my co-worker with diabetes, of a friend with chronic fatigue syndrome, of an aunt struggling with clinical depression, and a classmate with ulcerative colitis. I have acquaintances living with HIV.

I think of my own incomplete recovery. To pray for "complete healing" for those whose ailments cannot or will not ever be completely "healed" or "cured" seems audacious and perhaps even offensive. My co-workers, colleagues, family, friends, and I will negotiate medications, doctor's appointments, dietary needs, and fears for the rest of our lives. We will face unanticipated side effects, professional and personal repercussions from our special needs, and stigma from many well-meaning strangers every day. Our everyday reality is one of incomplete health; yet we are not entirely sick, either.

I believe we need a new congregational prayer that acknowledges the reality of chronic illness, asking God for the strength to persist even in the face of challenges that may seem insurmountable. Such a prayer might ask that we be granted the courage to continue in life even as we face the reality of our death; to rage and to praise, to bless and to curse, to accept and to reject diagnoses simultaneously.

Fragments of this prayer exist already in our liturgical and scriptural inheritance. The creation of a new prayer, modeled upon and paralleling the traditional *Mi Sheberakh*, is a liturgical process of midrash. In our traditional *Mi Sheberakh*, we invoke blessings upon the ill people in the names of our biblical ancestors. Abraham, Isaac and Jacob, Sarah, Rebecca, Rachel and Leah are invoked less for any particular connection to healing and health, and more because of our general tradition to turn to their memories in prayer as a reminder to God of *zekhut avot*, "the merits of our ancestors," for which we ought to receive special grace.

Moses, Aaron, David, and Solomon may also be invoked for *zekhut avot*, but some of them are associated in their respective texts with healing and prayers for healing. Thus, the idea comes that a prayer for persistence might do well to invoke those individuals, families, and groups of people whose narratives we read in the *Tanakh* (Hebrew Bible) and whose struggles with obstacles that seemed to be insurmountable.

There is a tradition of invoking names from the tradition that are associated with experiences of ill health and recovery.[1] To borrow the language of comparative midrash, just as we invoke David for healing prayers, even so we may invoke him (and Jonathan, his companion) for persistence in love and loyalty in the face of persecution; just as we invoke there Moses, a prophet, for healing prayers, even so we invoke here Daniel, a prophet, for persistence of faith in the face of danger; even as we invoke there Solomon, a king, in our healing prayer, even so we invoke here Tamar, ancestress of kings, for her persistence in the face of injustice and discommodation; just as we invoke there Aaron, the High Priest, for his healing remedies, even so we invoke here Hannah, who was blessed by the High Priest, for her persistence in the face of despair.

We may choose to invoke their names as our spiritual, emotional, and psychological ancestors, in whose name God might bring peace, comfort, strength, and courage to us. In doing so, we create parallels with the traditional prayer for healing; we establish a chain of linkage between the one prayer and the other. This makes clear that these are potentially two liturgical texts in relationship to one another. It also provides a certain pattern of familiarity, such that (one hopes) the new prayer "feels" traditional to the average congregant, and seems like a natural liturgical response to their life situation.

Praying in the name of Jacob,[2] Jonathan and David,[3] Daniel,[4] Tamar,[5] and Hannah,[6] here is one possible construct for a new *Mi Sheberakh* for an individual who is chronically ill—if not simply used in the traditional congregational setting, possibly best used in a pastoral setting, quietly, with that person present in the room:

May the One who blessed our fathers and our mothers, bless _____, son/daughter of _____: strengthen his/her heart and raise up his/her hand, with the blessings you gave to Jacob, to Jonathan and David, to Daniel the Prophet, to Tamar mother of Peretz, and to Hannah.

May God give to him/her grace, compassion, and loving-kindness; might to his/her hand, wisdom to his/her heart, and the strength to live a life of honor and peace.

Speedily, *Adonai* our God, hear our voices, take up our prayers, and watch over his/her life force, spirit, and soul. With respect to your power, your loving-kindness, and your great compassion, behold we say to him/her: be strong and of good courage; only be strong and of good courage.[7] May the Source of all Blessing bless him/her, and bless all the People Israel quickly and for the good, and let us say: amen.

The prayer can also be adjusted according to the type of illness or the particular wishes of that specific person for whom the prayer is being offered. (Example: "May the One who blessed our foremother Hannah, who struggled so bitterly with infertility and misunderstanding, also be with our friend, *Esther, daughter of Reuven v'Elisheva*, with the blessing of a satisfying resolution to her struggle, and the support she needs from others.")

In a nonpastoral setting or as part of a normative synagogue service, another option is to alter the prayer slightly to shift this individual prayer to the plural. This means that all of those members of a community will be therein blessed, without calling undue attention to them as individuals (and to avoid the problem of praying for each individual who is chronically ill for the rest of their lives).

Another liturgical inclusion in a congregational blessing for those struggling with chronic illness might be the following:

> As we complete one book of the Torah and proceed to the next, it is traditional to stand and to say aloud, in unison, *chazak, chazak, v'nitchazek*, meaning "Strength! Strength! And we shall all be strengthened." Let us append this wish to the end of this blessing, adding it to our *Amen*.

These original liturgical forms are particularly well suited to the synagogue communities that Richard Address has so often helped create and inspire.

These are only a few of the potential sources we might use to create a prayer for those who struggle with illnesses that *cannot* be fully and completely healed. Advances in modern medicine have made it possible to live many weeks, months, and years while still engaged in the realities of chronic illness and pain. Jewish tradition is ripe with resources of comfort, of supplication, and of hope that might bring light into the world of those who suffer. It is our obligation to help to make a renewed Jewish practice, using the midrashic and liturgical tools of our tradition, to create new experiences and devices that nonetheless resonate with traditional Jewish rite and ritual.

Rabbi Richard Address, DMin, serves as the specialist-consultant on the synagogue as a caring community and on Jewish family issues for the Union for Reform Judaism. He teaches at Hebrew Union College–Jewish Institute of Religion in New York. As part of his work on "sacred aging," he created and edits the website www.jewishsacredaging.com.

The Human Body and the Body Politic

Rabbi Richard Address, DMin

Jewish tradition urges us to take care of our bodies. Our literature is filled with calls to be careful what we eat and to practice proper hygiene. The foundation for this concern was to enable us to stand in a more healthy relationship with God. In this way, it was not our contemporary understanding of health that was the primary motivation to care for our bodies. Regardless of the motivation, the concern with health and the role it plays in our relationships with self and God remains a legitimate religious concern. The following classic midrash demonstrates this point:

> A story is told of Hillel that when he had finished a lesson with his pupils, he accompanied them from the classroom. They said, "Master, where are you going?" He answered, "To perform a religious duty." "Which duty is that?" they asked. "To bathe in the bathhouse," replied Hillel. The students asked, "Is this a religious obligation?" Hillel replied, "If somebody is appointed to scrape and clean the statues of the king that are set up in the theaters and circuses and is paid to do the work, and furthermore, associates with the nobility, how much the more so should I, who am created in the divine image and likeness, take care of my body."
>
> LEVITICUS RABBAH 34:3

The intersection of Judaism and health, both physical and mental, dates from the *Tanakh* (Hebrew Bible), and obligations to God have taken on different contours with each age of Jewish history. They are reflected in halakhic rulings and in prayer. One need look no further than the morning blessing upon going to the bathroom, which gives thanks that everything that needs to open does open. The veins and arteries work and so we are able to stand in life before God for another day.

> *Blessed is* Adonai *our God, Sovereign of the universe*
> *With divine wisdom You have made our bodies*
> *Combining veins, arteries, and vital organs*
> *Into a finely balanced network.*
> *Wondrous Maker and sustainer of life,*
> *Were one of these to fail—how well we are aware!—*
> *We would lack the strength to stand in life before You.*
> *Blessed are You,* Adonai
> *Source of our health and strength.*

As this beautiful blessing affirms, it is a "miracle" that the intricately balanced network of our bodies works as well as it does. We are aware that if that which is supposed to open does not, or that which is supposed to close does not, we would be in pain. The "miracle" is a testament to God's wisdom, and thus the harmonious working of our bodies allows us to be in a fundamental relationship with God.

Concerns about health exist as a major motif throughout Jewish history. The intimate relationship between medicine and Judaism has been detailed at great length. Often the great contributions of Jewish physicians had to be measured against the host Christian and Islamic cultures. This relationship between Judaism, medicine, and healing has, at times, even been used, in a manipulative and political manner, to support anti-Semitism. In a fascinating little book titled *The Healthy Jew*, author Mitchell B. Hart traces how the Jewish involvement with health was sometimes used against a Jewish community. Hart notes that images of the Jews were often portrayed by anti-Semitic writers and officials as associated with disease and unhealthy conditions. He notes, however, that this involvement with medicine, health, and healing formed curious relationships between Jewish communities and their Diaspora hosts. The Jews survived persecutions and "they repay their persecutors by giving the gift of knowledge, by caring for the health of their kings, queens, princes, and popes; by translating ancient medical texts; and in the modern period, by contributing to medical research and practice to a degree far beyond what might be expected from such a numerically insignificant minority group."[1]

Our Present Condition

For many if not most Jews in the West, survival has been replaced by new existential challenges. The search for meaning and purpose seems to have emerged as possibly *the* existential challenge of our time.

I suggest that the fundamental factor in this reality is based on one of the great texts from our tradition. In Genesis 3:9 God roams the Garden of Eden looking for Adam and Eve but cannot find them (they are in hiding after eating the fruit of the Tree of Knowledge). God searches and calls to them: *Ayekah?* "Where are you?" Abraham Joshua Heschel put it beautifully when he wrote, "To the Biblical mind man is not only a creature who is constantly in search of himself, but also a *creature God is constantly in search of.* Man is a creature in search of meaning because there is meaning in search of him, because there is God's beseeching question, 'Where art thou?'"[2]

Part of this search is being played out in an increased interest on the part of scholars in the impact of and linkage between Judaism and health. But even more important, I believe, is the slow but steady rise in interest in these subjects not by the academic community, but by the so-called people in the pews. This growing interest relates not only to the social and political realities of today but also to the demographic realities that have emerged with the American Jewish community in the post–World War II era. Our community is tending to be older, more diverse, and more individualistic. But we are simultaneously becoming more interested in community and the importance of personal relationships—perhaps as an antidote to the individualistic trends. The relative security of our community has given rise to the development of a Jewish community in transition. The impact of modernity has helped move us into a transition that in some ways speaks to the tensions between the individual and the demands of community, between reason and spirit. Arnold Eisen examines some of this tension in his essay "Choose Life: American Jews and the Quest for Healing."[3] Eisen traces the role of modernity and its impact upon our community and cites a mainstream belief that, for the most part, modernity has been good for the Jews. One of the themes that emerges from Eisen's essay is that the security of the modern Jewish community may be freeing us to look at issues of faith, spirituality, and health in new ways. The worship of reason as the foundation of our future may be wanting, and we seem to desire, perhaps need, something beyond reason.

We are reminded of the themes in the High Holy Day prayer *Unetaneh Tokef*. This prayer, central to the High Holy Day liturgy, reminds us that we are not in control of much of life. It is what I call the "randomness factor" of our existence. We live in a society that creates the mythology that we can control much of our lives. Yet, the major issues of "who shall live and who shall die" reside outside of our control. The language of the prayer, its metaphorical imagery, is a lesson in humility and, in a way, hearkens back to God's call to us in Genesis 3. Where are we? What really matters in our life? We are reminded that "illness and pain force us to recognize that we are less than entirely rational agents, plagued not only by doubt or the diseases of philosophy but by death and the manifold diseases of body and psyche.... The emerging self-conception, aided and abetted by the triumphs of medicine, the resultant longer life spans, and our greater exposure to illness and its treatment, features the body prominently as both a friend who accompanies us well into ripe old age and as an adversary who afflicts us even in youth."[4]

Part of the gift of modernity has been the invitation to focus more on the self and how that human self experiences health and illness. Eisen notes that security and modernity have allowed us to begin to examine "the complex and problematic nature of the selves who need healing and who provide that healing."[5] If we were to answer the question, "Where are you?" we would have to say that we are simultaneously more alone while seeking community and more scientific while seeking some sort of spiritual anchor. Concerns with health and healing are a reflection of those apparent opposites.

Eisen and coauthor Steven Cohen began to observe this trend of individualism over a decade ago:

American Jews have drawn the activity and significance of their group identity into the subjectivity of the individual, the activities of the family, and the few institutions (primarily the synagogue), which are seen as extensions of this intimate sphere. At the same time, relative to their parents' generation, today's American Jews in their thirties, forties, and early fifties are finding less meaning in mass organizations, political activity, philanthropic endeavor, and attachment to the State of Israel. In broad strokes, that which is personally meaningful has gained at the expense of that which is peoplehood-oriented.[6]

I suggest that the gift of time is a major contributor to the emphasis or concern with the personal. We are living longer and living better. Life spans in the twentieth century in the United States have doubled. Economic security and acceptance have combined with expanded life spans and health to produce what is the longest living and healthiest Jewish community in our history. Ultimately, modernity's greatest gift to us will be the gift of time—longer lives, more time with family, and more time as members of the community. Time has allowed us greater opportunities to reflect on God's "Where are you?" call. What shall we do with this gift of time? What can it mean? Key to this question is the desire to maintain health. Thus, in this emerging age of transition, health becomes a powerful tool in which to seek our own meaning, sustain relationships, and support community.

Eisen also sees that the concern with death has contributed to our new awareness of health issues. It makes sense on a variety of levels. After all, with more time, we have more opportunities to contemplate life's meaning, our meaning, our legacy, and our purpose. But I am convinced that there is another factor in this shift. The baby boomers are the first generation that will have the opportunity to participate, over an extended period of time, in the death of their parents. The first cohort of baby boomers is turning sixty-five. In many cases, these people are still involved in caring for one or both parents. The "art" of caregiving has become a major influence in changing personal, communal, and political attitudes toward end-of-life issues and has helped raise awareness of health issues in general. There have always been older children who have cared for parents. However, never before have so many had the opportunity to care for their older parents for such an extended period of time. The continual involvement of adult children with their parents, sometimes for years and sometimes over decades, is impacting how that generation, and their children's generation, view health and healing—especially in the last third of life. The baby boomers, try as they might to delay aging, are now participating in it, with elder loved ones, in ways never before experienced. This generation is also becoming more aware of the importance of and fragility of good health. In this way, through our role as caregivers, do we also think more about our own ends.

The emergence of an emphasis on the personal journey, the security of modern life, and the challenges of the gift of time are part of a spiritual revolution that I also feel is a direct result of the aging of the baby boom generation. This has been a generation, for Jews and non-Jews alike, that filtered things through their own personal prism. The social contexts of the 1960s and 1970s that helped shape so much of the early and middle boomer waves have found their way into adult life and into contemporary Jewish communal life as well. I have no doubt that the recent surge in recovering and recapturing spirituality is a result of the boomers' search for their own place in the universe. The rise in personal expressions of Judaism, independent *chavurot* and *minyanim*, sometimes combining religious experiences and rituals from a variety of sources and cultures, are current representations of this personal search. For the majority of the liberal Jewish community, there is no allegiance to an authoritative text. Torah and tradition are there to serve as a guide. The recent increase in observance of kashrut can serve as an example. I wonder how much of this renewed interest is based on the need to fulfill the command of God, as opposed to suggesting that there is more of a desire to seek out a healthy lifestyle and to honor a growing awareness of food consciousness within a supportive community.

Community concerns also speak to the gift of time and the subtle and often subconscious contemplation of our own mortality. Community is powerful and needed. Perhaps in reaction to the mechanistic and often nonpersonal secular world, interest in smaller, relational communities is growing. We do not want to be alone. We do not want to die alone. We do not want to be lost in an institution where our own soul or person becomes just a bar code. The desire for community and personal contact and validation is, I believe, one of the challenges facing contemporary synagogues. How do we make them intimate and caring, so that each person, regardless of background, is cared for and supported? Once again, the genius and power of Judaism and our tradition can make an impact, for Judaism can evolve a holistic approach to health.

The discussions and research surrounding the "discovery" of the holistic approach to health are fascinating. In recent decades we have seen the emergence of journals, university and government departments, and countless books that speak to the issue of integrated medicine. The mind, body, and spirit interconnection has been "discovered." Gradually, we are seeing a quiet revolution in conversations around health and illness that see mind, body, and soul as part of a "well-connected dance" that, when in balance, creates a sense of wholeness, or, just like our bodies in that morning blessing, *shleimut*. Dr. Herbert Benson, an early pioneer of this holistic approach, wrote of the need to foster integrated discussions and awareness: "And my sense is that physicians and pastors, scientists and religious believers, health enthusiasts and the spiritually inclined have far more in common than we typically think, insights that, when shared and exchanged, could help transform humankind."[7] Dr. Jeff Levin, in his *God, Faith, and Health*, expands this integrated approach:

> Decades of research have shown that personality styles and patterns of behavior, as well as specific beliefs about the world and about health, strongly influence our health-related behavior, use of health care, and actual health. Our personalities and belief systems condition how we define health, respond to health crises, relate to the health care system, and take care of ourselves to prevent illness and promote wellness. Who we are psychologically, and how we relate to the world is especially potent for heart disease and depression. Religious beliefs, through effects on health beliefs and psychological characteristics, are potential sources of illness and health.[8]

Perhaps we can date the genesis of this new awareness and approach to health and healing to a paper given to the American Medical Association by Abraham Joshua Heschel in 1964. In "The Patient as a Person,"

Heschel called for a new type of relationship between physician and patient, one rooted in the grandeur and mystery of healing, health, and faith. "The doctor," wrote Heschel, "is God's partner in the struggle between life and death. Religion is medicine in the form of a prayer; medicine is prayer in the form of a deed.... It is a grievous mistake to keep a wall of separation between medicine and religion. There is a division of labor but a unity of spirit. The act of healing is the highest form of *imitatio Dei*. To minister to the sick is to minister to God. Religion is not the assistant of medicine but the secret of one's passion for medicine."[9]

Judaism's approach to health and wellness is rooted in the understanding that everything we are is interconnected. One of the contemporary mainstays of this holistic approach, Dr. Andrew Weil, seemed to be channeling Maimonides when he wrote, "In taking a history from a new patient, I ask many questions about lifestyle, about relationships, hobbies, ways of relaxing, patterns of eating and exercising, sex and spiritual interests."[10]

Maimonides understood the interconnection of mind, body, and soul. His holistic approach to health and healing has been outlined as follows:

> First, the physician needs to obtain a clear understanding of the patient's subjective world and secure a diagnosis of the patient's psychological distress. Even if psychological stress is not manifest, it is assumed to exist, and the physician is required to search for it. Only after this "psychological workup" can the physician begin with a medical intervention. Of the patient, Maimonides demands a willingness to undertake an introspective process and adhere strictly to the regimen that the physician would formulate. Once the patient and the physician embark upon a carefully directed program which includes an examination of thoughts, feelings, a partial or total cure is likely. Maimonides expects that the patient's "spirits would be raised and depressive and self-defeating thoughts would decrease in frequency and vanish."[11]

Our increased awareness of and interest in a more holistic approach to our own health and healing, coupled with the psychospiritual restlessness of so many, have helped re-enliven attention to Maimonides.

Contemporary Practice

In my work for the Union for Reform Judaism, I have seen the gradual development in recent years of community and synagogue-based programs that have focused on issues of health and healing. Most of us are aware of and have participated in the weekly prayer for healing, the *Mi Sheberakh*, long a part of traditional liturgy, but which has recently become a standard part of Reform services. We are observing the reintroduction of the *gomel* blessing in increasing numbers of progressive congregations. This traditional blessing gives thanks that someone has come through a difficult time. Its origins may have been in the fact that people survived dangerous journeys. Now, so many of us have come through difficult surgeries or life-threatening situations that we desire to have that journey recognized within the context of a sacred community. For example, one Rosh Hashanah several years ago, during the Torah service, a congregation called forward a young man who had been in a terrible automobile accident. For close to a year he struggled to regain some sense of his self, his mobility, and his life. On this particular morning, he was called to the Torah so that he and the congregation could recite the *gomel* blessing, giving thanks that he had come through this terrible ordeal and that he had retaken his place within the community. The reintroduction of this prayer caused some turmoil within the congregation but led to many valuable discussions about ritual and religion. Such discussions are invitations to engage in meaningful and rich conversations about how faith and texts can affect people in their most powerful moments, thus demonstrating the impact and centrality of community.

Perhaps no issue has opened more doors to intense and personal conversations about health than end-of-life decisions. The extension of life spans and the dramatic accomplishments of medical technology have provided opportunities for congregations to guide congregants through the labyrinth of decision making at the end of life. Many congregations have developed their own guides on death customs and rituals that usually include an overview of Jewish traditions regarding decision making, customs and rituals associated with death and bereavement, appropriate texts from the tradition, and even location-specific information dealing with funeral homes and other resources.

Some of these guides, produced by a congregation and distributed to its members, are simple booklets, and some, like the more comprehensive material from Rodeph Sholom in New York City, have given rise to a series of educational and support programs. These congregation-wide educational programs teach Jewish rites and customs regarding end-of-life issues and often will include discussions not only with the rabbi, but also with elder-care lawyers, funeral directors, physicians, and social workers. It is in this context and in keeping with the desire for more personal and intimate religious communal experiences that we are now seeing, in the non-Orthodox community, a slow but steady rise in interest and development of the traditional *chevra kaddisha* program. This traditional *mitzvah*, which involves caring for a body before burial, has become the subject of an annual seminar that also examines laws associated with death, burial, and bereavement. Likewise, increasing numbers of congregations, as part of their caring community programs, have trained lay leaders to lead shivah *minyanim* as well as to create ongoing bereavement support groups.

Medical technology has also provided us with the reality of living with diseases that would have spelled death for some just a few years ago. The growing number of individuals who have survived cancer are also finding the need for comfort and support within the context of their faith community. In a recent discussion with cancer survivors, the members of the group spoke of the impact that the congregation had upon their situation. There was a sense of comfort and psychological and spiritual support from knowing that they had been prayed for. They understood firsthand how interrelated the mind, body, and spirit are, especially when dealing with illnesses such as theirs.

The psychological aspect of health and healing has led to a dramatic increase in the number of congregations and communities that have begun to deal with issues of mental health. In the past several years, increasing numbers of clergy and congregations have begun to create programs that have been designed to reduce the stigma of mental illness. Often these conversations have taken the form of community-wide educational programs that teach the Jewish texts on mental health and explore the impact of Jewish values on individuals and families. Special healing services have been created and even, in one community, a Passover seder. Denominations and agencies have created resources for communities and congregations in this area such as the Union for Reform Judaism's Committee on Jewish Family Concerns's *Refuat HaNefesh* and the Bay Area Jewish Healing Center's resource guide. Often one of the intended consequences of these conferences is the fact that they give "permission" for individuals and families who are dealing with significant mental health concerns to find comfort and support as well as to feel that they are not alone.

It was through just these types of programs that many congregations have now developed support programs for families dealing with Alzheimer's disease. The profound spiritual issues raised by this illness are finding their way into congregational life. With the longevity revolution of extended life spans now at hand, it is important that our community begin to seek out ways to support the increasing numbers of families that will deal with aspects of dementia and Alzheimer's in the coming decades. With so many of our people, of all ages, dealing with mental health issues, the increase in awareness and involvement in areas of mental health is a welcome symbol of reducing stigma by creating communities of caring and acceptance.

Community-based health education is also beginning to become a reality. In past generations, one hardly associated the synagogue as a center for health and wellness. That is changing. Scan the program offerings of many synagogues and Jewish community centers and you will find increasing instances of programs that look at various aspects of health—from yoga to meditation, to nutrition and exercise. The Union for Reform Judaism has produced a four-page "Health Audit" for congregational and personal use that includes checklists based on classic texts that speak to things that can be done to highlight health and wellness. Slowly, some communities are experimenting with the concept of a congregation-based health worker or congregational nurse who does everything from direct visitations to members in their homes to educating religious school children on issues of health. Indeed, one of the ongoing challenges to expanding the concept of health and wellness will be to provide educational opportunities for all ages within congregations and communities that teach Jewish texts and their relationship to health and wellness.

The emerging awareness of health and wellness is one of the most exciting aspects of contemporary American Judaism, and a developing source of interest in these issues seems to be emerging from seminary students. In two recent classes at the Hebrew Union College–Jewish Institute of Religion campus in New York, a striking number of students saw health and wellness as the highest priority of their religious studies.

These developments are part of a growing trend within our community to examine the richness of Jewish tradition as it relates to health and wellness, spirituality, and medicine. The embrace of a more holistic approach to these issues reflects well on the fact that we are part of a religious tradition and heritage that has understood for centuries that what we think affects how we feel. Our minds and bodies and souls do operate as a finely balanced integrated system, and when that balance is upset, illness results. The importance of our tradition's teaching and the power of our community to care and support each of us as a reflection of the Divine can serve as a meaningful antidote to a sense of isolation and searching that is so present in society today. We can only see this "new" awareness of health as another attempt on our part to seek meaning and purpose in a world that is so often hostile and frustrating.

In the end, this "new" awareness may be what Judaism has always achieved—the adaptation of tradition to new realities in the search to answer God's question of Genesis 3: *Ayekah?* "Where are you?"

NOTES

PREFACE

1. Arthur Green, "Mystical Sources of the Healing Movement," in *Healing and the Jewish Imagination: Spiritual and Practical Perspectives on Judaism and Health*, ed. William Cutter (Woodstock, Vt.: Jewish Lights, 2007), pp. 51–62.
2. Tamara Eskenazi, "Reading the Bible as a Healing Text," in Cutter, ibid., p. 77.
3. Tracey Kite and Susan Rosenthal, "Bridges to Wholeness: Jewish Family Services and Jewish Healing," *Journal of Jewish Communal Service*, 82, no. ½ (Winter/Spring 2007): 7–14.
4. Julie Pelc and Elliot Kukla, "Tilling Our Souls," May 2009, www.huc.edu/kalsman/Midrash-and-Medicine.
5. Ibid.
6. Ibid.
7. *Siddur Sim Shalom: A Prayerbook for Shabbat, Festivals, and Weekdays* (New York: Rabbinical Assembly, 1984).

1   METAPHORS AND SIDE EFFECTS

L'Mashal: Metaphor and Meaning in Illness

1. *As You Like It*, act 2, scene 7.
2. Mardy Grothe, *I Never Metaphor I Didn't Like: A Comprehensive Compilation of History's Greatest Analogies, Metaphors, and Similes* (New York: Harper-Collins, 2008), p. 4.
3. An *Amora* of the third century, elsewhere lauded and rewarded for studying Torah with the highly stigmatized sufferers of the horrible disease known as *ra'atan*; see Babylonian Talmud, *Ketubot* 77b.
4. See, e.g., the classic narratives of Babylonian Talmud, *Berakhot* 5b.
5. A well-known and oft-cited quotation of Menachem Mendl of Kotzk (1787–1859).
6. Hebrew, *HaEl HaNe'eman.*
7. Most handily, Exodus 21:19, which refers to liability for medical expenses.

From Heaven to Hypochondria: Metaphors of Jewish Healing

1. Woody Allen, "Conversations with Helmholtz," in *Getting Even* (New York: Random House, 1971; New York: Vintage, 1978), p. 91. Citations are to the Vintage edition.

2. Moses Maimonides, *A Maimonides Reader*, ed. Isadore Twersky (New York: Behrman House, 1972), p. 409.
3. Alter Druyanov, *Sefer HaBedikha VeHaKhidud* [The Book of Jokes and Wit], 3 vols. (Tel Aviv: Dvir, 1991).
4. Ibid., vol. *aleph*, joke 918.
5. Susan Sontag, *Illness as Metaphor* (New York: Farrar, Straus & Giroux, 1978), pp. 84–85.
6. Adolf Hitler, *Mein Kampf*, "Years of Study and Suffering in Vienna," accessed at www.englishatheist.org/mein/Chapter2.htm.
7. Robert N. Proctor, *The Nazi War on Cancer* (Princeton, N.J.: Princeton University Press, 1999), 46.
8. Sontag, *Illness as Metaphor*, pp. 84–85.
9. Leon Pinsker, "Auto-Emancipation," 1882, trans. D. S. Blondheim (1916), accessed at www.mideastweb.org/autoemancipation.htm.
10. Ibid.
11. Theodor Herzl, "The Family Affliction," in *Zionist Writings: Essays and Addresses*, vol. 2, *1898–1904*, trans. Harry Zohn (New York: Herzl Press, 1975; originally published in *American Hebrew*, January 13, 1899).

2   THE NARROW PLACE FROM WHICH HEALING COMES, AND THE EXPANSIVE EDGE OF THE CONTINENT

Surviving the Narrow Places: Judah and Joseph and the Journey to Wholeness

1. Robert Alter, *The Art of Biblical Narrative* (New York: Basic Books, 1981), p. 114.
2. It is poignant that Joseph was said to have spent three years in the Egyptian prison as a result of his encounter with Potiphar's wife, which parallels the three days he languished in the pit in Dothan, and the prison itself is referred to as a *bor*, "a pit" (Genesis 40:14–15).
3. Avivah Zornberg, *The Murmuring Deep: Reflections on the Biblical Unconscious* (New York: Schocken Books, 2009), p. 319.
4. The biblical text goes out of its way to emphasize that the pit did not have a drop of water. See Genesis 37:24.
5. Steven Kepnes, *The Text as Thou: Martin Buber's Dialogical Hermeneutics and Narrative Theology* (Bloomington: Indiana University Press, 1992), p. 76.
6. Genesis 37:31–32. Some of what follows in this article is based on Norman J. Cohen, *Self, Struggle and Change: Family Conflict Stories in Genesis and Their Healing Insights for Our Lives* (Woodstock, Vt.: Jewish Lights, 1995), pp. 162–82.
7. See *Midrash HaGadol* to Genesis 38:1 in this regard.
8. Aside from the passage in *Midrash HaGadol*, see also *Genesis Rabbah* 85:1.
9. Genesis 38:7–10. This is called levirate marriage. See, in this regard, Deuteronomy 25:5.

10. Genesis 38:11. Tamar was literally bound to Sheilah—she was in a state of *zikkah*, tied to Sheilah, dependent on him.

11. The midrash emphasizes this in noting in several texts that both ascent and descent are mentioned in connection with Timnah—in Judges 14:1, Samson "went down [*va-yeired*] to Timnah," while contrastingly here in Genesis, Judah "ascended [*va-ya'al*] to Timnah." At Timnah, Samson was seduced by Delilah, which led to his death; at Timnah, Judah came to recognize himself, and as a result, he was worthy of being the progenitor of the line of King David. See, for example, *Genesis Rabbah* 85:6.

12. Genesis 38:17. This is reminiscent of Genesis 37:31 when the brothers dipped Joseph's coat in the blood of a kid in order to fool their father. It is another indicator in the biblical narrative of the connection between Genesis 37 and 38, the stories of Joseph and Judah.

13. Tamar had forced Judah into performing the levirate duties of the younger brother!

14. See, in this regard, the *Mekhilta D'Rabbi Yishmael, Massekhta D'Beshallach*, *parashah* 6, and its many parallels.

15. Peretz is the first name in the genealogy in the book of Ruth (4:18).

16. Similarly Rahab, another non-Israelite prostitute who lived in the wall of Jericho, saved Israel by protecting the spies in Joshua 2:18. According to the Rabbis, the scarlet line that she placed in her window to identify her when Israel crossed the Jordan was given to her by Peretz's twin, Zerach. It was the thread that the midwife placed on his hand indicating that he was the firstborn. The tradition emphasized that Rahab's progeny included the prophets Ezekiel and Jeremiah. There is also a tradition preserved in the book of Matthew 1:26 that Rahab was the mother of Boaz; thus she, too, is associated with the line of King David in the book of Ruth.

17. See, among several texts, the *Mekhilta D'Rabbi Yishmael, Massekhta D' Beshallach*, *parashah* 6.

18. E.g., Joseph placed the brothers in prison for three days, claiming they were spies, just as he had spent three days in the pit in Dothan, according to several midrashim on Genesis 37.

19. See, in this regard, *Genesis Rabbah* 93:2, in which the confrontation between the two brothers is pictured as a battle between two kings.

20. *Massekhta D'Beshallach*, *parashah* 6.

3   Lyric and Community
The Midrashic Impulse in Poems, Our Dialogue with Ecclesiastes, and Other Lyrical Interpretations

1. Shelley's "A Defence of Poetry" and Keats's *Fall of Hyperion* are available in numerous anthologies or in collections of the writings of each romantic great. The Keats was suggested to me by Jonathan Cohen.

2. I believe that the poem was called "December 27, 1966," but it is not included in either of his two important anthologies.

3. For John Updike's poetry on the end of his own life, see *Endpoint and Other Poems* (New York: Knopf, 2009).

4. Rafael Campo, *The Healing Art* (New York: W. W. Norton, 2003), p. 31.

5. A brief listing of significant narrative prose would include *The Death of Ivan Ilych* (Leo Tolstoy), *The Dying Animal* (Philip Roth), *The Death of the Old Man* (A. B. Yehoshua), *As I Lay Dying* (William Faulkner), *The Year of Magical Thinking* (Joan Didion), *A Death in the Family* (James Agee), *The Interpreter of Maladies* (Jhumpa Lahiri), and countless more in which illness or death at the end of illness serves as the center of a broader aesthetic vision that encompasses human response, taboo, and cultural meaning. See Sandra Gilbert, *Death's Door: Modern Dying and the Ways We Grieve* (New York: W. W. Norton, 2006). I realize that most of these examples include death—and not just the experience of illness. The illness and narrative movement, which has been fostered by many clinical leaders today, is most vividly expressed in the work of Dr. Rita Charon, the founder of the journal *Literature and Medicine*, which has given so much both to clinicians and to teachers of literature. Dr. Charon's work with medical students at Columbia University has become legendary.

6. Marc J. Straus, "Like Me," in *Symmetry* (Evanston, Ill.: Northwestern University Press, 2000), p. 54.

7. Straus, "Eleventh Floor," in *Symmetry*, p. 47.

8. A paraphrase from Abba Kovner, *Sloan-Kettering* [Hebrew] (Tel Aviv: HaKibbutz HaMe'uhad, 1987), p. 18.

9. Benjamin Kukoff, unpublished poem.

10. Yehuda Amichai, "A Man in His Life," in *Yehuda Amichai: A Life of Poetry*, ed., trans. Benjamin Harshav and Barbara Harshav (New York: HarperCollins, 1989), p. 356.

11. Zelda, "When the Woman," in *The Spectacular Difference*, trans. Marcia Falk (Cincinnati: Hebrew Union College Press, 2004), p. 247.

12. T. Carmi, "Poems against My Will, #3," in *Shirim, 1951–1994* (Tel Aviv: Dvir, 1994), p. 316; translation mine.

13. In an unpublished essay, the late Henry Samuel Levinson (to whom this book is dedicated) argued that a very ill person may only legitimately hope for something that can happen. Thus, in his homey example, a severely restricted patient with multiple sclerosis may hope for a good martini at the end of the day, but not that he will suddenly walk unaided.

14. Meron Isaacson, "A Time to Give Birth," in *Et Levakesh* (Tel Aviv: HaKibbutz HaMe'uhad, 1989), p. 35; translation mine.

15. Dan Pagis, "Pages in an Album," in *Kol haShirim* (Tel Aviv: HaKibbutz HaMe'uhad, 1991), p. 99.

16. William Shakespeare, *As You Like It* 2.7.

17. Eric Berk and William Cutter, paper to appear in *Hebrew Studies*.

18. M. H. Abrams, *The Mirror and the Lamp: Romantic Theory and the Critical Tradition* (New York: Oxford University Press, 1971).

19. Carmi, "Poems against My Will, #3."

20. Kovner, *Sloan-Kettering*, p. 18.

21. Lea Goldberg, "Meshorer Zaken," in *Shirim*, vol. 2 [Hebrew] (Tel Aviv: Sifriat Poalim, 2002); translation mine.

22. Haim Gouri, *Eival* [Hebrew] (Tel Aviv: HaKibbutz HaMe'uhad, 2009); translation mine.

23. I am indebted to the work and teaching of Dr. Robert Carroll, who introduced me to the world of poetry therapy. The poem "This Much," from his recent collection *Amazing Change* (Los Angeles: Bombshelter Press, 2009), is only one of hundreds of his poetic narratives that contains the simple surprise that poetry makes possible.

24. Yehuda Amichai, "The Precision of Pain ...," in *Open Closed Open*, trans. Chana Bloch and Chana Kronfeld (New York: Harcourt, 2000).

"Psalms, Songs & Stories": Midrash and Music at the Jewish Home of San Francisco

1. The original songs based on the psalms that are cited in this essay were composed by the Singers and Songwriters of the Jewish Home of San Francisco with Judith-Kate Friedman and Rabbi Sheldon Marder as part of the "Psalms, Songs & Stories" project.

2. Musician/songwriter Judith-Kate Friedman and Rabbi Sheldon Marder are the cofounders and coleaders of "Psalms, Songs & Stories," which began at the Jewish Home of San Francisco in 2002. I am grateful to Judith-Kate Friedman for her friendship, generosity, creative spirit, and steadfast commitment to the residents of the Jewish Home. The vision of this project could not have been realized without her.

3. Adin Steinsaltz, *The Thirteen Petalled Rose*, trans. Yehuda Hanegbi (New York: Basic Books, 1980), pp. 125–26.

4. Dennis Sylva, *Psalms and the Transformation of Stress: Poetic-Communal Interpretation and the Family*, Louvain Theological & Pastoral Monographs 16 (Grand Rapids, Mich.: W. B. Eerdmans, 1994), p. 4.

5. Kathleen Norris, *The Cloister Walk* (New York: Riverhead Books, 1996), pp. 96, 104.

6. Leonard B. Meyer, *Emotion and Meaning in Music* (Chicago: University of Chicago Press, 1956), pp. 23–25.

7. Kathryn Shattuck, obituary of Leonard B. Meyer, *New York Times*, January 2, 2008.

8. Meyer, *Emotion and Meaning*, pp. 28–29.

9. William Cutter, *R'fuah Sh'leimah/Songs of Jewish Healing* (New York: Synagogue 2000 / Transcontinental Music, 2002), p. 5. I am grateful to William Cutter for

enriching my life's work with his encouragement, advice, and teaching over many years. He is a true mentor.

10. Words and music of this and all other songs cited in this essay are by residents of the Jewish Home of San Francisco, Judith-Kate Friedman, and Sheldon Marder.

11. Jenny Rose's name is used by permission of her son.

12. Nissim Ezekiel, "At 62," in *Collected Poems, 1952–1988* (Delhi: Oxford University Press, 1989), p. 273.

13. Barbara Myerhoff, *Remembered Lives: The Work of Ritual, Storytelling, and Growing Older*, ed. Marc Kaminsky (Ann Arbor: University of Michigan Press, 1992), p. 240.

14. Edmund Sherman, *Reminiscence and the Self in Old Age* (New York: Springer, 1991), p. 119.

15. Jonathan Magonet, *A Rabbi Reads the Psalms* (London: SCM Press, 1994), p. 52.

16. Barry W. Holtz, *Back to the Sources: Reading the Classic Jewish Texts* (New York: Summit Books, 1984), p. 179.

17. Theresa A. Allison, "Songwriting and Transcending Institutional Boundaries in the Nursing Home," in *The Oxford Handbook of Medical Ethnomusicology*, ed. Benjamin D. Koen (New York: Oxford University Press, 2008), p. 222.

18. Ibid., p. 223.

19. Ibid., p. 243.

20. Ibid., p. 233. In his book *The Psalms: An Introduction* (Grand Rapids, Mich.: Wm. B. Eerdmans, 2001), p. 96, James L. Crenshaw explains chiastic structure as follows: "In this particular pattern, which resembles the [Greek] letter X, A is followed by B, and the two are then reversed to achieve a sequence of ABB'A'. The possibilities of this scansion seem limitless, for one can apply it on either the macro-level or on the micro-level. Interpreters stress broad concepts like humankind and animal, land and sea, earthly and heavenly, good and bad, gem and flower, masculine and feminine. They emphasize single letters and words or phrases; moreover, they mark units of greater or lesser scope by means of this feature." The relationship of health and wealth, in the song based on Psalm 126, seems a worthy addition to James Crenshaw's list of examples.

21. A similar appeal to musical authenticity on the part of the musician/songwriter who coleads the groups can have the same outcome but is a less reliable tool for reaching consensus than the Bible.

22. The door painting, by Misha Taratuta, appeared on the cover of a magazine called *Forum on the Jewish People, Zionism and Israel* (Spring 1988). It accompanied the article "Don't Cry for Me, San Francisco," about the painter's family who immigrated to Israel after fifteen years as refusenik-dissidents in Leningrad.

23. The Yiddish word *freylach* is an adjective that means "happy." The songwriters invoked poetic license in using it here as a noun.

24. Allison, "Songwriting and Transcending," p. 234.

25. Seamus Heaney, *The Redress of Poetry* (New York: Noonday Press, 1995), p. 158.

26. The cost of skilled nursing care at the Jewish Home is largely funded by Medi-Cal (California's Medicaid program) and Medicare reimbursement, and by individual donations and foundation grants. The Jewish Home is a beneficiary agency of the Jewish Community Federation of San Francisco, the Peninsula, and Marin and Sonoma Counties.

27. Edward Hirsch, *How to Read a Poem* (New York: Harcourt Brace, 1999), pp. 304–5.

28. Robert Alter, *The Book of Psalms: A Translation with Commentary* (New York: W. W. Norton, 2007), pp. 148–49.

29. Robert Alter, *The Art of Biblical Poetry* (New York: Basic Books, 1985), pp. xxvii, 21.

30. James L. Kugel, *The Idea of Biblical Poetry: Parallelism and Its History* (Baltimore: Johns Hopkins University Press, 1981), pp. 49–58.

31. Adele Berlin, *The Dynamics of Biblical Parallelism* (Bloomington: Indiana University Press, 1985); Walter Brueggemann, *The Message of the Psalms: A Theological Commentary* (Minneapolis: Augsburg, 1984).

32. Sigmund Mowinckel, *The Psalms in Israel's Worship*, vol. 2, trans. D. R. Ap-Thomas (Grand Rapids, Mich.: William B. Eerdmans, 2004), p. 166.

33. *The Midrash on Psalms*, vol. 1, trans. William G. Braude (New Haven: Yale University Press, 1959), p. 33.

34. Allison, "Songwriting and Transcending," p. 241.

35. Judith-Kate Friedman, "Freeing the Voice Within," *Signpost* 8, no. 3 (February 2004): www.signpostjournal.org.uk.

4 GOD IN THE DOCTOR'S OFFICE: SOME MIDRASHIC ELABORATIONS

Talking to Physicians about Talking about God: A Midrashic Invitation

1. Chaim Nachman Bialik, "Levadi," 1902. The most accessible version of the poem is contained in Stanley Burnshaw, et al., *The Modern Hebrew Poem Itself* (Detroit: Wayne State University Press, 1996).

2. A short list of such writer-healers would include Dr. Rita Charon, professor at Columbia Unviersity, who has famously introduced aspects of narrative into her clinical work and who encourages her students to study narratives of illness and healing as part of their growth. Dr. Charon is one of the founders of the journal *Literature and Medicine*. The other physician-writers mentioned in the body of my essay are well-known writers for various magazines in the American treasury of popular high culture. I am particularly grateful to Professor Shlomith Rimmon-Kenan, one of the world's truly important narrative theorists, who shifted her career from pure theory to a greater interest in medicine and literature as a consequence of her personal experience with health. In that, she has been my personal scholarly model for the past decade. See S. Rimmon-Kenan, "What Can Narrative

Theory Learn from Illness Narratives?" *Literature and Medicine* 25, no. 2 (Fall 2006): 241–54.

3. Jerome Groopman, "God on the Brain," *New Yorker*, September 10, 2001.

4. John Donne, *Devotions upon Emergent Occasions and Death's Duel* (New York: Random House, 1999), p. 118—one of the many expostulations in this collection.

5. Nachman of Breslov was a Hasidic master of the third generation of Hasidic rabbis who established a "school" that fostered no single "rebbe" after his death. His career divided broadly into a period of preaching highly elaborate and sophisticated *derashot* (sermons) and—near the end of his life—complex narratives that embodied his particular kabbalistic ideology. The best study of his life is Arthur Green, *Tormented Master: The Life and Spiritual Quest of Rabbi Nahman of Bratslav* (reprint, Woodstock, Vt.: Jewish Lights, 1992).

6. Nell Burger Kirst, "Medical Care That Transcends Words," *New York Times*, January 4, 2010.

7. For a fairly comprehensive exploration of narrative in clinical environments (specifically in the settings of occupational therapy), see Cheryl Mattingly, *Healing Dramas and Clinical Plots: The Narrative Structure of Experience* (New York: Cambridge University Press, 1998).

A Physician's Response to the Midrashic Invitation

1. Adapted from M. Stern, ed., *Daily Prayers* (New York: Hebrew Publishing, 1928), p. 13.

2. Joseph H. Herz, trans., *Sayings of the Fathers* (New York: Behrman House, 1945).

5   Contexts of Suffering, Contexts of Hope

Neither Suffering nor Its Rewards: A Story about Intimacy and Dealing with Suffering and with Death

1. This essay is taken from Ruhama Weiss's book *Mithayevet B'Nafshi* (Committing My Soul) [Hebrew], translated and adapted here by William Cutter.

2. Ephraim Urbach, *The World of the Sages* [Hebrew] (Jerusalem: Magnes Press, 2002), pp. 437–58.

3. These references are to chapters in Weiss's *Mithayevet B'Nafshi*.

4. Julius Theodor and Chanoch Albeck, eds., *Midrash Bereshit Rabba* [English] (Jerusalem: Wahrmann, 1965), p. 572.

5. Elisabeth Kübler-Ross, *Death Is Essential to Life*, trans. Y. Bar-Kokhba [Hebrew] (Jerusalem: Keter, 2002), pp. 100–101.

6. *Translator's note:* The author concludes this chapter with two codas that apply more generally to her book: (1) the story of two young women meeting in high school and B'nei Akiva movements and working their way toward serious Talmudic study, which, in addition to its genuine intrinsic value for them, represented a major break for women among the Orthodox communities in which they

were raised; and (2) a discussion of *mithayevet b'nafshi*, "to commit my soul," and what that means in terms of ultimate concerns. For Weiss, it means living in the present, studying that present through Talmud, and associating herself with the Underground against Suffering.

The Experience of Suffering: A Response to Ruhama Weiss

1. It seems that Bar Kokhba's name was Bar Kusba, which is about all we know about him.
2. Roland Barthes, *S/Z*, trans. Richard Miller (New York: Hill and Wang, 1974; originally published in 1970).
3. Abraham J. Heschel, *Heavenly Torah as Refracted through the Generations*, trans. Gordon Tucker (New York: Continuum, 2004).
4. There is no reason to posit that these understandings did not recede back into the biblical period, but Heschel did not deal with biblical material per se, perhaps because of pietistic anxieties.

6 MIDRASHIC RENDERINGS OF AGE AND OBLIGATION

After the Life Cycle: The Moral Challenges of Later Life

1. Henri Nouwen and Walter Gaffney, *Aging: The Fulfillment of Life* (New York: Bantam Doubleday Dell, 1976).
2. Ibid., p. 13.
3. Charles Taylor, *Sources of the Self: The Making of the Modern Identity* (Cambridge, Mass.: Harvard University Press, 1989), pp. 11–14.
4. Nouwen and Gaffney, *Aging*, p. 14.
5. Ibid., p. 13.
6. In Thomas R. Cole, *The Journey of Life: A Cultural History of Aging in America* (New York: Cambridge University Press, 1991), p. xxxii.
7. Erik Erikson, *Identity: Youth and Crisis* (New York: Norton, 1968), pp. 142, 114.
8. Erik Erikson, *Childhood and Society* (reprint, New York: W. W. Norton, 1986).
9. Erikson, *Identity*, p. 133.
10. Cole, *The Journey of Life*, chap. 1.
11. Alasdair MacIntyre, *After Virtue: A Study in Moral Theory*, 2nd ed. (Notre Dame, Ind: University of Notre Dame Press, 1984).
12. Harry R. Moody, "The Meaning of Life and the Meaning of Old Age," in *What Does It Mean to Grow Old? Reflections from the Humanities*, ed. Thomas R. Cole and Sally Gadow (Durham, N.C.: Duke University Press, 1986), pp. 11–40.
13. Cole, *The Journey of Life*, p. 240.
14. Richard Nelson Bolles, *The Three Boxes of Life and How to Get Out of Them: An Introduction to Life/Work Planning* (Berkeley, Calif.: Ten Speed Press, 1978).
15. Anthony Giddens, *Modernity and Self-Identity: Self and Society in the Late Modern Age* (Stanford, Calif.: Stanford University Press, 1991).
16. Ibid., p. 147.

17. Harry R. Moody, *Abundance of Life: Human Development Policies for an Aging Society* (New York: Columbia University Press, 1988).

18. In Chris Phillipson, *Reconstructing Old Age* (London: Sage, 1998), p. 49.

19. Erikson, *Identity*, p. 132.

20. MacIntyre, *After Virtue*.

21. Charles Taylor, *The Ethics of Authenticity* (Cambridge, Mass.: Harvard University Press, 1992), 28–29.

22. Ibid., pp. 40–41.

23. Erikson, *Childhood and Society*, p. 380.

24. Leopold Rosenmayr, *Die späte Freiheit* (Paris: Edition Atelier, 1990).

25. Alex Comfort, *The Joy of Sex* (London: Quartet Books, 1974); Alex Comfort, *A Good Age* (New York: Crown, 1976).

26. William F. May, "The Virtues and Vices of Aging," in *What Does it Mean to Grow Old?* ed. Cole and Gadow, p. 45.

27. AAMC Task Force, 1999, report 3.

28. Ronald Blythe, *The View in Winter: Reflections on Old Age* (New York: Harcourt, 1998).

29. Moody, *Abundance of Life*, pp. 4–5.

30. Zalman Schachter-Shalomi, *From Age-ing to Sage-ing: A Profound New Vision of Growing Older*, with Ronald S. Miller (New York: Warner Books, 1995).

31. Marc Freedman, *The Kindness of Strangers: Adult Mentors, Urban Youth, and the New Voluntarism* (San Francisco: Jossey-Bass, 1993).

32. John Cowper Powys, *The Art of Growing Old* (London: Cape, 1944).

33. Florida Scott-Maxwell, *The Measure of My Days* (London: Penguin Books, 1978).

34. Wendy Lustbader, *Counting on Kindness: The Dilemmas of Dependency* (New York: Free Press, 1991), p. 15.

35. Ibid., p. 18.

36. Ibid., p. 30.

37. Ibid., p. 34.

38. May, "The Virtues and Vices of Aging," p. 50.

39. Ibid., p. 51.

40. Ibid.

41. Ibid., pp. 52–53.

42. Ibid., p. 53.

43. Ibid., p. 59.

44. Ibid., p. 49.

45. Sara Ruddick, "Virtues and Age," in *Mother Time: Women, Aging, and Ethics*, ed. Margaret Urban Walter (Lanham, Md.: Rowman and Littlefield, 1999), p. 45. Interestingly, Ruddick does not cite William May's piece, "The Virtues and Vices of Aging."

46. Ibid., p. 46.

47. Ibid., p. 50.

48. Ibid., p. 53.

49. Ibid., p. 54.

50. Theodore Roszak, *America the Wise: The Longevity Revolution and the True Wealth of Nations* (Boston: Houghton Mifflin, 1998).

51. Scott-Maxwell, *The Measure of My Days*, pp. 24–25.

The Journey of Later Life: Moses as Our Guide

1. Richard Wolf, "A 'Fiscal Hurricane' on the Horizon," *USA Today*, November 14, 2005.

2. Ronald Manheimer, "The Paradox of Beneficial Retirement: A Journey into the Vortex of Nothingness," *Journal of Aging, Humanities and the Arts* 2, no. 2 (April 2008): 93.

3. George Santayana, *The Life of Reason* (New York: Charles Scribner's Sons, 1906), p. 6.

4. Biblical translations by Everett Fox, *The Five Books of Moses* (New York: Schocken Books, 1995).

5. See *Netivot Shalom*, the Slonimer Rebbe's Torah commentary, *Parashat Shemot*, in which he cites the Kobriner Rebbe, who suggests that the possibility for renewal and redemption exists as long as a person does not accept the inevitability of the status quo, saying, "That is just the way things are."

6. Sara Lawrence-Lightfoot, *The Third Chapter: Passion, Risk, and Adventure in the 25 Years after 50* (New York: Farrar, Straus & Giroux, 2008), p. 244.

7. Hayim Nahman Bialik and Yehoshua Hana Ravnitzky, eds., *The Book of Legends/Sefer ha-Aggadah: Legends from the Talmud and Midrash*, trans. William G. Braude (New York: Schocken Books, 1992), chap. 5.

8. Daniel 7:13. In the *Zohar*, God is also called *Atika Kaddisha*, "the Holy Ancient One."

9. See Zalman Schachter-Shalomi, *From Age-ing to Sage-ing: A Profound New Vision of Growing Older*, with Ronald S. Miller (New York: Warner Books, 1995).

10. See Maggie Kuhn, *No Stone Unturned: The Life and Times of Maggie Kuhn*, with Christina Long and Laura Quinn (New York: Ballantine Books, 1991).

11. "Maggie Kuhn: Being Outrageous on Behalf of the Elderly," *Toledo Blade,* April 6, 1985.

12. *Yalkut Shimoni, Chukkat* 763. As the Israelites complain bitterly against Moses for not providing water after the death of Miriam, God upbraids him and Aaron: "Leave this place quickly. My children are near death with thirst, and you sit here mourning for that old woman [Miriam]."

13. Perhaps Moses responded to his losses in a manner akin to Aaron's wordless grief for his sons (Leviticus 10:3).

14. Elisabeth Kübler-Ross, *On Death and Dying* (New York: Scribner, 1997). Just as later scholars have argued that dying individuals pass back and forth through the stages outlined by Kübler-Ross, so too the midrashic Moses cycles through them numerous times in the midrashic account.

15. In Adolph Jellinek, *Beit HaMidrash* (Jerusalem: Sifrei Wahrmann, 1967), pp. 124–25; my translation.

16. Translation adapted from Louis Ginzberg, *The Legends of the Jews* (Philadelphia: Jewish Publication Society, 1966), p. 465.

17. Ibid.

18. It may be fruitful to explore other biblical models for complex aging. For example, Jacob had to find generativity amid decline and despair. It would be interesting to think of what we might learn from the aged King David, who lost his virility and his grip, or from Abraham, who left the known world behind as an old man and who experienced unbelievable late-life fecundity.

19. William H. Thomas, *What Are Old People For? How Elders Will Save the World* (Acton, Mass.: VanderWyk & Burnham, 2007).

20. Shirley Brown in a talk for Hiddur: The Center for Aging and Judaism of the Reconstructionist Rabbinical College, April 2009.

21. The Assets Based Community Development (ABCD) approach to community organizing recommends mapping assets in a community as a strategy for fostering growth and change. See Luther Snow, *The Power of Asset Mapping: How Your Congregation Can Act on Its Gifts* (Herndon, Va.: Alban Institute, 2004).

22. Ellen M. Gee and Gloria M. Gutman, eds., *The Overselling of Population Aging: Apocalyptic Demography, Intergenerational Challenges, and Social Policy* (New York: Oxford University Press, 2000).

23. See Thomas, *What Are Old People For?*

8 The Dilemmas of Psychotherapy; the Healing Response of Midrash

The Danger of Cure, the Value of Healing: Toward a Midrashic Way of Being

1. Philip Rieff, *The Triumph of the Therapeutic: Uses of Faith after Freud* (Chicago: University of Chicago Press, 1966); T. J. Jackson Lears, "From Salvation to Self-realization: Advertising and the Therapeutic Roots of the Consumer Culture, 1880–1930," in *The Culture of Consumption: Critical Essays in American History, 1880–1980*, ed. R. W. Fox and T. J. Jackson Lears (New York: Pantheon Press, 1983), pp. 3–38.

2. See, among others, Christopher Lasch, *The Culture of Narcissism: American Life in an Age of Diminishing Expectations* (New York: W. W. Norton, 1979).

3. See A. Scull, *The Most Solitary of Afflictions: Madness and Society in Britain, 1700–1900* (New Haven: Yale University Press, 1993); G. F. Drinka, *The Birth of Neurosis: Myth, Malady, and the Victorians* (New York: Simon and Schuster,

1984); E. Shorter, *From Paralysis to Fatigue: A History of Psychosomatic Illness in the Modern Era* (New York: Free Press, 1992); E. Showalter, *The Female Malady: Women, Madness, and English Culture, 1830–1980* (New York: Pantheon, 1985); R. C. Fuller, *Mesmerism and the American Cure of Souls* (Philadelphia: University of Pennsylvania Press, 1982); J. Kovel, "The American Mental Health Industry," in *Critical Psychiatry: The Politics of Mental Health*, ed. D. Ingleby (New York: Pantheon Books, 1980), pp. 72–101; Philip Cushman, *Constructing the Self, Constructing America: A Cultural History of Psychotherapy* (Reading, Mass.: Addison Wesley, 1995); I. Prilleltensky, *The Morals and Politics of Psychology: Psychological Discourse and the Status Quo* (Albany: SUNY Press, 1994); E. E. Sampson, "Cognitive Psychology as Ideology," *American Psychologist* 36, no. 7 (July 1981): 730–43.

4. William Cutter, ed., *Healing and the Jewish Imagination: Spiritual and Practical Perspectives on Judaism and Health* (Woodstock, Vt.: Jewish Lights, 2007), p. 4.

5. P. Cushman and P. Gilford, "Will Managed Care Change Our Way of Being?" *American Psychologist* 55, no. 9 (September 2000): 985–96.

6. Susan Bordo, *Unbearable Weight: Feminism, Western Culture, and the Body* (Berkeley: University of California Press, 1993).

7. For examples of this, see M. Brettschneider, *The Narrow Bridge: Jewish Views on Multiculturalism* (New Brunswick, N.J.: Rutgers University Press, 1996); and D. Biale, M. Galchinsley, and S. Heschel, eds., *Insider/Outsider: American Jews and Multiculturalism* (Berkeley: University of California Press, 1998).

8. Lasch, *Culture of Narcissism*.

9. Karen Brodkin, *How Jews Became White Folks and What That Says about Race in America* (New Brunswick, N.J.: Rutgers University Press, 1998); Noel Ignatief, *How the Irish Became White* (New York: Routledge, 1995).

10. Robert Crawford, "Health as a Meaningful Social Practice," *Health: An Interdisciplinary Journal for the Social Study of Health, Illness and Medicine* 10, no. 4 (October 2006): 404.

11. Ibid., p. 419.

12. S. A. Mitchell and L. Aron, *Relational Psychoanalysis* (Hillsdale, N.J.: Analytic Press, 1999). See also D. Orange, "Toward the Art of Living Dialogue: Between Constructivisim and Hermeneutics in Psychoanalytic Thinking," in *Beyond Postmodernism: New Dimensions in Clinical Theory and Practice*, ed. R. Frie and D. Orange (New York: Routledge, 2009); I. Z. Hoffman, "Doublethinking Our Way to Scientific Legitimacy: The Desiccation of Human Experience," *Journal of the American Psychoanalytic Association* 57, no. 5 (October 2009): 1043–69; D. B. Stern, *Partners in Thought: Working with Unformulated Experience, Dissociation, and Enactment* (New York: Routledge, 2010).

13. H.-G. Gadamer, *Truth and Method* (New York: Crossroads, 1989), suggests the most creative interpretive approach to texts in general, which seem—at the same time—particularly suited to midrashic method. See also P. Ochs and N. Levene,

eds., *Textual Reasonings: Jewish Philosophy and Text Study at the End of the Twentieth Century* (Grand Rapids, Mich.: William B. Eerdmans, 2002).

14. Ira Stone, *Reading Levinas/Reading Talmud* (Philadelphia: Jewish Publication Society, 1998).

15. Hoffman, "Doublethinking Our Way to Scientific Legitimacy"; Stern, *Partners in Thought*; R. Stolorow, G. Atwood, and D. Orange, *Worlds of Experience* (New York: Basic Books, 2002).

16. Ochs and Levene, eds., *Textual Reasonings*; David Stern, *Midrash and Theory: Ancient Jewish Exegesis and Contemporary Literary Studies* (Evanston, Ill.: Northwestern University Press, 1996).

17. Charles Taylor, *Sources of the Self: The Making of the Modern Identity* (Cambridge, Mass.: Harvard University Press, 1989).

18. Gershom Scholem, *On the Kabbalah and Its Symbolism* (New York: Schocken Books, 1965), especially pp. 29–31.

19. E.g., D. Fox and I. Prilleltensky, eds., *Critical Psychology: An Introduction* (Thousand Oaks, Calif.: Sage, 1997); Tod S. Sloan, *Damaged Life: The Crisis of the Modern Psyche* (New York: Routledge, 1996).

20. Intertextuality has become of increasing interest in the past three decades. Few scholars have been as influential in the growth of its discussion than Daniel Boyarin. See particularly D. Boyarin, *Intertextuality and the Reading of Midrash* (Bloomington: Indiana University Press, 1990).

21. E. Fromm, *You Shall Be as Gods: A Radical Interpretation of the Old Testament and Its Traditions* (New York: Holt, Rinehart and Winston, 1966); Karl Marx, *Capital*, vol. 1 (London: Lawrence and Wishart, 1976; based on the original of 1867).

22. Stern, *Midrash and Theory*, p. 29.

23. Philip Cushman, "Iron Fists / Velvet Gloves: Recruitment-Indoctrination Processes in a Mass Marathon Psychology Training Program," *Psychotherapy* 26 (Spring 1989): 23–39.

24. Rachel Cowan, editorial in *The Outstretched Arm*, the newsletter of the National Jewish Healing Center, Fall 1991.

Midrashic Thinking: An Appreciation and a Caution

1. A serious controversy has erupted recently over the question of whether psychoanalysis and psychology are nonscientific and are as effective as other modes of therapy. Significant criticism of psychoanalysis and psychology can be found in Timothy B. Baker, Richard M. McFall, and Varda Shoham, "Current Status and Future Prospects of Clinical Psychology: Toward a Scientifically Principled Approach to Mental and Behavioral Health Care," *Psychological Science in the Public Interest* 9, no. 2 (2008): 67–103. For a major response, see Jonathan K. Shedler, "The Efficacy of Psychodynamic Psychotherapy," *American Psychologist* 65, no. 2 (February/March 2010): 98–109. The controversy has been noted in the press, e.g., Sharon Begley, "Ignoring the Evidence: Why Do Psychologists Reject Science?" *Newsweek*,

October 12, 2009; Eric Jaffe, "Of Two Minds," *Los Angeles Times*, January 11, 2010, as well as numerous other sources.

2. Frank M. Lachmann, *Transforming Narcissism: Reflections on Empathy, Humor and Expectations* (New York: Analytic Press, 2008), especially chap. 5, "Through the Lens of Humor," pp. 87–109. The interest in humor goes back to the founder of modern psychoanalysis, Sigmund Freud. "Humour," in *The Standard Edition of the Complete Psychological Works of Sigmund Freud (1927–1931)*, vol. 21, *The Future of an Illusion, Civilization and Its Discontents and Other Works* (1927), pp. 159–66.

3. See Béatrice Beebe and Frank M. Lachmann, *Infant Research and Adult Treatment: Co-constructing Interactions* (New York: Analytic Press, 2002); Daniel N. Stern, *The Interpersonal World of the Infant: A View from Psychoanalysis and Developmental Psychology* (New York: Basic Books, 1985; rev. ed., 2000); and David J. Wallin, *Attachment in Psychotherapy* (New York: Guilford, 2007).

4. See Gerald Edelman, *Wider Than the Sky* (New Haven: Yale University Press, 2004); and Allan N. Shore, *Affect Regulation and the Origin of Self: The Neurobiology of Emotional Development* (New York: W. W. Norton, 2003).

5. Translations of *Pesikta D'Rav Kahana* in this article follow William G. Braude and Israel J. Kapstein, trans., *Pesikta De-Rab Kahanah* (Philadelphia: Jewish Publication Society, 1975), with minor modifications.

6. Translation from *Tanakh: The Holy Scriptures* (Philadelphia: Jewish Publication Society, 1985).

7. M. Cary, *A History of Rome* (London: Macmillan, 1957), pp. 744–46.

8. For example, for the phrase "the partner of God in the act of Creation," see *Mekhilta D'Rabbi Yishmael: Yitro, Masekhet D'Amalek*, chap. 2, *Pesikta Zutreta (Lekach Tov)*, Numbers, p. 136b. These citations have to do with proper judging and offering sacrifices.

9 THE NARRATIVE TURN IN JEWISH BIOETHICS
Aggadah and Midrash: A New Direction for Bioethics?

1. Immanuel Jakobovits, *Jewish Medical Ethics: A Comparative and Historical Study of the Jewish Religious Attitude to Medicine and Its Practice* (New York: Bloch, 1959), p. xxxv.

2. Ibid., p. 93.

3. Steven H. Miles, *The Hippocratic Oath and the Ethics of Medicine* (New York: Oxford University Press, 2004), pp. 3–4.

4. A typical translation of the Hippocratic oath, by W. H. S. Jones, in *The Doctor's Oath* (Cambridge: Cambridge University Press, 1924), as reprinted in *British Medical Journal* 2 (1948): 616: "I swear by Apollo Physician, by Aesculapius, by Health (Hygieia), by Heal-all (Panacea), and by all the gods and goddesses, making them

witnesses, that I will carry out, according to my ability and judgment, this oath and this indenture: ... I will use treatment to help the sick according to my ability and judgment, but I will never use it to injure or wrong them. I will not give poison to anyone though asked to do so, nor will I suggest such a plan. Similarly I will not give a pessary to a woman to cause abortion. But in purity and in holiness I will guard my life and my art. I will not use the knife on sufferers from stone, but I will give place to such as are craftsmen therein. Into whatsoever houses I enter, I will do so to help the sick, keeping myself free from all intentional wrongdoing and harm, especially from fornication with woman or man, bond or free. Whatsoever in the course of practice I see or hear (or even outside my practice in social intercourse) that ought never to be published abroad, I will not divulge, but consider such things to be holy secrets. Now if I keep this oath, and break it not, may I enjoy honor, in my life and art, among all men for all time; but if I transgress and forswear myself, may the opposite befall me."

5. The oath of Asaph and Yochanan (*Sefer HaRefuot*), as translated by Shlomo Pines, "The Oath of Asaph the Physician and Yohanan Ben Zabda. Its Relation to the Hippocratic Oath and the Doctrina Duarum Viarum of the Didache," *Proceedings of the Israel Academy of Sciences and Humanities* 9 (1975): pp. 223–64: "[1] This is the pact which Asaph ben Berakhyahu and Yochanan ben Zabda made with their pupils, and they adjured them with the following words: [2] Do not attempt to kill any soul by means of a potion of herbs, [3] Do not make a woman [who is] pregnant [as a result of] whoring take a drink with a view to causing abortion, [4] Do not covet beauty of form in women with a view to fornicating with them, [5] Do not divulge the secret of a man who has trusted you.... [14] Now [then] put your trust in the Lord, your God, [who is] a true God, a living God, [15] For [it is] He who kills and makes alive, who wounds and heals.... [33] As for you, be strong, do not let your hands be weak, for your work shall be rewarded, [34] The Lord is with you, while you are with Him, [35] If you keep His pact, follow His commandments, cleaving to them, [36] You will be regarded as His saints in the eyes of all flesh, and they will say: [37] Happy the people whose [lot] is such, happy the people whose God is the Lord...."

6. In David L. Freeman and Judith Z. Abrams, eds., *Illness and Health in the Jewish Tradition* (Philadelphia: Jewish Publication Society, 1999), p. 158.

7. See Richard Walzer, *Galen on Christians and Jews* (London: Oxford University Press, 1949).

8. Jakobovits, *Jewish Medical Ethics*, p. xxxiii.

9. Ariel Bar-Sela, Hebbel E. Hoff, and Elias Farias, "Moses Maimonides: Two Treatises on the Regimen of Health," *American Philosophical Society* 54, no. 4 (1964): 24–27, quoted in Freeman and Abrams, eds., *Illness and Health*, p. 149.

10. Elliot N. Dorff, *Matters of Life and Death: A Jewish Approach to Modern Medical Ethics* (Philadelphia: Jewish Publication Society, 1998), p. 15.

11. J. David Bleich, "The Obligation to Heal in the Judaic Tradition," in *Jewish Bioethics*, ed. Fred Rosner and J. David Bleich (Jersey City, N.J.: Ktav, 2000), p. 21.

12. Michael Chernick, "Ownership, Stewardship, and Justice," in *Living Torah: Selections from Seven Years of Torat Chayim*, ed. Elaine Glickman (New York: URJ Press, 2005), pp. 296–97.

13. John Locke, "Two Treatises of Government, Ch. 2," cited in *Biomedical Ethics*, ed. Thomas Mappes and David DeGrazia (New York: McGraw-Hill, 1996), p. 379; Immanuel Kant, *Lectures on Ethics*, trans. Louis Infield (New York: Harper & Row, 1963), cited in Mappes and DeGrazia, eds., *Biomedical Ethics*, p. 378; Bleich, "Obligation to Heal," p. 20.

14. One need only consider the landmark cases of Nancy Cruzan or Karen Quinlan to realize the differences between a patient's or a family's ideas of nonmaleficence and those of the medical profession. These cases were brought by the families of comatose women to force the physicians caring for them to discontinue their treatment. In recent years we may have come full circle and physicians are now asking courts to allow them to discontinue treatment they consider to be futile (and typically very expensive and a waste of scarce resources) but that the family wants to maintain.

15. It was right around the time Jakobovits was working on his dissertation, 1954, that Joseph Murray and his team performed the world's first successful kidney transplantation between identical twin brothers. Murray was awarded the Nobel Prize for this achievement in 1990 and recalled in his acceptance speech the moral dilemma posed by performing a risky operation on an individual (the donating brother) that was not for his own benefit.

16. Miles, *Hippocratic Oath*, p. 5.

17. Rita Charon and Martha Montello, eds., *Stories Matter: The Role of Narrative in Medical Ethics* (New York: Routledge, 2002), p. xi.

18. See William Cutter's discussion and analysis of this story in "Rabbi Judah's Handmaid," in *Death and Euthanasia in Jewish Law: Essays and Responsa*, ed. Walter Jacob and Moshe Zemer (Pittsburgh: Rodef Shalom Press, 1994), pp. 61–87; and "Do the Quality of Stories Influence the Quality of Life? Some Perspectives on the Limitations and Enhancements of Narrative Ethics," in *Quality of Life in Jewish Bioethics*, ed. Noam Zohar (Lanham, Md.: Lexington Books, 2006), pp. 55–66. See also the discussion by Peter Knobel in "An Expanded Approach to Jewish Bioethics: A Liberal/Aggadic Approach," in *Healing and the Jewish Imagination: Spiritual and Practical Perspectives on Judaism and Health*, ed. William Cutter (Woodstock, Vt.: Jewish Lights, 2007), pp. 171–82, and Louis Newman, "The Narrative and the Normative: The Value of Stories for Jewish Ethics," pp. 183–92, in the same volume.

19. References to Rabbi Yehudah HaNasi in the Talmud refer to him simply as Rabbi. That is the convention I will follow in this discussion. I have added in brackets {}

a coda found in the Talmud but often not quoted when the story is retold in bioethics literature.

20. *Tosafot* (s.vv. *umanah tefillin*) point out that someone with an intestinal illness is not required to wear tefillin, but Rabbi was used to maintaining himself in an elevated state of holiness.

21. Cutter, "Do the Quality of Stories," p. 62.

22. Often translated as "in the throes of dying," or "in his death throes," the classical understanding is that a *goseis* is a dying person who is expected to die within three days. Perhaps a better understanding in our times is what is referred to as "actively dying." There is extensive discussion of this concept in modern medical literature arising out of hospice care. It is not specifically time dependent, although patients typically die within hours to a day or two once they enter this stage. This is the time when families tend to be called and maintain vigil by their loved one. It is characterized by specific physical findings and is generally recognizable to those who regularly care for dying patients. Although many, perhaps most, patients never go through this stage, once a patient enters this stage there is nothing to be done to alter the outcome. Rabbi, in the story, is not "actively dying," and I would argue, as I do above, is not a *goseis* by classical or modern definition.

23. Arnold Eisen, "Choose Life: American Jews and the Quest for Healing," in *Healing and the Jewish Imagination*, ed. Cutter, p. 35.

24. Knobel, "Expanded Approach to Jewish Bioethics," p. 172.

25. Newman, *Healing and the Jewish Imagination*, ed. Cutter, p. 186.

26. Cutter, "Do the Quality of Stories," p. 68.

27. See, for examples of works that illustrate this tension, J. David Bleich, "Treatment of the Terminally Ill," in *Bioethical Dilemmas: A Jewish Perspective* (Hoboken, N.J.: Ktav, 1998), pp. 61–112; J. David Bleich, "Euthanasia," in *Judaism and Healing: Halakhic Perspectives* (Hoboken, N.J.: Ktav, 1981), pp. 134–45; and Avram Reisner, "A Halakhic Ethic of Care for the Terminally Ill," Responsa of the Committee on Jewish Law and Standards of the Conservative Movement, YD 339:1.1990a.

28. There is, in fact, a substantial literature on the actively or imminently dying. See, e.g., K. A. Moneymaker, "Understanding the Dying Process: Transitions during Final Days to Hours," *Journal of Palliative Medicine* 8, no. 5 (October 2005): 1079; and M. Lynch and C. M. Dahlin, "The National Consensus Project and National Quality Forum Preferred Practices in Care of the Imminently Dying," *Journal of Hospice & Palliative Nursing* 9, no. 6 (December 2007): 316–22. See also J. L. Hallenbeck, "The Final 48 Hours," in *Palliative Care Perspectives* (New York: Oxford University Press, 2003).

29. Leonard Sharzer, "Organ Donation after Cardiac Death," Responsa of the Committee on Jewish Law and Standards of the Conservative Movement, YD 367:1.2010, Fn 44.

30. Newman, *Healing and the Jewish Imagination*, ed. Cutter, p. 185.

31. Abraham J. Heschel, "The Patient as Person," in *The Insecurity of Freedom* (Philadelphia: Jewish Publication Society, 1966), p. 37.

32. Charon and Montello, *Stories Matter*, p. xi.

Jewish Bioethics: Between Interpretation and Criticism

1. For recent contributions to this debate, see Peter Knobel, "An Expanded Approach to Jewish Bioethics: A Liberal/Aggadic Approach," and Louis E. Newman, "The Narrative and the Normative: The Value of Stories for Jewish Ethics," in *Healing and the Jewish Imagination*, ed. William Cutter (Woodstock, Vt.: Jewish Lights, 2007), pp. 171–92; William Cutter, "Does the Quality of Stories Influence the Quality of Life? Arguments from Jewish Bioethics," in *Quality of Life in Jewish Bioethics*, ed. Noam Zohar (Lanham, Md.: Lexington Books, 2006).

2. Geoffrey H. Hartman, *Saving the Text* (Baltimore: Johns Hopkins University Press, 1981), pp. 138–39.

3. An example for such hurt that Hartman adduces is the purported insult suffered by Jean Genet. Here, he recalls Sartre, who suggests that Genet's literary genius was spurred by injurious words directed at him when he was a child. To the purported insult that unleashed the dramatist's genius we may add our own, no less real example. In his autobiographical notes and comments, Akibah Ernst Simon traces his Jewish and Zionist paths. Simon testifies that in order to become a Zionist, he first needed to become a Jew. He also intimates that he was unaware of his Judaism until the seventh year to his life. In a German primary school, halfway through the first decade of the twentieth century, a classmate had invited him to his birthday party and later cancelled the invitation, explaining that his parents did not allow him to invite home a Jew. Perplexed, Simon asked his father that evening whether it was true that he was Jewish. His father replied "Yes you are, and you should be proud of it!" (Y. Amir, "A. E. Simon's Judaism," in *Akiba Ernst Simon: Educator in Thought and Action* [Jerusalem: School of Education of the Hebrew University/Ministry of Education and Culture, Magnes Press, 1980], p. 13). Years later, he recalls, when he was drafted into the Imperial Army to serve Germany in World War I, he was "an agnostic and ignorant Jew; an assimilated *maskil* with an aesthetic sensibility." Yet, within less than three years, he "was a Zionist who was open to addressing questions of faith." Part of this transformation he attributes to overhearing one of his sergeant major's orders during hostilities. While assigning positions to the troops, the sergeant major uttered, "There, among the bushes—that is a particularly dangerous spot. Send Simon there, the little Jew" (A. E. Simon, *Chapters in My Life: Building in the Time of Destruction* [Tel Aviv: Sifriat Poalim, Leo Baeck Institute, 1986], pp. 42–43). Simon resolved to abandon progress toward an academic career in Germany and dedicated himself to the task of education among Israel.

4. Hartman, *Saving the Text*, pp. 120–23.

5. Leibowitz's argument was published in "Judaism, Humanism, and Universalism" [*Yahadut, Am Yehudi, u-Medinat Yisarel*] (Tel Aviv: Schocken, 1975), p. 314. The volume was translated into English as *Judaism, Human Values, and the Jewish State*, ed. E. Goldman (Cambridge, Mass.: Harvard University Press, 1992). Menahem Kellner makes a similar argument in his "Reflections on the Impossibility of Jewish Ethics," *Bar Ilan Annual* 22–23 (Moshe Schwarcz Memorial Volume, 1987), pp. 45–52. Toward the conclusion of his analysis, he states, "[Jewish] ethic must be seen as divinely revealed.... But if it is revealed, we must cope with the question of the autonomy or heteronomy of such an ethic. If we assume its autonomy, then we are back at square one: God is irrelevant to any truly autonomous ethic ... no autonomous ethic could be a truly Jewish ethic. But if normative Jewish ethics is not autonomous, it must be heteronomous and, according to the consensus of moral philosophy since Kant, impure" (p. 50).
6. Hartman, *Saving the Text*, p. 139.
7. Ibid.
8. Ibid., pp. 140–41.
9. Ibid., p. 141.
10. Kellner, "Impossibility of Jewish Ethics," p. 46.
11. Robert Cover, *Narrative, Violence, and the Law: The Essays of Robert Cover*, ed. Martha Minow, Michael Ryan, and Austin Sarat (Ann Arbor: University of Michigan Press, 1995), p. 203.
12. See Tom L. Beauchamp and James F. Childress, *Principles of Biomedical Ethics* (Oxford: Oxford University Press, 1979).
13. Especially in the aftermath of the publication of Michel Foucault's *Folie et déraison: Histoire de la folie à l'âge classique* in 1961, abridged and translated as *Madness and Civilization: A History of Insanity in the Age of Reason* (New York: Random House, 1965); and retranslated in full as *History of Madness* (London: Routledge, 2006).
14. Michel Foucault, *The Birth of the Clinic*, trans. A. M. Sheridan (London: Routledge Classics, 2003). One similarity between the provision of mental health treatment and other health care regards the association between health and normality. Foucault writes, "It might be said that up to the end of the eighteenth century medicine related much more to health than to normality; it did not begin by analyzing a 'regular' functioning of the organism and go on to seek where it had deviated.... It referred, rather, to qualities of vigour, suppleness, and fluidity, which were lost in illness and which it was the task of medicine to restore. Nineteenth century medicine ... was regulated more in accordance with normality than with health ... and physiological knowledge—once marginal and purely theoretical for the doctor—was to be established ... at the very center of medical reflexion" (p. 40).
15. Especially in ibid., pp. 48–9.

16. A recent airing of the metamedical issues that arise in the discussion on the allocation of scarce resources occurred in response to the report of the Task Force for Mass Critical Care presented in a series of documents in a supplement to the May 2008 edition of *Chest*, http://chestjournal.chestpubs.org/content/133/5_suppl.

17. Cover, *Narrative, Violence, and the Law*, ed. Minow, Ryan, and Sarat, p. 224.

18. Wayne C. Booth, *The Company We Keep* (Berkeley: University of California Press, 1988), pp. 227–29. Booth cites examples like that of the poet Infante attempting to commit suicide on a plane following his reading of Malcolm Lowry's *Under a Volcano*, or of youngsters who experiment with drugs after reading Kerouac's *On the Road*.

19. Booth, *The Company We Keep*, p. 187 (emphasis in the original).

20. Ibid., chap. 13.

10 What Takes Place and What Can Be Changed

A Midrash on the *Mi Sheberakh*: A Prayer for Persisting

1. Avraham Yaari, *"Tefilot Misheberakh"* ["The Misheberakh Prayers"], *Kiryat Sefer* 33 (1958): pp. 118–130. See also *Kiryat Sefer* 36 (1961).

2. Jacob struggled with an invisible being in the night, emerging with a limp. He would not cease his wrestling until he also emerged with a blessing from his adversary (Genesis 32).

3. Jonathan was the rightful inheritor of his father Saul's throne but desired instead to yield leadership to his beloved friend, David. Because he refused to abandon his deeply held convictions, he fought against his father and died in battle defending his companion and his beliefs. David, in his turn, did not slay Saul, nor purge the families of his rival dynasty, even at the risk of his own life and throne, in honor of Jonathan his beloved friend (Samuel 2 and Kings 1).

4. Daniel's enemies threw him into the lion's den, by order of the king (Daniel 6).

5. Tamar was twice widowed, childless, and then denied both levirate remarriage and release from bond by her father-in-law because he feared that she would somehow cause the death of a third husband were she to be allowed to marry again (Genesis 38–39).

6. Hannah was infertile, wished desperately for a child, was mocked by her co-wife about it, and received little understanding from her husband. She invented silent prayer, received the blessing of Eli the High Priest, and became pregnant with Samuel the prophet (Judges 13).

7. As Moses passes the mantle of leadership to the next generation, he says, *Chazak v'ematz*, meaning "May you be strong and courageous" (Deuteronomy 31–32).

The Human Body and the Body Politic

1. Mitchell B. Hart, *The Healthy Jew: The Symbiosis of Judaism and Modern Medicine* (New York: Cambridge University Press, 2007), p. 11.

2. Abraham J. Heschel, *Between God and Man* (New York: Free Press, 1959), pp. 238–39.

3. Arnold Eisen, "Choose Life: American Jews and the Quest for Healing," in *Healing and the Jewish Imagination: Spiritual and Practical Perspectives on Judaism and Health*, ed. William Cutter (Woodstock, Vt.: Jewish Lights, 2007), pp. 15–41.

4. Ibid., pp. 27–28.

5. Ibid., p. 17.

6. Arnold Eisen and Steven Cohen, *The Jew Within: Self, Family, and Community in America* (Bloomington: Indiana University Press, 2000), p. 184.

7. Herbert Benson, *Timeless Healing* (New York: Scribner, 1996), p. 287.

8. Jeff Levin, *God, Faith, and Health: Exploring the Spirituality-Healing Connection* (New York: John Wiley, 2001), p. 99.

9. Abraham J. Heschel, *The Insecurity of Freedom* (New York: Schocken, 1979), p. 33.

10. Andrew Weil, *Spontaneous Healing* (New York: Knopf, 1995), p. 97.

11. Fred Rosner and Samuel S. Kottek, eds., *Moses Maimonides: Physician, Scientist, and Philosopher* (Northvale, N.J.: Jason Aronson, 1993), p. 167.

CREDITS

"A Man in His Life" from *Yehuda Amichai: A Life of Poetry, 1948–1994* by Yehuda Amichai, translated by Benjamin and Barbara Harshav. Copyright © 1994 by HarperCollins Publishers Inc. Hebrew-language version copyright © 1994 by Yehuda Amichai. Reprinted by permission of HarperCollins Publishers.

Eitan Fishbane, selections from *Shadows in Winter* (Syracuse: Syracuse University Press) © 2011 by Eitan Fishbane.

From "Hallelu (after Psalms 117 and 134)" © 2004 Composing Together Works. Words and music by elders of the Jewish Home San Francisco Psalms, Songs and Stories™ Project, Rabbi Sheldon Marder, and Judith-Kate Friedman. All rights reserved. Reprinted with permission. Contact: Songwriting Works™ Educational Foundation, www.songwritingworks.org, 360-385-1160.

From "Love Everlasting" © 2003 Composing Together Works. Words and music by elders of the Jewish Home San Francisco Psalms, Songs and Stories™ project with Judith-Kate Friedman and Rabbi Sheldon Marder. All rights reserved. Reprinted with permission.

From "Psalm 128" © 2004 Composing Together Works. Words and music by elders of the Jewish Home San Francisco Psalms, Songs and Stories™ Project, Rabbi Sheldon Marder, and Judith-Kate Friedman. All rights reserved. Reprinted with permission. Contact: Songwriting Works™ Educational Foundation, www.songwritingworks. org, 360-385-1160.

Marc J. Straus, "Eleventh Floor" and "Like Me," in *Symmetry* (Evanston, Ill.: Northwestern University Press/TriQuarterly Books, 2000), pp. 47, 54 © 2000 by Marc J. Straus. Published 2000. All rights reserved.

From "Tears, Dreamers" © 2007 Composing Together Works. Words and music by elders of the Jewish Home San Francisco Psalms, Songs and Stories™ project with Judith-Kate Friedman and Rabbi Sheldon Marder. All rights reserved. Reprinted with permission.

"When the Woman" from *The Spectacular Difference: Selected Poems of Zelda*, translated from the Hebrew, with an introduction and notes by Marcia Falk (Hebrew Union College Press, 2004). Copyright © 2004 by Marcia Lee Falk. Reprinted by permission of the translator.

Congregation Resources

Empowered Judaism: What Independent Minyanim Can Teach Us about Building Vibrant Jewish Communities
By Rabbi Elie Kaunfer; Foreword by Prof. Jonathan D. Sarna
Examines the independent minyan movement and the lessons these grassroots communities can provide. 6 x 9, 224 pp, Quality PB, 978-1-58023-412-2 **$18.99**

Spiritual Boredom: Rediscovering the Wonder of Judaism *By Dr. Erica Brown*
Breaks through the surface of spiritual boredom to find the reservoir of meaning within. 6 x 9, 208 pp, HC, 978-1-58023-405-4 **$21.99**

Building a Successful Volunteer Culture
Finding Meaning in Service in the Jewish Community
By Rabbi Charles Simon; Foreword by Shelley Lindauer; Preface by Dr. Ron Wolfson
Shows you how to develop and maintain the volunteers who are essential to the vitality of your organization and community. 6 x 9, 192 pp, Quality PB, 978-1-58023-408-5 **$16.99**

The Case for Jewish Peoplehood: Can We Be One?
By Dr. Erica Brown and Dr. Misha Galperin; Foreword by Rabbi Joseph Telushkin
6 x 9, 224 pp, HC, 978-1-58023-401-6 **$21.99**

Inspired Jewish Leadership: Practical Approaches to Building Strong Communities
By Dr. Erica Brown 6 x 9, 256 pp, HC, 978-1-58023-361-3 **$24.99**

Jewish Pastoral Care, 2nd Edition: A Practical Handbook from Traditional & Contemporary Sources *Edited by Rabbi Dayle A. Friedman, MSW, MAJCS, BCC*
6 x 9, 528 pp, Quality PB, 978-1-58023-427-6 **$30.00**; HC, 978-1-58023-221-0 **$40.00**

Rethinking Synagogues: A New Vocabulary for Congregational Life
By Rabbi Lawrence A. Hoffman, PhD 6 x 9, 240 pp, Quality PB, 978-1-58023-248-7 **$19.99**

The Spirituality of Welcoming: How to Transform Your Congregation into a Sacred Community *By Dr. Ron Wolfson* 6 x 9, 224 pp, Quality PB, 978-1-58023-244-9 **$19.99**

Children's Books

What You Will See Inside a Synagogue
By Rabbi Lawrence A. Hoffman, PhD, and Dr. Ron Wolfson; Full-color photos by Bill Aron
A colorful, fun-to-read introduction that explains the ways and whys of Jewish worship and religious life. 8½ x 10½, 32 pp, Full-color photos, Quality PB, 978-1-59473-256-0 **$8.99**
For ages 6 & up (A book from SkyLight Paths, Jewish Lights' sister imprint)

Because Nothing Looks Like God
By Lawrence Kushner and Karen Kushner Introduces children to the possibilities of spiritual life. 11 x 8½, 32 pp, Full-color illus., HC, 978-1-58023-092-6 **$17.99** *For ages 4 & up*
Board Book Companions to Because Nothing Looks Like God
5 x 5, 24 pp, Full-color illus., SkyLight Paths Board Books *For ages 0–4*

How Does God Make Things Happen? 978-1-893361-24-9 **$7.95**

What Does God Look Like? 978-1-893361-23-2 **$7.99**

Where Is God? 978-1-893361-17-1 **$7.99**

The Book of Miracles: A Young Person's Guide to Jewish Spiritual Awareness
Written and illus. by Lawrence Kushner
6 x 9, 96 pp, 2-color illus., HC, 978-1-879045-78-1 **$16.95** *For ages 9 & up*

In God's Hands *By Lawrence Kushner and Gary Schmidt* 9 x 12, 32 pp, Full-color illus., HC, 978-1-58023-224-1 **$16.99**

In Our Image: God's First Creatures *By Nancy Sohn Swartz*
9 x 12, 32 pp, Full-color illus., HC, 978-1-879045-99-6 **$16.95** *For ages 4 & up*

Also Available as a Board Book: **How Did the Animals Help God?**
5 x 5, 24 pp, Full-color illus., Board Book, 978-1-59473-044-3 **$7.99** *For ages 0–4*
(A book from SkyLight Paths, Jewish Lights' sister imprint)

The Kids' Fun Book of Jewish Time
By Emily Sper 9 x 7½, 24 pp, Full-color illus., HC, 978-1-58023-311-8 **$16.99**

What Makes Someone a Jew? *By Lauren Seidman*
Reflects the changing face of American Judaism.
10 x 8½, 32 pp, Full-color photos, Quality PB, 978-1-58023-321-7 **$8.99** *For ages 3–6*

Social Justice

There Shall Be No Needy
Pursuing Social Justice through Jewish Law and Tradition
By Rabbi Jill Jacobs; Foreword by Rabbi Elliot N. Dorff, PhD; Preface by Simon Greer
Confronts the most pressing issues of twenty-first-century America from a deeply Jewish perspective.
6 x 9, 288 pp, Quality PB, 978-1-58023-425-2 **$16.99**; HC, 978-1-58023-394-1 **$21.99**
Also Available: **There Shall Be No Needy Teacher's Guide**
8½ x 11, 56 pp, PB, 978-1-58023-429-0 **$8.99**

Conscience: The Duty to Obey and the Duty to Disobey
By Rabbi Harold M. Schulweis
This clarion call to rethink our moral and political behavior examines the idea of conscience and the role conscience plays in our relationships to government, law, ethics, religion, human nature, God—and to each other.
6 x 9, 160 pp, Quality PB, 978-1-58023-419-1 **$16.99**; HC, 978-1-58023-375-0 **$19.99**

Judaism and Justice: The Jewish Passion to Repair the World
By Rabbi Sidney Schwarz; Foreword by Ruth Messinger
Explores the relationship between Judaism, social justice and the Jewish identity of American Jews.
6 x 9, 352 pp, Quality PB, 978-1-58023-353-8 **$19.99**; HC, 978-1-58023-312-5 **$24.99**

Spiritual Activism: A Jewish Guide to Leadership and Repairing the World
By Rabbi Avraham Weiss; Foreword by Alan M. Dershowitz
6 x 9, 224 pp, Quality PB, 978-1-58023-418-4 **$16.99**; HC, 978-1-58023-355-2 **$24.99**

Righteous Indignation: A Jewish Call for Justice
Edited by Rabbi Or N. Rose, Jo Ellen Green Kaiser and Margie Klein; Foreword by Rabbi David Ellenson, PhD
Leading progressive Jewish activists explore meaningful intellectual and spiritual foundations for their social justice work.
6 x 9, 384 pp, Quality PB, 978-1-58023-414-6 **$19.99**; HC, 978-1-58023-336-1 **$24.99**

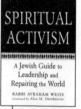

Spirituality/Women's Interest

New Jewish Feminism: Probing the Past, Forging the Future
Edited by Rabbi Elyse Goldstein; Foreword by Anita Diamant
Looks at the growth and accomplishments of Jewish feminism and what they mean for Jewish women today and tomorrow.
6 x 9, 480 pp, HC, 978-1-58023-359-0 **$24.99**

The Divine Feminine in Biblical Wisdom Literature
Selections Annotated & Explained
Translation & Annotation by Rabbi Rami Shapiro
5½ x 8½, 240 pp, Quality PB, 978-1-59473-109-9 **$16.99**
(A book from SkyLight Paths, Jewish Lights' sister imprint)

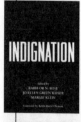

The Quotable Jewish Woman: Wisdom, Inspiration & Humor from the Mind & Heart
Edited by Elaine Bernstein Partnow 6 x 9, 496 pp, Quality PB, 978-1-58023-236-4 **$19.99**

The Women's Haftarah Commentary: New Insights from Women Rabbis on the 54 Weekly Haftarah Portions, the 5 Megillot & Special Shabbatot
Edited by Rabbi Elyse Goldstein Illuminates the historical significance of female portrayals in the Haftarah and the Five Megillot.
6 x 9, 560 pp, Quality PB, 978-1-58023-371-2 **$19.99**

The Women's Torah Commentary: New Insights from Women Rabbis on the 54 Weekly Torah Portions
Edited by Rabbi Elyse Goldstein
Over fifty women rabbis offer inspiring insights on the Torah, in a week-by-week format.
6 x 9, 496 pp, Quality PB, 978-1-58023-370-5 **$19.99**; HC, 978-1-58023-076-6 **$34.95**

See Passover for *The Women's Passover Companion: Women's Reflections on the Festival of Freedom* and *The Women's Seder Sourcebook: Rituals & Readings for Use at the Passover Seder.*

Pastoral Care Resources
LifeLights/™אורות החיים

LifeLights/™אורות החיים are inspirational, informational booklets about challenges to our emotional and spiritual lives and how to deal with them. Offering help for wholeness and healing, each *LifeLight* is written from a uniquely Jewish spiritual perspective by a wise and caring soul—someone who knows the inner territory of grief, doubt, confusion and longing.

In addition to providing wise words to light a difficult path, each *LifeLight* booklet provides suggestions for additional resources for reading. Many list organizations, Jewish and secular, that can provide help, along with information on how to contact them.

Categories/Sample Topics:
Health & Healing
Caring for Yourself When You Are Caring for Someone Who Is Ill
Facing Cancer as a Family
Recognizing a Loved One's Addiction, and Providing Help
Loss / Grief / Death & Dying
Coping with the Death of a Spouse
From Death through *Shiva*: A Guide to Jewish Grieving Practices
Taking the Time You Need to Mourn Your Loss
Talking to Children about Death
Judaism / Living a Jewish Life
Bar and Bat Mitzvah's Meaning: Preparing Spiritually with Your Child
Yearning for God
Family Issues
Grandparenting Interfaith Grandchildren
Talking to Your Children about God
Spiritual Care / Personal Growth
Easing the Burden of Stress
Finding a Way to Forgive
Praying in Hard Times

Now available in hundreds of congregations, health-care facilities, funeral homes, colleges and military installations, these helpful, comforting resources can be uniquely presented in *LifeLights* display racks, available from Jewish Lights. **Each *LifeLight* topic is sold in packs of twelve for $9.95.** General discounts are available for quantity purchases.

Visit us online at **www.jewishlights.com** for a complete list of titles, authors, prices and ordering information, or call us at (802) 457-4000 or toll free at (800) 962-4544.

Holidays/Holy Days

Who by Fire, Who by Water—Un'taneh Tokef
Edited by Rabbi Lawrence A. Hoffman, PhD
Examines the prayer's theology, authorship and poetry through a set of lively essays, all written in accessible language.
6 x 9, 272 pp, HC, 978-1-58023-424-5 **$24.99**

Rosh Hashanah Readings: Inspiration, Information and Contemplation
Yom Kippur Readings: Inspiration, Information and Contemplation
Edited by Rabbi Dov Peretz Elkins; Section Introductions from Arthur Green's These Are the Words
An extraordinary collection of readings, prayers and insights that will enable you to enter into the spirit of the High Holy Days in a personal and powerful way, permitting the meaning of the Jewish New Year to enter the heart.
Rosh Hashanah: 6 x 9, 400 pp, Quality PB, 978-1-58023-437-5 **$19.99**
Yom Kippur: 6 x 9, 368 pp, Quality PB, 978-1-58023-438-2 **$19.99**

Jewish Holidays: A Brief Introduction for Christians
By Rabbi Kerry M. Olitzky and Rabbi Daniel Judson
5½ x 8½, 176 pp, Quality PB, 978-1-58023-302-6 **$16.99**

Reclaiming Judaism as a Spiritual Practice: Holy Days and Shabbat
By Rabbi Goldie Milgram 7 x 9, 272 pp, Quality PB, 978-1-58023-205-0 **$19.99**

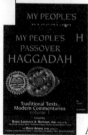

7th Heaven: Celebrating Shabbat with Rebbe Nachman of Breslov
By Moshe Mykoff with the Breslov Research Institute
5⅛ x 8¼, 224 pp, Deluxe PB w/ flaps, 978-1-58023-175-6 **$18.95**

Shabbat, 2nd Edition: The Family Guide to Preparing for and Celebrating the Sabbath *By Dr. Ron Wolfson*
7 x 9, 320 pp, Illus., Quality PB, 978-1-58023-164-0 **$19.99**

Hanukkah, 2nd Edition: The Family Guide to Spiritual Celebration
By Dr. Ron Wolfson 7 x 9, 240 pp, Illus., Quality PB, 978-1-58023-122-0 **$18.95**

The Jewish Family Fun Book, 2nd Edition: Holiday Projects, Everyday Activities, and Travel Ideas with Jewish Themes *By Danielle Dardashti and Roni Sarig; Illus. by Avi Katz*
6 x 9, 304 pp, 70+ b/w illus. & diagrams, Quality PB, 978-1-58023-333-0 **$18.99**

The Jewish Lights Book of Fun Classroom Activities: Simple and Seasonal Projects for Teachers and Students *By Danielle Dardashti and Roni Sarig*
6 x 9, 240 pp, Quality PB, 978-1-58023-206-7 **$19.99**

Passover

My People's Passover Haggadah
Traditional Texts, Modern Commentaries
Edited by Rabbi Lawrence A. Hoffman, PhD, and David Arnow, PhD
A diverse and exciting collection of commentaries on the traditional Passover Haggadah—in two volumes!
Vol. 1: 7 x 10, 304 pp, HC, 978-1-58023-354-5 **$24.99**
Vol. 2: 7 x 10, 320 pp, HC, 978-1-58023-346-0 **$24.99**

Leading the Passover Journey: The Seder's Meaning Revealed, the Haggadah's Story Retold *By Rabbi Nathan Laufer*
Uncovers the hidden meaning of the Seder's rituals and customs.
6 x 9, 224 pp, Quality PB, 978-1-58023-399-6 **$18.99**; HC, 978-1-58023-211-1 **$24.99**

The Women's Passover Companion: Women's Reflections on the Festival of Freedom
Edited by Rabbi Sharon Cohen Anisfeld, Tara Mohr and Catherine Spector; Foreword by Paula E. Hyman
6 x 9, 352 pp, Quality PB, 978-1-58023-231-9 **$19.99**; HC, 978-1-58023-128-2 **$24.95**

The Women's Seder Sourcebook: Rituals & Readings for Use at the Passover Seder
Edited by Rabbi Sharon Cohen Anisfeld, Tara Mohr and Catherine Spector
6 x 9, 384 pp, Quality PB, 978-1-58023-232-6 **$19.99**

Creating Lively Passover Seders: A Sourcebook of Engaging Tales, Texts & Activities
By David Arnow, PhD 7 x 9, 416 pp, Quality PB, 978-1-58023-184-8 **$24.99**

Passover, 2nd Edition: The Family Guide to Spiritual Celebration
By Dr. Ron Wolfson with Joel Lurie Grishaver 7 x 9, 416 pp, Quality PB, 978-1-58023-174-9 **$19.95**

Life Cycle
Marriage/Parenting/Family/Aging

The New Jewish Baby Album: Creating and Celebrating the Beginning of a Spiritual Life—A Jewish Lights Companion
By the Editors at Jewish Lights; Foreword by Anita Diamant; Preface by Rabbi Sandy Eisenberg Sasso
A spiritual keepsake that will be treasured for generations. More than just a memory book, *shows you how—and why it's important*—to create a Jewish home and a Jewish life. 8 x 10, 64 pp, Deluxe Padded HC, Full-color illus., 978-1-58023-138-1 **$19.95**

The Jewish Pregnancy Book: A Resource for the Soul, Body & Mind during Pregnancy, Birth & the First Three Months *By Sandy Falk, MD, and Rabbi Daniel Judson, with Steven A. Rapp* Medical information, prayers and rituals for each stage of pregnancy. 7 x 10, 208 pp, b/w photos, Quality PB, 978-1-58023-178-2 **$16.95**

Celebrating Your New Jewish Daughter: Creating Jewish Ways to Welcome Baby Girls into the Covenant—New and Traditional Ceremonies *By Debra Nussbaum Cohen; Foreword by Rabbi Sandy Eisenberg Sasso* 6 x 9, 272 pp, Quality PB, 978-1-58023-090-2 **$18.95**

The New Jewish Baby Book, 2nd Edition: Names, Ceremonies & Customs—A Guide for Today's Families *By Anita Diamant* 6 x 9, 336 pp, Quality PB, 978-1-58023-251-7 **$19.99**

Parenting as a Spiritual Journey: Deepening Ordinary and Extraordinary Events into Sacred Occasions *By Rabbi Nancy Fuchs-Kreimer, PhD*
6 x 9, 224 pp, Quality PB, 978-1-58023-016-2 **$16.95**

Parenting Jewish Teens: A Guide for the Perplexed
By Joanne Doades Explores the questions and issues that shape the world in which today's Jewish teenagers live and offers constructive advice to parents.
6 x 9, 176 pp, Quality PB, 978-1-58023-305-7 **$16.99**

Judaism for Two: A Spiritual Guide for Strengthening and Celebrating Your Loving Relationship *By Rabbi Nancy Fuchs-Kreimer, PhD, and Rabbi Nancy H. Wiener, DMin; Foreword by Rabbi Elliot N. Dorff*
Addresses the ways Jewish teachings can enhance and strengthen committed relationships. 6 x 9, 224 pp, Quality PB, 978-1-58023-254-8 **$16.99**

The Creative Jewish Wedding Book, 2nd Edition: A Hands-On Guide to New & Old Traditions, Ceremonies & Celebrations *By Gabrielle Kaplan-Mayer*
9 x 9, 288 pp, b/w photos, Quality PB, 978-1-58023-398-9 **$19.99**

Divorce Is a Mitzvah: A Practical Guide to Finding Wholeness and Holiness When Your Marriage Dies *By Rabbi Perry Netter; Afterword by Rabbi Laura Geller*
6 x 9, 224 pp, Quality PB, 978-1-58023-172-5 **$16.95**

Embracing the Covenant: Converts to Judaism Talk About Why & How
By Rabbi Allan Berkowitz and Patti Moskovitz 6 x 9, 192 pp, Quality PB, 978-1-879045-50-7 **$16.95**

The Guide to Jewish Interfaith Family Life: An InterfaithFamily.com Handbook
Edited by Ronnie Friedland and Edmund Case
6 x 9, 384 pp, Quality PB, 978-1-58023-153-4 **$18.95**

A Heart of Wisdom: Making the Jewish Journey from Midlife through the Elder Years
Edited by Susan Berrin; Foreword by Rabbi Harold Kushner
6 x 9, 384 pp, Quality PB, 978-1-58023-051-3 **$18.95**

Introducing My Faith and My Community: The Jewish Outreach Institute Guide for the Christian in a Jewish Interfaith Relationship
By Rabbi Kerry M. Olitzky 6 x 9, 176 pp, Quality PB, 978-1-58023-192-3 **$16.99**

Making a Successful Jewish Interfaith Marriage: The Jewish Outreach Institute Guide to Opportunities, Challenges and Resources *By Rabbi Kerry M. Olitzky with Joan Peterson Littman*
6 x 9, 176 pp, Quality PB, 978-1-58023-170-1 **$16.95**

A Man's Responsibility: A Jewish Guide to Being a Son, a Partner in Marriage, a Father and a Community Leader *By Rabbi Joseph B. Meszler*
6 x 9, 192 pp, Quality PB, 978-1-58023-435-1 **$16.99**

So That Your Values Live On: Ethical Wills and How to Prepare Them
Edited by Rabbi Jack Riemer and Rabbi Nathaniel Stampfer
6 x 9, 272 pp, Quality PB, 978-1-879045-34-7 **$18.99**

Inspiration

The Seven Questions You're Asked in Heaven: Reviewing and Renewing Your Life on Earth *By Dr. Ron Wolfson*
An intriguing and entertaining resource for living a life that matters.
6 x 9, 176 pp, Quality PB, 978-1-58023-407-8 **$16.99**

Happiness and the Human Spirit: The Spirituality of Becoming the Best You Can Be *By Rabbi Abraham J. Twerski, MD*
Shows you that true happiness is attainable once you stop looking outside yourself for the source. 6 x 9, 176 pp, Quality PB, 978-1-58023-404-7 **$16.99**; HC, 978-1-58023-343-9 **$19.99**

A Formula for Proper Living: Practical Lessons from Life and Torah
By Rabbi Abraham J. Twerski, MD
Gives you practical lessons for life that you can put to day-to-day use in dealing with yourself and others. 6 x 9, 144 pp, HC, 978-1-58023-402-3 **$19.99**

The Bridge to Forgiveness: Stories and Prayers for Finding God and Restoring Wholeness *By Rabbi Karyn D. Kedar* 6 x 9, 176 pp, HC, 978-1-58023-324-8 **$19.99**

The Empty Chair: Finding Hope and Joy—Timeless Wisdom from a Hasidic Master, Rebbe Nachman of Breslov *Adapted by Moshe Mykoff and the Breslov Research Institute*
4 x 6, 128 pp, Deluxe PB w/ flaps, 978-1-879045-67-5 **$9.99**

The Gentle Weapon: Prayers for Everyday and Not-So-Everyday Moments—Timeless Wisdom from the Teachings of the Hasidic Master, Rebbe Nachman of Breslov *Adapted by Moshe Mykoff and S. C. Mizrahi, together with the Breslov Research Institute*
4 x 6, 144 pp, Deluxe PB w/ flaps, 978-1-58023-022-3 **$9.99**

God Whispers: Stories of the Soul, Lessons of the Heart *By Rabbi Karyn D. Kedar*
6 x 9, 176 pp, Quality PB, 978-1-58023-088-9 **$15.95**

God's To-Do List: 103 Ways to Be an Angel and Do God's Work on Earth
By Dr. Ron Wolfson 6 x 9, 144 pp, Quality PB, 978-1-58023-301-9 **$16.99**

Jewish Stories from Heaven and Earth: Inspiring Tales to Nourish the Heart and Soul *Edited by Rabbi Dov Peretz Elkins* 6 x 9, 304 pp, Quality PB, 978-1-58023-363-7 **$16.99**

Life's Daily Blessings: Inspiring Reflections on Gratitude and Joy for Every Day, Based on Jewish Wisdom *By Rabbi Kerry M. Olitzky* 4½ x 6½, 368 pp, Quality PB, 978-1-58023-396-5 **$16.99**

Restful Reflections: Nighttime Inspiration to Calm the Soul, Based on Jewish Wisdom
By Rabbi Kerry M. Olitzky and Rabbi Lori Forman 4½ x 6½, 448 pp, Quality PB, 978-1-58023-091-9 **$15.95**

Sacred Intentions: Daily Inspiration to Strengthen the Spirit, Based on Jewish Wisdom
By Rabbi Kerry M. Olitzky and Rabbi Lori Forman 4½ x 6½, 448 pp, Quality PB, 978-1-58023-061-2 **$15.95**

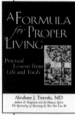

Kabbalah/Mysticism

Ehyeh: A Kabbalah for Tomorrow
By Rabbi Arthur Green, PhD 6 x 9, 224 pp, Quality PB, 978-1-58023-213-5 **$18.99**

The Flame of the Heart: Prayers of a Chasidic Mystic
By Reb Noson of Breslov; Translated and adapted by David Sears, with the Breslov Research Institute
5 x 7¼, 160 pp, Quality PB, 978-1-58023-246-3 **$15.99**

The Gift of Kabbalah: Discovering the Secrets of Heaven, Renewing Your Life on Earth
By Tamar Frankiel, PhD 6 x 9, 256 pp, Quality PB, 978-1-58023-141-1 **$16.95**

Kabbalah: A Brief Introduction for Christians
By Tamar Frankiel, PhD 5½ x 8½, 208 pp, Quality PB, 978-1-58023-303-3 **$16.99**

The Lost Princess & Other Kabbalistic Tales of Rebbe Nachman of Breslov
The Seven Beggars & Other Kabbalistic Tales of Rebbe Nachman of Breslov
Translated by Rabbi Aryeh Kaplan; Preface by Rabbi Chaim Kramer
Lost Princess: 6 x 9, 400 pp, Quality PB, 978-1-58023-217-3 **$18.99**
Seven Beggars: 6 x 9, 192 pp, Quality PB, 978-1-58023-250-0 **$16.99**

Seek My Face: A Jewish Mystical Theology *By Rabbi Arthur Green, PhD*
6 x 9, 304 pp, Quality PB, 978-1-58023-130-5 **$19.95**

Zohar: Annotated & Explained *Translation & Annotation by Dr. Daniel C. Matt; Foreword by Andrew Harvey* 5½ x 8½, 176 pp, Quality PB, 978-1-893361-51-5 **$15.99**
(A book from SkyLight Paths, Jewish Lights' sister imprint)

See also *The Way Into Jewish Mystical Tradition* in The Way Into... Series.

Spirituality

Repentance: The Meaning and Practice of *Teshuvah*
By Dr. Louis E. Newman; Foreword by Rabbi Harold M. Schulweis; Preface by Rabbi Karyn D. Kedar
Examines both the practical and philosophical dimensions of *teshuvah*, Judaism's core religious-moral teaching on repentance, and its value for us—Jews and non-Jews alike—today. 6 x 9, 256 pp, HC, 978-1-58023-426-9 **$24.99**

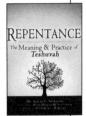

Tanya, the Masterpiece of Hasidic Wisdom
Selections Annotated & Explained
Translation & Annotation by Rabbi Rami Shapiro; Foreword by Rabbi Zalman M. Schachter-Shalomi
Brings the genius of *Tanya*, one of the most powerful books of Jewish wisdom, to anyone seeking to deepen their understanding of the soul.
5½ x 8½, 240 pp, Quality PB, 978-1-59473-275-1 **$16.99**
(A book from SkyLight Paths, Jewish Lights' sister imprint)

Aleph-Bet Yoga: Embodying the Hebrew Letters for Physical and Spiritual Well-Being
By Steven A. Rapp; Foreword by Tamar Frankiel, PhD, and Judy Greenfeld; Preface by Hart Lazer
7 x 10, 128 pp, b/w photos, Quality PB, Lay-flat binding, 978-1-58023-162-6 **$16.95**

A Book of Life: Embracing Judaism as a Spiritual Practice
By Rabbi Michael Strassfeld 6 x 9, 544 pp, Quality PB, 978-1-58023-247-0 **$19.99**

Bringing the Psalms to Life: How to Understand and Use the Book of Psalms
By Rabbi Daniel F. Polish, PhD 6 x 9, 208 pp, Quality PB, 978-1-58023-157-2 **$16.95**

Does the Soul Survive? A Jewish Journey to Belief in Afterlife, Past Lives & Living with Purpose *By Rabbi Elie Kaplan Spitz; Foreword by Brian L. Weiss, MD*
6 x 9, 288 pp, Quality PB, 978-1-58023-165-7 **$16.95**

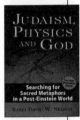

First Steps to a New Jewish Spirit: Reb Zalman's Guide to Recapturing the Intimacy & Ecstasy in Your Relationship with God *By Rabbi Zalman M. Schachter-Shalomi with Donald Gropman* 6 x 9, 144 pp, Quality PB, 978-1-58023-182-4 **$16.95**

Foundations of Sephardic Spirituality: The Inner Life of Jews of the Ottoman Empire
By Rabbi Marc D. Angel, PhD 6 x 9, 224 pp, Quality PB, 978-1-58023-341-5 **$18.99**

God & the Big Bang: Discovering Harmony between Science & Spirituality
By Dr. Daniel C. Matt 6 x 9, 216 pp, Quality PB, 978-1-879045-89-7 **$16.99**

God in Our Relationships: Spirituality between People from the Teachings of Martin Buber *By Rabbi Dennis S. Ross* 5½ x 8½, 160 pp, Quality PB, 978-1-58023-147-3 **$16.95**

The Jewish Lights Spirituality Handbook: A Guide to Understanding,
Exploring & Living a Spiritual Life *Edited by Stuart M. Matlins*
What exactly is "Jewish" about spirituality? How do I make it a part of my life? Fifty of today's foremost spiritual leaders share their ideas and experience with us.
6 x 9, 456 pp, Quality PB, 978-1-58023-093-3 **$19.99**

Judaism, Physics and God: Searching for Sacred Metaphors in a Post-Einstein World
By Rabbi David W. Nelson 6 x 9, 352 pp, Quality PB, inc. reader's discussion guide,
978-1-58023-306-4 **$18.99**; HC, 352 pp, 978-1-58023-252-4 **$24.99**

Meaning and Mitzvah: Daily Practices for Reclaiming Judaism through Prayer, God, Torah, Hebrew, Mitzvot and Peoplehood *By Rabbi Goldie Milgram*
7 x 9, 336 pp, Quality PB, 978-1-58023-256-2 **$19.99**

Minding the Temple of the Soul: Balancing Body, Mind, and Spirit through Traditional Jewish Prayer, Movement, and Meditation *By Tamar Frankiel, PhD, and Judy Greenfeld*
7 x 10, 184 pp, Illus., Quality PB, 978-1-879045-64-4 **$16.95**

One God Clapping: The Spiritual Path of a Zen Rabbi *By Rabbi Alan Lew with Sherril Jaffe*
5½ x 8½, 336 pp, Quality PB, 978-1-58023-115-2 **$16.95**

The Soul of the Story: Meetings with Remarkable People
By Rabbi David Zeller 6 x 9, 288 pp, HC, 978-1-58023-272-2 **$21.99**

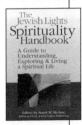

There Is No Messiah ... and You're It: The Stunning Transformation of Judaism's Most Provocative Idea *By Rabbi Robert N. Levine, DD*
6 x 9, 192 pp, Quality PB, 978-1-58023-255-5 **$16.99**

These Are the Words: A Vocabulary of Jewish Spiritual Life
By Rabbi Arthur Green, PhD 6 x 9, 304 pp, Quality PB, 978-1-58023-107-7 **$18.95**

Meditation

Jewish Meditation Practices for Everyday Life
Awakening Your Heart, Connecting with God
By Rabbi Jeff Roth
Offers a fresh take on meditation that draws on life experience and living life with greater clarity as opposed to the traditional method of rigorous study.
6 x 9, 224 pp, Quality PB, 978-1-58023-397-2 **$18.99**

The Handbook of Jewish Meditation Practices
A Guide for Enriching the Sabbath and Other Days of Your Life
By Rabbi David A. Cooper Easy-to-learn meditation techniques.
6 x 9, 208 pp, Quality PB, 978-1-58023-102-2 **$16.95**

Discovering Jewish Meditation: Instruction & Guidance for Learning an Ancient Spiritual Practice *By Nan Fink Gefen, PhD* 6 x 9, 208 pp, Quality PB, 978-1-58023-067-4 **$16.95**

Meditation from the Heart of Judaism: Today's Teachers Share Their Practices, Techniques, and Faith *Edited by Avram Davis*
6 x 9, 256 pp, Quality PB, 978-1-58023-049-0 **$16.95**

Ritual/Sacred Practices

The Jewish Dream Book: The Key to Opening the Inner Meaning of
Your Dreams *By Vanessa L. Ochs, PhD, with Elizabeth Ochs; Illus. by Kristina Swarner*
Instructions for how modern people can perform ancient Jewish dream practices and dream interpretations drawn from the Jewish wisdom tradition.
8 x 8, 128 pp, Full-color illus., Deluxe PB w/ flaps, 978-1-58023-132-9 **$16.95**

God in Your Body: Kabbalah, Mindfulness and Embodied Spiritual Practice
By Jay Michaelson
The first comprehensive treatment of the body in Jewish spiritual practice and an essential guide to the sacred.
6 x 9, 272 pp, Quality PB, 978-1-58023-304-0 **$18.99**

The Book of Jewish Sacred Practices: CLAL's Guide to Everyday &
Holiday Rituals & Blessings *Edited by Rabbi Irwin Kula and Vanessa L. Ochs, PhD*
6 x 9, 368 pp, Quality PB, 978-1-58023-152-7 **$18.95**

Jewish Ritual: A Brief Introduction for Christians
By Rabbi Kerry M. Olitzky and Rabbi Daniel Judson
5½ x 8½, 144 pp, Quality PB, 978-1-58023-210-4 **$14.99**

The Rituals & Practices of a Jewish Life: A Handbook for Personal Spiritual
Renewal *Edited by Rabbi Kerry M. Olitzky and Rabbi Daniel Judson*
6 x 9, 272 pp, Illus., Quality PB, 978-1-58023-169-5 **$18.95**

The Sacred Art of Lovingkindness: Preparing to Practice
By Rabbi Rami Shapiro 5½ x 8½, 176 pp, Quality PB, 978-1-59473-151-8 **$16.99**
(A book from SkyLight Paths, Jewish Lights' sister imprint)

Science Fiction/Mystery & Detective Fiction

Criminal Kabbalah: An Intriguing Anthology of Jewish Mystery &
Detective Fiction *Edited by Lawrence W. Raphael; Foreword by Laurie R. King*
All-new stories from twelve of today's masters of mystery and detective fiction—sure to delight mystery buffs of all faith traditions.
6 x 9, 256 pp, Quality PB, 978-1-58023-109-1 **$16.95**

Mystery Midrash: An Anthology of Jewish Mystery & Detective Fiction
Edited by Lawrence W. Raphael; Preface by Joel Siegel
6 x 9, 304 pp, Quality PB, 978-1-58023-055-1 **$16.95**

Wandering Stars: An Anthology of Jewish Fantasy & Science Fiction
Edited by Jack Dann; Introduction by Isaac Asimov
6 x 9, 272 pp, Quality PB, 978-1-58023-005-6 **$18.99**

More Wandering Stars: An Anthology of Outstanding Stories of Jewish Fantasy and
Science Fiction *Edited by Jack Dann; Introduction by Isaac Asimov*
6 x 9, 192 pp, Quality PB, 978-1-58023-063-6 **$16.95**

Spirituality/Prayer

Making Prayer Real: Leading Jewish Spiritual Voices on Why Prayer Is Difficult and What to Do about It *By Rabbi Mike Comins*
A new and different response to the challenges of Jewish prayer, with "best prayer practices" from Jewish spiritual leaders of all denominations.
6 x 9, 320 pp, Quality PB, 978-1-58023-417-7 **$18.99**

Witnesses to the One: The Spiritual History of the *Sh'ma*
By Rabbi Joseph B. Meszler; Foreword by Rabbi Elyse Goldstein
6 x 9, 176 pp, Quality PB, 978-1-58023-400-9 **$16.99**; HC, 978-1-58023-309-5 **$19.99**

My People's Prayer Book Series: Traditional Prayers, Modern Commentaries *Edited by Rabbi Lawrence A. Hoffman, PhD*
Provides diverse and exciting commentary to the traditional liturgy. Will help you find new wisdom in Jewish prayer, and bring liturgy into your life. Each book includes Hebrew text, modern translations and commentaries from all perspectives of the Jewish world.

Vol. 1—The *Sh'ma* and Its Blessings
  7 x 10, 168 pp, HC, 978-1-879045-79-8 **$24.99**
Vol. 2—The *Amidah* 7 x 10, 240 pp, HC, 978-1-879045-80-4 **$24.95**
Vol. 3—*P'sukei D'zimrah* (Morning Psalms)
  7 x 10, 240 pp, HC, 978-1-879045-81-1 **$24.95**
Vol. 4—*Seder K'riat Hatorah* (The Torah Service)
  7 x 10, 264 pp, HC, 978-1-879045-82-8 **$23.95**
Vol. 5—*Birkhot Hashachar* (Morning Blessings)
  7 x 10, 240 pp, HC, 978-1-879045-83-5 **$24.95**
Vol. 6—*Tachanun* and Concluding Prayers
  7 x 10, 240 pp, HC, 978-1-879045-84-2 **$24.95**
Vol. 7—*Shabbat at Home* 7 x 10, 240 pp, HC, 978-1-879045-85-9 **$24.95**
Vol. 8—*Kabbalat Shabbat* (Welcoming Shabbat in the Synagogue)
  7 x 10, 240 pp, HC, 978-1-58023-121-3 **$24.99**
Vol. 9—Welcoming the Night: *Minchah* and *Ma'ariv* (Afternoon and
  Evening Prayer) 7 x 10, 272 pp, HC, 978-1-58023-262-3 **$24.99**
Vol. 10—Shabbat Morning: *Shacharit* and *Musaf* (Morning and
  Additional Services) 7 x 10, 240 pp, HC, 978-1-58023-240-1 **$24.99**

Spirituality/Lawrence Kushner

The Book of Letters: A Mystical Hebrew Alphabet
Popular HC Edition, 6 x 9, 80 pp, 2-color text, 978-1-879045-00-2 **$24.95**
Collector's Limited Edition, 9 x 12, 80 pp, gold-foil-embossed pages, w/ limited-edition silkscreened print, 978-1-879045-04-0 **$349.00**

The Book of Miracles: A Young Person's Guide to Jewish Spiritual Awareness
6 x 9, 96 pp, 2-color illus., HC, 978-1-879045-78-1 **$16.95** *For ages 9–13*

The Book of Words: Talking Spiritual Life, Living Spiritual Talk
6 x 9, 160 pp, Quality PB, 978-1-58023-020-9 **$16.95**

Eyes Remade for Wonder: A Lawrence Kushner Reader *Introduction by Thomas Moore*
6 x 9, 240 pp, Quality PB, 978-1-58023-042-1 **$18.95**

Filling Words with Light: Hasidic and Mystical Reflections on Jewish Prayer
By Rabbi Lawrence Kushner and Rabbi Nehemia Polen
5½ x 8½, 176 pp, Quality PB, 978-1-58023-238-8 **$16.99**; HC, 978-1-58023-216-6 **$21.99**

God Was in This Place & I, i Did Not Know: Finding Self, Spirituality and Ultimate Meaning 6 x 9, 192 pp, Quality PB, 978-1-879045-33-0 **$16.95**

Honey from the Rock: An Introduction to Jewish Mysticism
6 x 9, 176 pp, Quality PB, 978-1-58023-073-5 **$16.95**

Invisible Lines of Connection: Sacred Stories of the Ordinary
5½ x 8½, 160 pp, Quality PB, 978-1-879045-98-9 **$15.95**

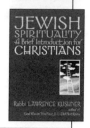

Jewish Spirituality: A Brief Introduction for Christians
5½ x 8½, 112 pp, Quality PB, 978-1-58023-150-3 **$12.95**

The River of Light: Jewish Mystical Awareness
6 x 9, 192 pp, Quality PB, 978-1-58023-096-4 **$16.95**

The Way Into Jewish Mystical Tradition
6 x 9, 224 pp, Quality PB, 978-1-58023-200-5 **$18.99**; HC, 978-1-58023-029-2 **$21.95**

Theology/Philosophy/The Way Into... Series

The Way Into... series offers an accessible and highly usable "guided tour" of the Jewish faith, people, history and beliefs—in total, an introduction to Judaism that will enable you to understand and interact with the sacred texts of the Jewish tradition. Each volume is written by a leading contemporary scholar and teacher, and explores one key aspect of Judaism. The Way Into... series enables all readers to achieve a real sense of Jewish cultural literacy through guided study.

The Way Into Encountering God in Judaism
By Rabbi Neil Gillman, PhD
For everyone who wants to understand how Jews have encountered God throughout history and today.
6 x 9, 240 pp, Quality PB, 978-1-58023-199-2 **$18.99**; HC, 978-1-58023-025-4 **$21.95**
Also Available: **The Jewish Approach to God:** A Brief Introduction for Christians
By Rabbi Neil Gillman, PhD
5½ x 8½, 192 pp, Quality PB, 978-1-58023-190-9 **$16.95**

The Way Into Jewish Mystical Tradition
By Rabbi Lawrence Kushner
Allows readers to interact directly with the sacred mystical texts of the Jewish tradition. An accessible introduction to the concepts of Jewish mysticism, their religious and spiritual significance, and how they relate to life today.
6 x 9, 224 pp, Quality PB, 978-1-58023-200-5 **$18.99**; HC, 978-1-58023-029-2 **$21.95**

The Way Into Jewish Prayer
By Rabbi Lawrence A. Hoffman, PhD
Opens the door to 3,000 years of Jewish prayer, making anyone feel at home in the Jewish way of communicating with God.
6 x 9, 208 pp, Quality PB, 978-1-58023-201-2 **$18.99**

Also Available: **The Way Into Jewish Prayer Teacher's Guide**
By Rabbi Jennifer Ossakow Goldsmith
8½ x 11, 42 pp, PB, 978-1-58023-345-3 **$8.99**
Download a free copy at www.jewishlights.com.

The Way Into Judaism and the Environment
By Jeremy Benstein, PhD
Explores the ways in which Judaism contributes to contemporary social-environmental issues, the extent to which Judaism is part of the problem and how it can be part of the solution.
6 x 9, 288 pp, Quality PB, 978-1-58023-368-2 **$18.99**; HC, 978-1-58023-268-5 **$24.99**

The Way Into *Tikkun Olam* (Repairing the World)
By Rabbi Elliot N. Dorff, PhD
An accessible introduction to the Jewish concept of the individual's responsibility to care for others and repair the world.
6 x 9, 304 pp, Quality PB, 978-1-58023-328-6 **$18.99**; 320 pp, HC, 978-1-58023-269-2 **$24.99**

The Way Into Torah
By Rabbi Norman J. Cohen, PhD
Helps guide you in the exploration of the origins and development of Torah, explains why it should be studied and how to do it.
6 x 9, 176 pp, Quality PB, 978-1-58023-198-5 **$16.99**

The Way Into the Varieties of Jewishness
By Sylvia Barack Fishman, PhD
Explores the religious and historical understanding of what it has meant to be Jewish from ancient times to the present controversy over "Who is a Jew?"
6 x 9, 288 pp, Quality PB, 978-1-58023-367-5 **$18.99**; HC, 978-1-58023-030-8 **$24.99**

Theology/Philosophy

Jewish Theology in Our Time: A New Generation Explores the Foundations and Future of Jewish Belief *Edited by Rabbi Elliot J. Cosgrove, PhD*
A powerful and challenging examination of what Jews can believe—by a new generation's most dynamic and innovative thinkers.
6 x 9, 272 pp, HC, 978-1-58023-413-9 **$24.99**

Maimonides, Spinoza and Us: Toward an Intellectually Vibrant Judaism
By Rabbi Marc D. Angel, PhD A challenging look at two great Jewish philosophers and what their thinking means to our understanding of God, truth, revelation and reason. 6 x 9, 224 pp, HC, 978-1-58023-411-5 **$24.99**

The Death of Death: Resurrection and Immortality in Jewish Thought
By Rabbi Neil Gillman, PhD 6 x 9, 336 pp, Quality PB, 978-1-58023-081-0 **$18.95**

Doing Jewish Theology: God, Torah & Israel in Modern Judaism *By Rabbi Neil Gillman, PhD*
6 x 9, 304 pp, Quality PB, 978-1-58023-439-9 **$18.99**; HC, 978-1-58023-322-4 **$24.99**

Ethics of the Sages: Pirke Avot—Annotated & Explained
Translation & Annotation by Rabbi Rami Shapiro 5½ x 8¼, 192 pp, Quality PB, 978-1-59473-207-2 **$16.99***

Hasidic Tales: Annotated & Explained *Translation & Annotation by Rabbi Rami Shapiro*
5½ x 8½, 240 pp, Quality PB, 978-1-893361-86-7 **$16.95***

A Heart of Many Rooms: Celebrating the Many Voices within Judaism
By Dr. David Hartman 6 x 9, 352 pp, Quality PB, 978-1-58023-156-5 **$19.95**

The Hebrew Prophets: Selections Annotated & Explained
Translation & Annotation by Rabbi Rami Shapiro; Foreword by Rabbi Zalman M. Schachter-Shalomi
5½ x 8½, 224 pp, Quality PB, 978-1-59473-037-5 **$16.99***

A Jewish Understanding of the New Testament *By Rabbi Samuel Sandmel;*
Preface by Rabbi David Sandmel 5½ x 8¼, 368 pp, Quality PB, 978-1-59473-048-2 **$19.99***

Jews and Judaism in the 21st Century: Human Responsibility, the Presence of God and the Future of the Covenant *Edited by Rabbi Edward Feinstein; Foreword by Paula E. Hyman*
6 x 9, 192 pp, Quality PB, 978-1-58023-374-3 **$19.99**; HC, 978-1-58023-315-6 **$24.99**

A Living Covenant: The Innovative Spirit in Traditional Judaism
By Dr. David Hartman 6 x 9, 368 pp, Quality PB, 978-1-58023-011-7 **$25.00**

Love and Terror in the God Encounter: The Theological Legacy of Rabbi Joseph B. Soloveitchik *By Dr. David Hartman* 6 x 9, 240 pp, Quality PB, 978-1-58023-176-3 **$19.95**

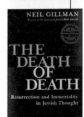

The Personhood of God: Biblical Theology, Human Faith and the Divine Image
By Dr. Yochanan Muffs; Foreword by Dr. David Hartman
6 x 9, 240 pp, Quality PB, 978-1-58023-338-5 **$18.99**; HC, 978-1-58023-265-4 **$24.99**

A Touch of the Sacred: A Theologian's Informal Guide to Jewish Belief
By Dr. Eugene B. Borowitz and Frances W. Schwartz
6 x 9, 256 pp, Quality PB, 978-1-58023-416-0 **$16.99**; HC, 978-1-58023-337-8 **$21.99**

Traces of God: Seeing God in Torah, History and Everyday Life *By Rabbi Neil Gillman, PhD*
6 x 9, 240 pp, Quality PB, 978-1-58023-369-9 **$16.99**

We Jews and Jesus: Exploring Theological Differences for Mutual Understanding *By Rabbi Samuel Sandmel; Preface by Rabbi David Sandmel* 6 x 9, 192 pp, Quality PB, 978-1-59473-208-9 **$16.99***

Your Word Is Fire: The Hasidic Masters on Contemplative Prayer
Edited and translated by Rabbi Arthur Green, PhD, and Barry W. Holtz
6 x 9, 160 pp, Quality PB, 978-1-879045-25-5 **$15.95**

I Am Jewish
Personal Reflections Inspired by the Last Words of Daniel Pearl
Almost 150 Jews—both famous and not—from all walks of life, from all around the world, write about many aspects of their Judaism.
Edited by Judea and Ruth Pearl 6 x 9, 304 pp, Deluxe PB w/ flaps, 978-1-58023-259-3 **$18.99**
Download a free copy of the *I Am Jewish Teacher's Guide* at www.jewishlights.com.

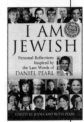

Hannah Senesh: Her Life and Diary, The First Complete Edition
By Hannah Senesh; Foreword by Marge Piercy; Preface by Eitan Senesh; Afterword by Roberta Grossman
6 x 9, 368 pp, b/w photos, Quality PB, 978-1-58023-342-2 **$19.99**

*A book from SkyLight Paths, Jewish Lights' sister imprint

About Jewish Lights

People of all faiths and backgrounds yearn for books that attract, engage, educate, and spiritually inspire.

Our principal goal is to stimulate thought and help all people learn about who the Jewish People are, where they come from, and what the future can be made to hold. While people of our diverse Jewish heritage are the primary audience, our books speak to people in the Christian world as well and will broaden their understanding of Judaism and the roots of their own faith.

We bring to you authors who are at the forefront of spiritual thought and experience. While each has something different to say, they all say it in a voice that you can hear.

Our books are designed to welcome you and then to engage, stimulate, and inspire. We judge our success not only by whether or not our books are beautiful and commercially successful, but by whether or not they make a difference in your life.

For your information and convenience, at the back of this book we have provided a list of other Jewish Lights books you might find interesting and useful. They cover all the categories of your life:

Bar/Bat Mitzvah	Life Cycle
Bible Study / Midrash	Meditation
Children's Books	Men's Interest
Congregation Resources	Parenting
Current Events / History	Prayer / Ritual / Sacred Practice
Ecology / Environment	Social Justice
Fiction: Mystery, Science Fiction	Spirituality
Grief / Healing	Theology / Philosophy
Holidays / Holy Days	Travel
Inspiration	Twelve Steps
Kabbalah / Mysticism / Enneagram	Women's Interest

Stuart M. Matlins, Publisher

Or phone, fax, mail or e-mail to: **JEWISH LIGHTS Publishing**
Sunset Farm Offices, Route 4 • P.O. Box 237 • Woodstock, Vermont 05091
Tel: (802) 457-4000 • Fax: (802) 457-4004 • www.jewishlights.com
Credit card orders: **(800) 962-4544** (8:30AM–5:30PM ET Monday–Friday)
Generous discounts on quantity orders. SATISFACTION GUARANTEED. Prices subject to change.

For more information about each book, visit our website at www.jewishlights.com